German Radio Plays

The German Library: Volume 86
Volkmar Sander, General Editor

GERMAN RADIO PLAYS

Edited by Everett Frost and

Margaret Herzfeld-Sander

CONTINUUM · NEW YORK

PT
1258
.G47
1991
15 4739
Feb. 1992

1991
The Continuum Publishing Company
370 Lexington Avenue, New York, NY 10017

The German Library
is published in cooperation with Deutsches Haus,
New York University.
This volume has been supported by a grant
from the funds of Stifterverband für die Deutsche Wissenschaft.

Printed in the United States of America

Library of Congress Cataloging-in-Publication Data

German radio plays / edited by Everett Frost and Margaret Herzfeld
-Sander,
    p.   cm. — (The German library ; v. 86)
    Contents: Introduction / Everett Frost and Margaret Herzfeld
-Sander — The outsider / Wolfgang Borchert — Dreams ; Don't go to
Al-Kuwaid! / Günter Eich — The good God of Manhattan / Ingeborg
Bachmann — Radio play / Peter Handke — Houses / Jürgen Becker —
Breakfast in Miami / Reinhard Lettau.
    ISBN 0-8264-0341-7 (cloth) — ISBN 0-8264-0342-5
(paperback)
    1. Radio plays, Germans—Translations into English.   2. Radio
plays, English—Translations from German.   I. Series.
PT1258.G47   1991
832'.02208—dc20   90-2553
                                            CIP

Contents

Introduction

American readers who think of radio drama as a form of popular entertainment cranked out by commercial radio in the 1940s and 1950s—suitable for nostalgia buffs, perhaps, but not a subject for serious study—may find themselves puzzled by the presence of a volume of plays written for the radio in an extended library of German literature and drama. But to Europeans (with their heavily subsidized noncommercial radio systems) radio drama means something quite different, and the reasons for including it would seem more self-evident. While there is plenty of what might be called "popular" stuff (mysteries, soap operas, light comedy) on the radio in Germany as well, *Hörspiel* (radio drama) is regarded as a significant art form created, without condescension, by serious artists. Indeed, there is hardly a major postwar author who has not written for or been produced by German radio at one time or another. Over the last forty years radio drama has established a rich and remarkable tradition in Germany and, though in recent years its practitioners have been increasingly on the defensive, radio drama continues to flourish as a major art form. As a result of this concentrated use of radio as a medium for drama—on the scale on which it has been done, in the dramaturgical intensity that has been applied to it, the outstanding quality and variety of the writing, and the level and diversity of invention it has inspired—the Hörspiel has exercised a major influence on the development of postwar German (and European) literature. As A. P. Frank has observed:

> With its many forms, radio drama extends into almost all genres of modern literature. It can perhaps only be fully appreciated by seeing its relationship to the modern stream-of-consciousness epic, to the short story, to the symbolist novels and narratives, and to the different forms of contemporary theater in which twentieth-century literature is so rich. (*Das Hörspiel*, p. 189)

Not surprisingly, radio drama prompts a good deal of interest in Germany: the general public takes a kind of civic pride in it, texts of radio plays are printed and anthologized, and the work is studied as a serious form of cultural activity. Hörspiel departments rival each other in their efforts to create major productions and discover new talent, and they compete energetically for international prizes. (The offices for the distinguished international prize, the Prix Futura, is located at Sender Freies Berlin.) I can still remember my surprise and delight more than a decade ago when I discovered that one could buy printed texts and anthologies and studies of radio plays in most self-respecting bookstores throughout the Federal Republic of Germany. And even the sparser shelves of the former GDR sported several editions and collections of radio plays and an annual anthology of the best scripts produced by GDR radio.

There are several reasons why such an astonishing level of creative activity has been able to flourish. These include the promising beginnings made in radio prior to 1933, the situation in Germany after World War II, and the structure and funding of German broadcasting that resulted from it.

German radio drama has its origins in the vigorous tradition of German theater that predates the invention of radio. From at least Lessing (1729–81) onward, classic German theater achieved a distinctive form, one that, as the internationally known critic and former head of Radio Drama at the BBC, Martin Esslin, remarks in the introduction to volume 83 of this series, "has become the model for the culture of most of the nations of Central and Eastern Europe." By the end of the nineteenth century, Schiller and Goethe had, according to Esslin, "established the claim of German drama, and hence German literature, to be the equal of the other great national literatures of Europe." In consequence, "the theater is seen as part of the educational infrastructure, on a level with museums, libraries, and universities, and accordingly . . . theater-going is regarded as an intellectual pursuit." With such a strong theatrical tradition already established, it is not surprising that the new medium of radio, with its unprecedented ability to extend voice, music, and sound over great distances, would be seen to open new possibilities for drama and literature. Seen from this point of view, radio drama came about as the marriage of a literary or theatrical genre (drama) with the technical means to broadcast it (radio). In this it resembles other art forms—like film or television or video—resulting from the combination of a technical invention and pre-established forms more than it does artistic forms that have evolved out of long gestation periods like drama, lyric poetry, or prose fiction. In the sense that it is wholly made out of sound, radio drama may be seen to resemble music as well. I leave others to debate whether or not, in Marshall McLuhan's famous phrase, "the medium is the message," but certainly, the medium very quickly became a part of it. One consequence of this has been that in both the practice and criticism of radio drama there has been an intersting and sometimes explosive struggle between an emphasis on the literary and dramatic forms that predate radio, and an emphasis on subordinating these to the exploitation of the unique technical capabilities and advantages of a medium restricted exclusively to sound. The former leads to the preeminence of text and story; the latter to stressing sound, the origins of language in sound, and the tremendous potential for the electronic manipulation of language and sound. Radical experiments of this kind date from the 1920s and include such things as the sound poems of Hugo Ball, the *Ursonate* of Kurt Schwitters, and the noise-as-art experiments of the Italian Futurist, Luigi Russolo. Perhaps the major tendency in the evolution of radio drama in Germany over the last half century is the successful and increasingly sophisticated attempt to define and develop a *radiophonic* art form in its own terms, fully exploiting the possibilities of the medium, equivalent to, but independent of the genres of literature and drama out of which it emerged. Increasingly it shows a concern to be an original rather than derivative art form—a "naughty child" free of the strictures and structures of a parent.

But initial attempts to take advantage of the tremendous opportunity suddenly offered would rely for its materials and structures on well-established antecedents such as prose fiction and stage drama. Early radio drama consisted almost entirely of adaptations of literary fiction and appropriations of stage drama. Bertolt Brecht's remark that "the possibilities of radio are limitless" is indicative of the enthusiasm felt by many artists of the time (*Radiotheorie: 1927–1932*, p. 120).

Radio could also include drama by going to drama and music events and transmitting them to a wider audience. Thus, for example, in 1929 technicians from Radio Berlin simply trooped out to Baden Baden to transmit the notorious annual music-theater festival. But the fact that the radio would—for the first time in history—be there prompted the participants, among them Bertolt Brecht, Paul Hindemith, Walter Benjamin, and Kurt Weill, to create something that was specifically meant for broadcast. Brecht and Hindemith began, and Brecht and Weill completed, a cantata for radio, *The Flight of Lindbergh,* subsequently subtitled, *A Didactic Radio Play for Boys and Girls.* The radio play dramatizes, and a chorus celebrates, the historic transatlantic flight of the American pilot, Charles Lindbergh, as he struggles to overcome the storms, the fog, the clouds above and the seas below, the weakness of his engine and the fragility of his plane, and, finally, sleep and human limitations themselves. Tracked by ships at sea, seen by an Irish fisherman as he enters Europe, and finally coming within sight of the control tower in Paris, his progress is reported via radio. Thus the very radio capabilities that had prompted the invention of the cantata become an element in its composition. In later versions, Brecht and Weill emphasized this by altering the title to *The Flight of the Lindberghs,* and they had the idea that the music could be given to children at home who would then sing along with the choral parts. (An early attempt at "interactive" radio, though I have found no evidence that they ever actually managed to attempt the experiment.) In the 1930s, Brecht again changed the title. Lindbergh's fascination with the technology of the Luftwaffe, and his anti-Semitic sentiments caused him to engage in some rather murky associations with the Nazis, and to become an "American Firster" spokesman, arguing against American involvement in the war against Fascism. Brecht removed his name from the play and renamed it *The Oceanflight.*

Brecht was quick to see the tremendous potential radio had for theater, and wrote and lectured, on and off the radio, about it. In his "Advice to Radio Station Directors," he urged them to

> bring your tape recorders closer to actual real-life happenings and not rely too much on trying to imitate it or refer to it. . . .
>
> Regarding radio drama: the "acoustic novel" now being tried out by Arnolt Bronnen should be tried by others. . . . But you should only hire the top people! Here's the address of the great epic writer, Alfred Döblin. . . .

The station directors must have listened, for in 1929 Döblin adapted his monumental novel, *Berlin Alexanderplatz,* for radio long before it became the remarkable television film directed by Rainer Werner Fassbinder.

In the mid-1930s, these promising beginnings were radically aborted by the Nazis, and had to be recreated after World War II. The Third Reich understood the emotional and persuasive power of the new medium of radio all too well and exploited it for demonic ends: from one point of view, Hitler's broadcasts were a kind of demented Hörspiel, effectively orchestrated, and an important tool for creating enthusiasm for the cult of leadership of Der Führer. But it is in the decades after World War II—the period represented by the radio plays gathered in this volume—that radio drama came into its own in the Federal Republic of Germany as a significant art form, with parallel developments in Austria and German-speaking Switzerland, and in somewhat different form in the former GDR. Several factors combined to make such a flourishing possible:

1. In the immediate postwar period, the German radio system had to be quickly refurbished by the occupying British, American, French, and Soviet armies in order to serve the exigencies of communication. To serve this function, it had to reach the entire nation. But the allies also wanted to insulate it from the possibility of takeover by another predator like Hitler, and so it was radically decentralized. Thus each Land, or region, has its own independent radio station, linked into a confederation with the other stations into the ARD (Arbeitsgemeinschaft der Rundfunkanstalten Deutschlands), but which is autonomous in administration and programming. As the system developed, the autonomy of each station has provided opportunities for several independent centers of radio drama to flourish simultaneously, and ultimately to rival each other in their claims for discovering artistic talent and producing new plays by significant authors. This rivalry has fueled a vigorous debate about the nature, aesthetic, and purposes of radio drama, such as the debate between traditional and *Neues Hörspiel* (roughly, narrative drama and acoustic art), which continues into the 1990s.

2. Broadly speaking, the radio system in Germany resulted from the conjunction of British design and American money—a well-funded "BBC" with a leather jacket rather than a bowler hat. Quite

aside from aesthetic questions of its desirability, the model suggested by commercial radio in the United States, which depended upon a functioning consumer economy, would have been simply impossible in the devastated circumstances of Germany in 1945. The British model of a subsidized, predominantly noncommercial use of the public trust of the airwaves proved not only more feasible but also more useful for the immediate and practical exigent ends that radio had to serve in the years immediately following the war. Thus the British reorganization of the primary radio station in its zone of occupation, Nordwestdeutscher Rundfunk (NWDR), Hamburg, served as a model. The United States had the only economy still intact enough to afford such an undertaking. It was willing to subsidize these initial efforts, at first through the army and subsequently through the Marshall Plan, as part of the developing struggle for hegemony in Europe with its erstwhile ally, the Soviet Union. As the German economy recovered, the German radio stations, like those of the BBC, came to be supported by a licensing fee charged for the use of each home radio receiver, much like the American practice of requiring automobiles to be licensed in order to be driven on public roads. As a result, German radio was designed along subsidized lines with each broadcasting house transmitting on two or three channels simultaneously (operating two or three "stations" we would say in America); with one or two channels reserved for light entertainment, popular music, and news and weather; and one channel, like the BBC "third programme," reserved for serious cultural programming: classical music, readings, lectures, and serious drama.

3. In addition to such grim and practical necessities as reading casualty lists, broadcasting news of the inconceivable horror of the death camps, identifying the location of displaced persons, reuniting families; transmitting news about food, water, and sanitation; and providing survival instructions, radio also had the tasks of lifting morale, representing Western democracy and freedom of speech as a more attractive alternative to that provided by Soviet totalitarianism, and reacquainting the German public with a cultural legacy that had been forbidden for a decade or more. It had, in short, the major task of contributing to the restoration of humane cultural life in Germany. In this undertaking radio drama played a crucial, even central

role. The theaters had been substantially destroyed in heavily bombed cities such as Berlin. Even where theater or caberets functioned, the virtual absence of public transportation made them difficult for more than an immediately local population to attend. And, as Lowell Bangarter has observed, the devastation of the publishing industry served as an incentive for the radio play:

> The situation at the end of the war initially made it difficult for literature to have a broad public impact. Publishing houses had to be rebuilt. Paper and other needed materials were scarce. Books were printed only in small editions. One consequence was an increased dissemination of literature through other media. . . . The limitations on resources for printing contributed to the development of the radio play. (*German Writing Since 1945*, New York, 1988, p. 3)

Radio, in its turn, contributed to the recovery and development of German literature and drama. In the days immediately following the collapse of the Third Reich, radio stations throughout Germany began daily fifteen- or thirty-minute readings from "Bücher die wir nicht lesen durften" (Books we were forbidden to read). Many stations began with Thomas Mann (whose return from exile was heavily covered on radio throughout Germany) and continued with Stefan Zweig, Vicki Baum, Franz Werfel, and Arthur Koestler among others. Almost immediately radio began attending and covering, then broadcasting, and finally commissioning authors from all the major literary colloquia, such as Group 47, which began to form in postwar Germany. Classic stage plays were adapted for radio and broadcast. In her book, *Die Westdeutsche Nachkriegszeit im literarischen Hörspiel*, Margaret Bloom includes a representative transcript of the program notes from the American-operated radio station in Frankfurt am Main:

> Das Buch ist aufgeschlagen." Each Tuesday at 21.45 we read for fifteen minutes from one of the great works of literature banned under the Nazis. At present we are offering Thomas Mann, *Joseph and His Brethren*, in a serialized form. . . . For some time to come, radio will be the only means of presenting the writing of their great exiles to the German people.
>
> Recently, Radio Frankfurt has begun its own production of Radio Plays. As in its literary shows, only plays are chosen that have either

been banned by the Nazis, or that convey a significant message for a democratic Germany. Up to now, two plays have been produced: *Tor und Tod* by Hugo von Hofmannsthal, and *Die Juden* by Lessing. Plays by Norman Corwin and Anton Chekhov are in preparation.

The substantial fees paid to authors for radio work also helped them to make a living from their work, "buying" time for them to pursue it, both in radio and in other venues.

One might think that literature and radio drama would have been among the least of the concerns of an occupying army. Therefore the acute sensitivity of British and American military officers and their German colleagues who directed the restoration of German broadcasting is all the more remarkable, and has to be identified among the reasons for the origins of such an extraordinary tradition of German radio drama. Henry Skornia, for example, who became deputy chief of radio in Berlin, and was in charge of US broadcasting interests in the developing Allied Control Authority, sent his "Ten Commandments for (West) German Broadcasting: 1948" to me, which were widely disseminated and used at the same time. It contained the admonition:

> Broadcasting must constantly be aware of its ability to attract attention to problems, situations, and otherwise abstract themes, often transforming and clarifying them with dramatic form. One minute of dramatized and illustrated material or pictures is often worth as much as a thousand words, written or spoken.

As Klaus Schöning, head of the Studio Akustische Kunst Westdeutscher Rundfunk, Cologne, remarked in an interview broadcast on KPFA, Berkeley, on October 1, 1984:

> At the end of the war, radio was the only public medium for a large sector of the population that was able to convey not only up-to-date information, but also cultural events. The theaters had all been destroyed, and the book trade and film industry were only beginning to reorient themselves. There was a great need to return to the point of pre-1933 artistic developments. . . . The audience's encouragement was extraordinary. The broadcast of a Hörspiel was a cultural event, drawing millions of listeners to the wireless set.

4. Television did not become a compelling national force in Germany until the mid-1960s, so that the art of radio had an opportunity to become a presence strong and respected enough to survive the impact of the advent of the younger medium. As a result, it is as true in the 1990s as it was in the 1960s that radio remains closer and more responsive to the nation's authors and literary movements than does TV, which has been, to a greater degree, captive to the influence of American commercial television.

For at least these four reasons—and there may be others—the Hörspiel has had an important place in German letters and culture from the postwar beginnings of the Federal Republic to the present day. Many of Germany's most noted writers, directors, dramaturgs, and filmmakers either trace their professional origins to radio or have done significant Hörspiel production along with their work for stage and film, and without condescension. But radio drama has not only responded and contributed to cultural life in Germany; it has played a signficant role in shaping that life as well:

> Almost all the well-known postwar German writers wrote radio plays. . . . [and] the fact that so many important postwar authors wrote radio plays guaranteed that this form became an accepted literary genre. Many writers conferences and meetings, such as those of Group 47, featured sessions devoted to hearing and discussing radio drama. Authors such as Max Frisch and Friedrich Dürenmatt used their work in radio as an opportunity to practice and experiment for their theatrical writing. (Bloom, p. 110)

This anthology spans a period of three decades (1947–77), and illustrates many of the developments and tendencies exhibited by the evolution of the *literarische Hörspiel*—literary radio drama—in postwar Germany. Three authors (Borchert, Eich, and Bachmann) represent the redefinition of the genre in the immediate postwar period and three authors (Handke, Becker, and Lettau) give an indication of its directions in the 1960s and 1970s.

After the Nazi period, radio tried to recover its wits, and radio drama continued to bear the strong imprint of its origins in literature and drama. Wolfgang Borchert's *The Outsider* was begun with the postwar cabaret theater in mind, but was finished as a radio play at the instigation of his friend, the actor Hans Quest (who played the lead in the original radio and stage productions, and to whom the play is dedicated) in response to the active revival of radio drama being superintended by the British at NWDR in Hamburg. Now generally considered to have been one of the first German plays to have been written after the war specifically for the radio, "the play that," in the words of its epigraph, "no theater wants to produce and no audience wants to see," premiered on NWDR on February 13, 1947, and became an overnight sensation: distributed throughout Germany and often repeated. It opened as a stage play in Hamburg on November 21 of the same year and was subsequently made into a movie under the title *Liebe 47*, directed by Wolfgang Liebeneiner.

In the early 1950s, Günter Eich played a major role in the maturation of the radio play as a significant genre in its own right:

> The beginning of the flowering of radio drama as a form of literature coincided more or less with the founding of the Federal Republic of Germany and lasted at least until the end of the 1950s. Many scholars date it from the year 1951 in which Günter Eich's *Traüme* *(Dreams)* was first broadcast by NWDR, Hamburg, which they consider the hour of birth of the German radio play. (Bloom, p. 109)

Eich's influence on radio drama and, more broadly, on European drama and literature in the 1950s cannot be overestimated. *Don't Go to Al-Kuwaid!* premiered on Bayerischer Rundfunk in 1950. Like *Dreams* and *The other Woman and I*, which would follow, it uses the disembodied theater of radio to explore the surreal boundary between a dream world and the world that adults call "real" when they are awake. Though many of his later plays would locate that mental or dream world in more realistic settings, *Al-Kuwaid* takes place "once upon a time" in the Middle East, an exotic and fairy-take realm from the point of view of Europeans, since it invokes such things as tales of a-thousand-and-one Arabian nights. (There is even a bandit in the play who quotes poetry and is called Omar.) The merchant, Mohallab, undergoes a Sisyphean labor, only to end up where he began. The ending of the play exactly repeats a portion of the dialogue from the beginning—the crucial scene in which Mohallab makes (again?) the very choice he has learned to regret and swears he would not repeat were it possible to live his life over again. Yet when it comes time, it is precisely this "wrong" choice that he makes:

And if I could begin it all over again, knowing what I know now, the result would be the same. And if I could begin again a third time, knowing what I would know then, the result would be the same. And if I could begin it all over again a hundred times, knowing each time a little more than the time before, the result would always be the same, and the hundredth life as the first, and the hundred lives as one. A cat's flux.

The passage quoted above is not from Eich's play, but from Samuel Beckett's novel, *Watt* (1953), one of many echoes of Eich in Beckett's work.

For all its exotic trappings and its skillful manipulation of the fantasies of the auditor, there is little to prevent or be lost in staging or filming *Don't Go to Al-Kuwaid!*. But in his next radio play, *Dreams*, the dreamworld is unsettlingly rooted in "ordinary" reality, though the play itself is a radical advance in the direction of radio as an autonomous art form: it could not be transposed to any other medium without leaving something of its essence behind. Eich is atypical of radio authors in that he not only wrote for radio, but was employed by it as well. Thus he was able to exploit its possibilities with precision.

Dreams illustrates that Günter Eich had an extraordinary gift for writing for the ear. Sound effects, for example, are minimal but exactly right. For example, popular radio drama had gone overboard on footsteps; in the days before stereo, it was a quick and easily understood way to indicate the movement and location of characters. Eich uses them with restraint. In the third dream, the indicated footsteps are the ones absolutely essential to the dramatic tension of the drama. The mastery with which the sound of the footsteps of the "monster" precede both the adults' denial of—and the child's insistence upon—their existence goes to the very heart of the episode. If the footsteps were not there, it would be the *child's* perception, not the adult's, that would be invalidated. In this play, sound itself becomes a character, an active part of the drama: the termites, and the thunder and its immersion in the climactic apocalyptic scream of the daughter/wife in Dream 5 convey the very essence of the drama through sound alone. The radio in Dream 5, like the train in Dream 1, the imagined monster in Dream 3, and the drums in Dream 4 are characters in the play that speak in a language of pure sound, conveying meaning not to the eye but to the ear of the audience alone. Of course it could be staged, but it is more powerful and more terrifying, heard, imagined, and absorbed. At one level the meaning seems to be that civilization is being driven, sacrificed, spooked, deprived of its reason and, finally, hollowed out and destroyed in a cacophony of increasingly mediated, increasingly technologized sound, culminating in the radio itself and the static-ridden broadcast of thunder. Of this, Eich had had firsthand experience: he had heard the trains (Dream 1) and "the little fellow" (Dream 3) drumming up (Dream 4)—Hitler had once referred to himself as Germany's drummer boy—his mind numbed and oblivious, Nazis drowning out contact with "reality" via the radio.

Ingeborg Bachmann is another major writer whose remarkable radio plays have not, until this volume and the SoundPlay series, been translated into English. Like Günter Eich, she was interested in exploring the dramatic possibilities in radio for telling a story, and she found in the drama of the theater of the mind an opportunity to explore the interior landscapes of emotion, particularly emotion when pushed to the extreme or in highly charged and irrational states such as those of the lovers in *The Good God of Manhattan*.

Bachmann takes full advantage of the opportunities provided by the radio medium. To present the Good God's squirrel henchmen, Frankie and Billie visually, would be to trivialize them and to risk making them comic. Imagined, they invoke an icon of New York (the Central Park squirrels) and appear menacing. The cacophonous soundscape of New York—its overpopulated streets, Grand Central Station, the Brooklyn Bridge, the subways—is carefully orchestrated to counterpoint and isolate the lyric absorption of the lovers. Radio directs attention to their language with its magnificent allusions to Tristan and Iseult, and the German romantic tradition in poetry.

The final three plays included in the anthology present a small sample of the flowering of the genre in the 1960s and 1970s. Peter Handke's *"Radio Play" (No. 1)* represents one of the major tendencies to emerge in radio drama in the 1960s: the attempt to create a dramatically compelling work that is, as one might now say, radically deconstructed, and not confined to the restrictions of a plot. Like its many parallels in the literature and drama of the period (one thinks, for example, of the later media works of Samuel Beckett, The

Living Theater of Julian Beck and Judith Malina, the dramas of Harold Pinter and Eugène Ionesco, and the emergence of Performance Art as a genre), it is apt to find itself accused of disorderly conduct.

The sound effects interwoven throughout deliberately call attention to the fact that the audience is hearing an artifically constructed play, not tuning in on the retelling of an actual event (the very kind of illusion that Bachmann or Borchert or Eich take such pains to create). Eich's footsteps intensify the drama, Handke's sound effects are used, he says, "to surprise, not to explain." Thus he intends that the director and technicians not spend the considerable energy usually employed to mix in sound effects that are as persuasive as possible, but to employ the conventional-stock-sound effects of radio drama, easily identifiable as such.

Jürgen Becker's *Houses* is an example of a radio play disentangled not only from the conventions of plot, but also from those of character as well. It is a play for voices that thematically orchestrates personalities or themes or points of view, not characters in a drama; and in this it resembles Dylan Thomas's 1950s voice play for radio, *Under Milkwood*. For this reason the Hörspiel is not even written as a dramatic script, but as a series of monologues and dialogues arranged in paragraphs without identifying specific speakers, thereby leaving a great deal of discretion to the radio director to weave the piece together. The German producer Raoul Wolfgang Schnell used sound motifs to denote certain emotions: for example, gunshots signal the aggressiveness of the tenants, and various bits of music from opera to top-40 rock and television ads signal the different moods and life-styles of the inhabitants of the houses.

Houses comes very close to simulating or documenting speech as it actually occurs in "realistic" living situations. As Becker has remarked, "The radio medium enables me to unlock the literary text. . . . The tape recorder is a medium necessary to my writing that allows me to *do* things that I can only *describe* in my prose" (Lermen, *Das Traditionelle und Neue Hörspiel*, p. 209). An obvious next step would be to move radio drama's tape recorders out of the recording studio and into the field, and Becker has been a formative influence on a subsequent form of radio drama—well equipped for the first time with high quality, lightweight,

portable recording equipment—which has done just that. It empha-
sizes radio drama's ability to develop creative works in sound from
Original Ton (original sound / field recordings), the compelling
drama of real people in real-life situations that had hitherto been the
recording province of radio journalists and documentarians. It has
been explored in such works as *Monologue: Terry Jo* by Ludwig
Harig and Max Bense (assembled from newspaper accounts of a
boating tragedy), *Gertrude* by Wolfgang Schiffer and Charles Dürr
(assembled from extensive field recordings of a mentally disturbed
woman), and *Moscow Time* and *San Paolo: Babylon* by Helmut
Kopetzky (documentaries about cities assembled from their sound-
scapes).

Reinhard Lettau's *Breakfast in Miami* uses documentation, provided in an appendix, to justify a political satire, thereby refusing to
let the play remain (in the manner of Peter Handke's play) as an
artifice of language, and trenchantly connecting it as a commentary
on actual events. Like Becker and certain aspects of Bachmann and
Handke (though to very different effect) it exploits radio's ability to
concentrate the attention of the listener on the elaborate, and highly
sophisticated, verbal play of the language. But for Lettau, language
is also a powerful weapon. In the merciless crucible of language he
distills characters out of the mental attitudes they represent (in this
case cynical, tyrannical, brutal, and foolish) and holds those attitudes up for scrutiny and judgment by his audience. And with the
world being the way it is, there is a sense in which the play can be
completed but not finished. After the Chinese massacre of its students in Tianamen Square in June 1989 and the events in Eastern
Europe the subsequent Fall, Lettau wrote a new scene for the *Sound-
Play* American radio production then in process (scene 15 in the
present volume: "About the Difficult of Throwing off Shackles").

The seven plays included here are chosen from among hundreds of
other, in many cases equally worthwhile, possibilities; and the
choice has not always been an easy one. Some authors who have
written significant radio plays, such as Bertolt Brecht, Heinrich Böll,
Max Frisch, and Friedrich Dürrenmatt, have been omitted because
their work is surveyed in other volumes of The German Library.
With the possible exception of Peter Handke's *"Radio Play" (No. 1)*,
which shows some tendencies in this direction, the anthology does

not include examples of *Neues Hörspiel*—the phrase does not translate well as "new, or avant-garde," radio drama, and is better thought of as experimental radio or acoustic art. Such plays are "realized" in a studio rather than performed from a script, and the electronics are as much a part of them as the words. Their "scripts" tend to resemble musical scores rather than plays and are less able to convey a sense of the work to a general audience. Over the last twenty-five years much of this remarkable activity has been commissioned, produced, described, defended, catalogued, broadcast, and distributed by Klaus Schöning, from his position as Chief Dramaturg and Head of the Hörspiel Studio Akustische Kunst at Westdeutscher Rundfunk in Cologne.

It is regrettable that so little of this activity is known in the United States, and that many remarkable Hörspiele remain untranslated, unproduced in English, and unstudied. It is hoped that the publication of this volume—and the 1991–92 *Soundplay:* Horspiel radio drama series that led to it—may mark the beginning of a remedy. With one exception, Günter Eich's *Don't Go to Al-Kuwaid!*, the radio plays included here are drawn from the *SoundPlay* radio drama series produced under my direction for broadcast throughout the public radio system in the United States in the fall of 1991. The plays by Günter Eich, Ingeborg Bachmann, Peter Handke, and Jürgen Becker were translated for the series and are printed in English for the first time in this anthology.

Neither the anthology nor the *SoundPlay* series from which it derives would have been possible without the generous help of Klaus Schöning, Erik Bauersfeld, and Faith Wilding; the assistance of the Goethe Institute and Ernst Schürmann, Manfred Triesch, Jürgen Ohlau, and Peter Seel; and the helpful advice of *SoundPlay* project consultants Peter Demetz, Frederic C. Tubach, Volkmar Sander, and my coeditor, Margaret Herzfeld-Sander. To them, one and all, I owe my thanks.

E. C. F.

GERMAN RADIO PLAYS

Wolfgang Borchert

Wolfgang Borchert was born in 1921 in Hamburg. He was trained as a bookseller and librarian, took acting lessons, and had a brief engagement as an actor before being drafted into the German army in 1941. In some of his letters he was critical of the Hitler regime. He was sent to the Russian front before they became public, but then was sentenced for these disloyal and subversive comments. Although injured, sick, and in pain he was transported from his hospital bed to prison and indicted for treason. Half a year later he was pardoned and sent back to the front in Russia. He was dismissed from the army because of his war injuries but was then betrayed by a fellow soldier for defeatist remarks against the National Socialists, and the war they had begun in 1939 against Poland and the Western world. He was sent back to prison in Berlin for another nine months. In the spring of 1945, he was transferred to another prison in Germany where he was finally liberated by American soldiers. At that point, he only had another nine months to live.

Back in Hamburg, Borchert became engaged in the effort to shape and build a better, more humane society. At an earlier stage he had written poems, experimenting with various forms and styles. His remarkable contribution of narrative prose and his play *The Outsider* were written after the war. There are over fifty impressive, gripping stories that excel through their exact observation, sensitive reflection, and a strong commitment to a compassionate and unsentimental attitude in life. Many of these stories, like those of his contemporary Heinrich Böll, were later incorporated in textbooks and read by practically every postwar German student. Representative of these

1

are *Die lange lange Straße (The Long, Long Street), Die Hundeblume (The Dandelion), An diesem Dienstag (This Tuesday), and Nachts schlafen die Ratten doch (The Rats Sleep at Night)*. He worked in the theater for a brief spell but soon had to spend a year in the hospital. There were no means to ameliorate his disease, which had become impossible to diagnose properly. He kept on writing about his experiences during the war years as a soldier and prisoner in his own country. As a dying man he was finally allowed to cross the German border to be admitted to a Swiss hospital. During his stay in Basel he gained new friends and supporters but died shortly after his arrival in 1947 at the age of twenty-six.

His brief life, his rebellious spirit, and search for an authentic voice of his generation may be compared to that of the nineteenth-century playwright Georg Büchner. He tried to capture the experience of a lost generation, the despair in an era of bleakness but also the hope and the need for responsible political action. He was in search of a precise and evocative language free from the bombast and manipulative distortions of the Third Reich. He wanted to write about and for a generation and their brutal and bitter years; of human failure and suffering; and the faint promise of a homecoming to an informed and responsible self, and a just society. He was unwilling to forget and wanted to remind his generation of their own involvement and guilt. His stories are superbly crafted, exposing and documenting the conditions and ambiguities of the German mind and by so doing transcending the borders of his country.

His play *The Outsider* became an instant success. Published in 1947, it was produced by every theater and radio station in West Germany as the most promising and effective expression of a young German writer. The dramatic action of the play is propelled by a barrage of accusations and denials, of constant reminders of the past war and the attempt to unveil the deliberate amnesia that had set in after the end of the Hitler era. *The Outsider* builds an episodic dramatic action around a man who will not forget. Beckmann returns from a prisoner-of-war camp in Russia to the German community to find that for him and many like him there is no homecoming. His wife has found another man. He tries to drown himself, but the river refuses to accept him and lifts him back onto the shore. Death, an overfed, belching undertaker, and God, an old man whom no one believes in anymore, look on indifferently. Beckmann has another chance to fight back. Haunted by the dead rising from their mass graves, Beckmann encounters the living whose inability to understand and to mourn frightens and isolates him from his own people. With horror he realizes that even his former colonel refuses to accept any kind of responsibility, speaking about the dead as necessary by-products of "a little touch of warfare." Beckmann feels responsible for the suicide of a crippled soldier. He finally offers his story to a theater producer who turns him down. He is told his story lacks charm, wit, and elegance, and above all, experience. His wife is lost to him, his parents are dead, their home taken over by a crude and loud-mouthed woman, and he sees his alter ego, his double, who had been trying to keep him alive, finally withdraw. All doors are shut and he stands accused by the dead of his own guilt. He asks himself in anguish how to go on living, with whom, and for what. In a final turn the playwright involves the listeners. Beckmann appeals to them to provide an answer although he is secretly afraid that there might be no answer at all. The play shifts from the real to the melodramatic, combines documentary material with allegorical references, enriches the factual with dreams and hallucinations. *The Outsider* is characterized by an emotional discourse and a didactic purpose. It calls for empathy and friendly action in a landscape of death, betrayal, and pain.

M.H.S.

THE OUTSIDER

For Hans Quest
A play that no theater will produce
and no audience will care to see

CHARACTERS

BECKMANN, *one of the many*
his WIFE, *who forgot him*
her BOYFRIEND, *who loves her*
a GIRL, *whose husband came home on one leg*
her HUSBAND, *who dreamt of her a thousand nights*
a COLONEL, *who is very jovial*
his WIFE, *who gets the chills in her own living room*
the MOTHER,
the SON-IN-LAW,
the DAUGHTER, *right in the middle of supper*
her smart HUSBAND
a CABARET PRODUCER, *who would like to be decent—but then decides against it*
MRS. KRAMER, *who is simply Mrs. Kramer, which is just what's so awful*
the OLD MAN, *in whom no one believes anymore*
the UNDERTAKER *with the hiccoughs*
a STREET CLEANER, *who isn't really one at all*
the OTHER ONE, *whom everyone knows*
the RIVER ELBE

A man comes home to Germany.

He's been away for a long time, this man. A very long time. Perhaps too long. And he returns looking a lot different from the way he did before. Outwardly he is a near relation of those figures that stand around in the fields to scare birds (and sometimes, at least at night, scaring people too). Inwardly—he's the same. He has waited outside a thousand days in the cold. And as the price of admission he's had to forfeit his kneecap. And after he's waited outside in the cold a thousand nights, he really finally comes home.

A man comes home to Germany.

And there he sits through rather an astonishing piece of film. He has to pinch his arm continually during the performance, because he doesn't know whether he's waking or sleeping. But then he notices to the right and the left of him other people all living through the same experience. So he thinks that all this must really be the truth. Yes: at the very end when he's standing in the street again with an empty stomach and cold feet, he realizes that it was really a perfectly ordinary, everyday film. About a man who comes to Germany, one of many. One of the many who come home, but then don't come home, because there's no home for them anymore. And their home starts being outside the door somewhere. Their Germany is outside the door somewhere, in the rain at night in the street.

That is their Germany.

Prologue

The wind moans. The Elbe laps against pilings. It is evening. The undertaker. Against the evening sky a man's silhouette.

UNDERTAKER *(punctuating his words with belches)*: Urp! Urp! Just like—Urp! Just like flies! Yes, just like flies! Ahah! There's one now, there on that dock over there. Looks as though he's wearing a uniform. Yes, that's an old army overcoat. He's got no cap—and his hair's short as the bristles of a brush. He's standing rather near the water. Almost too near the water, actually. That's suspicious. People who stand near the water in the darkness are either lovers or poets. Or else he's one of that great gray number who've simply had it—who throw in their hand and won't play anymore. Yes, he looks as if he were one of those, that one over there does. Standing dangerously near the water. And pretty much alone there. Not a lover, he'd have someone with him there, then. Nor a poet—poets have long hair. And this one here has hair like the bristles of a brush. Interesting case, this one, very interesting.

A loud, abrupt splash. The silhouette has vanished.

Urp! There! He's gone. Jumped in. Standing too close to the water. Got him down, no doubt. And now he's gone. Urp! A man dies. So what? So nothing. The wind goes on blowing. The Elbe goes on gurgling. Streetcar bells still ring. Whores still lie, soft and white, there in their windows. Mr. Kramer rolls over on his other side and goes on snoring. And not a single clock falters in its onward course! Urp! A man is dead. So what? So nothing. Only a few circles in the water prove that he was ever there. And even they quickly disappear. And when they're gone, he's forgotten, without a trace, as if he'd never even existed. And that's all. Ahah! I hear someone crying. Interesting. An old man just standing there and crying. Good evening!

OLD MAN (*not complainingly, but more or less totally crushed*): Children! Children! My children!

UNDERTAKER: What are you crying about, old man?

OLD MAN: Because there is nothing I can do, oh my, because there is nothing I can do.

UNDERTAKER: Urp! Pardon me! That's certainly awful, yes indeed— but you've certainly no reason for breaking down that way like an abandoned bride or something. Urp! Pardon me!

OLD MAN: Oh, my children! They're all my children, don't you see?

UNDERTAKER: Ahah! (*pause*) Who are you, anyway?

OLD MAN: The God in whom no one believes anymore.

UNDERTAKER: And you're crying because—? Urp! Pardon me!

OLD MAN: Because I can do nothing about it. They shoot themselves. They hang themselves. They drown themselves. They go on murdering themselves, today a hundred, tomorrow a hundred thousand. And I, I can do nothing about it.

UNDERTAKER: Rough, rough, old man. Very rough. But nobody believes in you anymore, that's the way it goes.

GOD: Bad, bad, very bad. I am God—the God in whom no one believes anymore. Very bad indeed. And I can do nothing about it, my children, I can do nothing about it. Bad, bad, very bad.

UNDERTAKER: Urp! Pardon me! Like flies! Urp! Dammit!

GOD: Why do you keep belching so disgustingly? It's absolutely dreadful!

UNDERTAKER: Yes, yes, it's terrible. Just terrible. Occupational disease. I'm an undertaker.

GOD: What—Death? Oh, you're in good shape. You're the new God. They believe in you. They love you. They fear you. You can't be deposed. You can't be denied. No one can blaspheme against you. Yes, you're in good shape, all right. You're the new God. No one can slip through your fingers. You're the new God, Death, but you've grown fat. I remember you as quite different. Much thinner, drier, bonier, but you've grown round and fat and good-tempered. Before, Death used to look so starved.

DEATH: Why, yes, I have put on a wee bit of weight this century. Business has been good. One war after another. Like flies! The dead hang on the walls of this century just like flies. Like flies they lie stiff and dry on the window sill of the era.

GOD: But this belching? Why all this hideous belching?

DEATH: Overeating. Plain overeating. That's all. You just can't keep from belching nowadays. Urp! Pardon me!

GOD: Children! Children! And I can do nothing about it. Children, my children! *(exit)*

DEATH: Ah me, good night then, old man. Go to sleep. And watch out you don't fall in the water too; we lost one just a moment ago. Take very good care, old man. It's dark now, very dark. Urp! Go home, old man. There's nothing you can do about it anymore. Don't cry over the one who just splashed in over there. The one with the bristly hair, in the old army overcoat. You'll cry yourself to pieces! All these people who stand by the water at night—they're no longer lovers or poets. The boy who was here before—he's just one of those who simply can't go on, and who won't go on. And those who simply can't go on, at night, somewhere or other, step quietly into the water. Plop. Done with. Forget him, old man, don't weep. You'll just weep yourself to pieces. He was only one of those who can't go on, one of the great gray company— only *one.*

The Dream

In the Elbe. *Monotonous lapping of little waves.*

BECKMANN: Where am I? My God, where am I?

ELBE: With me.

BECKMANN: With you? And—who are you?

ELBE: Who do you think I am, my little chickadee, when you throw yourself into the water from the landing stage at St. Pauli?

BECKMANN: The Elbe?

ELBE: **Yes,** that's who. The Elbe.

BECKMANN (*astounded*): The Elbe? You?

ELBE: Well, that's opened your baby blue eyes for you a little, anyway, right? I bet you thought I was a romantic young maiden with a pale green complexion—the Ophelia type, with water lilies amid her flowing hair, right? You thought that when the end came you could spend eternity in my sweet-scented lily white arms, right? That was a mistake, my boy, quite a mistake. I'm neither romantic nor sweet-scented. A decent river stinks. Yes indeed—of oil and fish. Now, what do you want in here?

BECKMANN: Sleep. I can't take it anymore up there. I'm through. I want to sleep and be dead. Be dead for life. And sleep. Sleep in peace at last. Sleep for ten thousand nights.

ELBE: You mean, what you want to do, you little baby you, is cut out! Is that right? You think you can't stick it out up there, right? You like to kid yourself that you've been through enough, right? How old are you? you fainthearted little tenderfoot you.

BECKMANN: Twenty-five. And now I want to sleep.

ELBE: Just think of that, twenty-five! And he wants to sleep away the rest of it. Twenty-five, and in the fog and darkness he steps into the water, because he can't take it anymore. Just what can't you take, you poor sad old thing?

BECKMANN: Everything. I can't bear anything up there anymore. I can't bear starving anymore. I can't bear limping around up there anymore and standing by my own bed; and then limping out of the house again because the bed's been taken. My leg, my bed, even my bread—I can't stick it out anymore, don't you understand?

ELBE: No. You snotty-nosed little suicide. No, do *you* understand? Do you really suppose that just because your wife won't go beddy-by with you anymore, because you've a limp and your stomach rumbles, you're entitled to creep in here under my skirts? To go jumping into the water—just like that? Listen, if everyone who's hungry decided to drown himself, our good old earth would be as bare as an old man's dome, just as bare and as bright and shiny. No, my boy, we can't allow that to happen. You won't get around me with that sort of excuse. You're not going to get taken on around here. You're asking for a smack on your bottom, my little one. Yes indeed—even if you were a soldier for six years. Everyone was. And they're all limping around somewhere. If your bed isn't vacant, find yourself another. I don't want your miserable little slice of life. You're small fry to me, baby. Listen to an old woman's advice: live a little first. Let them kick you around a bit—and then kick back! And when you're fed up, thoroughly fed up, fed up right to here, when you're trampled out flat and when your heart comes around crawling on all fours, then maybe we can take up your case once again. But no nonsense just yet, is that clear? And now, my pretty one, get out of my sight. Your little handful of life is *too* damned little for my purposes. Keep it. I just don't want it, babykins. And now, keep your mouth shut a moment for a change: I'm going to tell you something, very quietly, for your ear alone. Come here. Now: I shit on your suicide! You suckling. Just watch what I'm going to do with you. *(loudly)* Hey, boys! Throw this baby out on the sand here at Blankenese. He's going to have another go at it—he's just promised me. But be gentle, he says he's got a bad leg, the little rascal, the quitter, the little damp-behind-the-ears beginner!

Scene 1

Evening at Blankenese. The sound of wind and water. Beckmann. The Other One.

BECKMANN: Who goes there? In the middle of the night! Here by the water. Hello—who's there?

THE OTHER ONE: I am.

BECKMANN: Thanks a lot. And who's I?

THE OTHER: I am the other one.

BECKMANN: The other one? What other one?

THE OTHER: The one from yesterday. The one from long ago. The one from always. The one who says yes. The one who answers.

BECKMANN: The one from long ago?—and from always? You're the other one from the school bench, from the ice-skating rink? The one from the stairwell?

THE OTHER: The one from the snowstorm near Smolensk. And the one from the bunker at Gorodok.

BECKMANN: And the one—the one from Stalingrad, that one, are you that one too?

THE OTHER: That one too. And also the one from last night. And the one from tomorrow morning.

BECKMANN: Tomorrow. There is no tomorrow. Tomorrow has no you in it, in any case. Beat it. You've no face.

THE OTHER: You won't get rid of me. I am the other one, the one who is always here. Tomorrow. In the afternoons. In bed. During the night.

BECKMANN: Beat it. I have no bed. I'm lying here in the dirt.

THE OTHER: I am also the one from the dirt. I am always there. Escape from me is impossible.

BECKMANN: You have no face. Go away.

THE OTHER: You cannot escape me. I have a thousand faces. I am the voice that everyone understands. I am the other one, the one who is always here. The other self, the answerer. Who laughs while you weep. Who drives you on when you're tired, the slave driver; I am the secret, disturbing one. I am the optimist who sees good in evil itself and light in the deepest darkness. I am the one who believes, who laughs, who loves! I am the one who marches on, lame or not. And the one who says yes, when you say no, the yea-sayer. And the. . . .

BECKMANN: Say yes as much as you like. Go away. I don't want you. I say No. No. No. Go away. I say no. Do you hear me?

THE OTHER: I hear you. That's why I'm staying. Who are you, you nay-sayer, you pessimist?

BECKMANN: My name's Beckmann.

THE OTHER: Have you no Christian name, pessimist?

BECKMANN: No. Not since yesterday. Since yesterday my only name has been Beckmann. Just Beckmann. The way a table is called a table.

THE OTHER: Who calls you table?

BECKMANN: My wife. No, the woman who was my wife. You see, I was away for three years. In Russia. And yesterday I came home again. And that's where I went wrong. Three years is quite a while, you know. And my wife called me Beckmann. Beckmann—plain and simple. Three years—and Beckmann is what she called me, as one calls a table, Table. Beckmann. A piece of furniture. Put it away, that Beckmann over there. So you see, that's why I don't have a Christian name anymore. Do you understand?

THE OTHER: And why are you lying here on the sand? In the middle of the night? Here by the water?

BECKMANN: Because I can't get up. You see, I happen to have brought back a game leg with me. As a kind of souvenir. Souvenirs aren't a bad idea, you know; otherwise wars are forgotten so, so quickly . . . and I didn't want that to happen at any price. It was all just too, too beautiful. Oh my oh my was it beautiful!

THE OTHER: And that's why you're lying here in the middle of the night, beside the water?

BECKMANN: I fell.

THE OTHER: Oh! You fell. You mean you fell into the water?

BECKMANN: No, no! No—listen closely now: I decided to *let* myself fall in. Deliberately! Couldn't take it any more, all this lameness and all this sameness. And then that little matter of the woman who used to be my wife—just called me Beckmann, as you call a table, Table. And the other fellow, the one who was with her then—he just grinned. And then all these ruins. This rubbish heap at home. Here in Hamburg. And somewhere underneath lies my boy. A bit of mud and mortar and debris. Human mud, bone mortar. He was just one year old, and I'd never seen him. And now I see him every single night. Under ten thousand stones. Debris, nothing but a bit of debris. I couldn't bear it, I thought. And so I decided to let myself fall in. It would be very easy, I thought: Off the end of the dock—plop! Done for. Finished.

THE OTHER: Plop? Done for? Finished? You've been dreaming. You're lying right here in the sand.

BECKMANN: Dreaming? Yes. Dreaming out of hunger—out of longing. I dreamt that she spat me out again, the Elbe, that old . . . she didn't even want me. I ought to have another crack at things, she said. I had no right to what I wanted. I was too green, she said. I shit on your lousy little life, that's what she said. She whispered it in my ear: "I shit on your suicide." Shit, she said, that damned old bag—and she screeched like a fishwife. Life is so grand, she said, and here I am lying around in my wet rags on the shore at Blankenese, ice-cold. I'm always ice-cold. I had enough cold in Russia. I'm sick of this everlasting freezing. And that damned old Elbe, that miserable old *bag*—Oh yes, I've been dreaming out of hunger. *(pause)* What's that?

THE OTHER: Someone's coming. A girl or something. There now! There she is!

GIRL: Is anyone there? Just now someone was talking I'm sure— Hello! Is there anyone there?

BECKMANN: Yes, lying here. Here. Down by the water.

GIRL: What do you think you're doing there? Why don't you get up?

BECKMANN: As you can see, I'm lying here—half on land and half in the water.

GIRL: And whatever for? Stand up—I thought at first it was a dead man when I saw that dark heap by the water.

BECKMANN: Yes indeed, dark heap is right all right.

GIRL: You've a funny way of talking, you know? Well, actually there are often dead bodies lying down here in the evening by the water. Sometimes they're all swollen and slippery. And as white as ghosts. That's why I was so frightened. But you're still alive, thank God. You must be wet through and through, though.

BECKMANN: Right you are. Wet and cold like a genuine corpse.

GIRL: Well then, stand up now. Or have you hurt yourself?

BECKMANN: Yes I have. They stole my kneecap from me. In Russia. And now I have to go limping through life with a stiff leg. And it always seems to be going backward instead of forward on me. So there's no question of my ever getting up again.

GIRL: Come along, come along. I'll help you. Otherwise you might slowly start turning into a fish.

BECKMANN: If you think I won't start flopping off backward again, we might give it another try. Ah. Thank you.

GIRL: You see, you've even gone *upwards* now! But you're ice-cold and wet to the skin. If I hadn't come by, you really would have turned into a fish soon. And you *are* just about speechless. May I make a little suggestion? I live right around here. And I have some dry things back at the house. Will you come with me? Yes? Or are you too proud to let me change those damp clothes of yours for you. You semifish, you! You dumb, soggy fish, you!

BECKMANN: You'll take me with you?

GIRL: Yes, if you like. But only because you're so wet. I hope you're very ugly and unbothersome so I'll never have any cause to regret any of this. I'm only taking you with me because you're so wet and cold, is that clear? And since—

BECKMANN: Since? Since what? No—only since I'm so wet and cold. There's no other "since."

GIRL: But there is. There is indeed. Since your voice is so hopelessly sad. So colorless and disconsolate—oh, that's all nonsense, isn't it? Come on now, you, my dumb, soggy old fish.

BECKMANN: Hey—stop! You're running away from me. My leg can't keep up with me. Slowly!

GIRL: Oh yes, that's right—so then: slowly. Like two prehistoric, age-old, ice-cold, soggy fishes.

THE OTHER: They're gone now. That's how they are, these strange bipeds, these two-legged creatures. Really bizarre people live here in this world! First they let themselves drop into the water, dead set on dying. Then quite by accident along comes through the darkness, this one with a skirt, with a bosom and long hair. And then life is suddenly sweet and splendid again. Then nobody wants to die anymore. They want *never* to be dead, then. And just because of a few locks of hair, a white skin and the scent of a woman. Then they leap up from their deathbeds as good as new, like ten thousand sprightly stags in the springtime. Then even half-drowned bodies come to life again. All those people who really and truly couldn't stand it any more on this wretched, miserable, damned old globe. Drowned people start wriggling again—and all because of a pair of eyes, all because of a little softness and warmth and sympathy, all because of two little hands and a slender neck. Even the drowned! Those bipeds! Those bizarre people here on this earth—

Scene 2

A room. Evening. A door creaks and slams shut. Beckmann. The Girl.

GIRL: There! Now we'll see just what sort of a fish we've caught. Lights on! Well— *(she laughs)* Well, in heaven's name, what are those supposed to be?

BECKMANN: These? These are my glasses. Yes—just go on and laugh. These are my glasses. Unfortunately.

GIRL: You call those glasses? I do believe you're trying to be funny.

BECKMANN: Yes, my glasses. You're right: perhaps they do look a little funny, with these gray tin strips going around the lenses. And then these gray bands that you have to fix around your ears. And this other gray band right across the nose! You get a kind of gray, standardized face. A sort of tin robot's face. A sort of gasmask face. But then they're gas-mask glasses.

GIRL: Gas-mask glasses?

BECKMANN: Gas-mask glasses—for soldiers who wore glasses. So a soldier could see with a gas mask on.

GIRL: But what do you still go around in them for? Don't you have another pair somewhere?

BECKMANN: No. I did have a pair, but they were shot to pieces. No, they're not exactly pretty, but I'm glad I've at least got these. They're extraordinarily ugly—I know that. And it does make me sort of nervous when people laugh at me. But it can't be helped. I can't do without them—without them I'm hopelessly lost. Really, absolutely helpless without them.

GIRL: Oh? You're absolutely helpless without them? *(gaily, not at all unkindly)* Then give me those disgraceful things at once! There—now what do you say? No, you're not getting them back again until you have to go. In any case, it's more reassuring to me to know that you're absolutely helpless. Much more reassuring. And you know—without glasses you immediately look like a changed man to me. I really believe you make such a melancholy impression because you have to go around looking through these appalling gas-mask glasses.

BECKMANN: Everything's just a blur to me now. Come on—hand

them over. I can't see a thing. Even you seem to be far away. Absolutely blurry.

GIRL: Wonderful! That suits me perfectly. And it suits you much better too. With those glasses you look like a ghost.

BECKMANN: Perhaps I am a ghost. One from yesterday, whom nobody wants to see today. A ghost from the war, temporarily repaired for peace.

GIRL *(sympathetically and warmly)*: And what a grouchy, gray old ghost you are! I really think that you wear a pair of these gas-mask glasses inside you, too, you self-appointed fish. Leave the glasses with me. It's not at all a bad idea for you to see things a little blurrily for one evening. Do those trousers fit you at least? *(looks)* Well now—I guess they'll do. Here, take the jacket.

BECKMANN: Look at this, will you! You pull me out of the water and then you inundate me again. This jacket was made for an Olympic weight lifter. You must go around robbing giants.

GIRL: The giant is my husband—was my husband.

BECKMANN: Your husband?

GIRL: Yes. Did you think I ran a haberdashery here?

BECKMANN: Where is he? Your husband?

GIRL *(quietly, bitterly)*: Starved, frozen, killed—how should I know? He's been missing since Stalingrad. It's been three years.

BECKMANN *(stunned)*: Stalingrad? In Stalingrad, yes. Yes, many were killed in Stalingrad. But some come back again. And they put on the clothes of those who don't. The man who was your husband, the giant, who owns these clothes, he was left lying there. And I, I come back now and put them on. That's wonderful, isn't it? Isn't that wonderful? And his jacket's so big I practically drown in it. *(hurriedly)* I must take it off. Right. I must put on my own wet one. This jacket's killing me. It's choking me, this jacket. I'm a joke in this jacket. A dirty, vulgar joke, made by the war. No—I won't wear this jacket.

GIRL *(warmly, desperately)*: Be quiet, Fish. Keep it on, please. I like you this way, Fish. In spite of your funny haircut. You brought that from Russia with you too, didn't you? With the glasses and the leg. See—I thought so. You mustn't think I'm laughing at you, Fish. No, Fish, I'm really not. You look so wonderfully sad, you poor gray ghost: in that floppy jacket, with your hair and your stiff leg. Relax, Fish, relax—I don't think it's so funny. No, Fish, you look wonderfully sad. I could cry when you look at me with those unconsolable eyes. And you're so quiet. Say something, Fish, please. Say anything. It doesn't have to make sense, just anything at all. Say something, Fish, the world's so terribly quiet. Say something, then it won't seem so lonely here. Open your mouth, please, Fish Man. Don't stand there all night. Come. Sit down. Here, beside me. Not so far away, Fish. No harm in coming closer, you can only see me blurrily anyway. Come on; you can even close your eyes as far as I'm concerned. Come and say something, so there's something here. Don't you feel how horribly quiet it is?

BECKMANN *(confused)*: I like looking at you. Yes—you. But I'm afraid that any step I take is going to be backward. Very afraid.

GIRL: There you go again. Forward, backward. Upward, downward. Tomorrow we may all be lying in the water, white and fat, quiet and cold. But today we're still warm. Still warm, Fish—come on and say something, Fish. You're not going to swim away this evening. And don't talk so much: I don't believe a word. And now I think I'd better lock the door.

BECKMANN: Don't do that. I'm no fish, and you've no need to lock the door. No—God knows I'm no fish.

GIRL *(affectionately)*: Fish! Oh Fish! You gray, wet, patched-up ghost.

BECKMANN *(suddenly far off)*: Something's smothering me. I'm sinking. I'm strangling—it's because I can't see properly. It's all completely blurred to me now—and it's strangling me.

GIRL *(fearfully)*: What's the matter? What's the matter with you? What's happening?

BECKMANN *(with increasing horror)*: Now I'm slowly but surely going crazy. Give me my glasses. Quickly. It's happening because everything's so misty now. There! I have the feeling that a man is standing behind your back. He's been there from the start. A big man. Like a sort of athlete. Like a giant, you know. But that's only because I haven't got my glasses—and the giant has only one leg. He's coming nearer, the giant's coming nearer with one leg and two crutches. Do you hear them—tick, tock. Tick tock. That's the sound of the crutches. Now he's standing right in back of you. Don't you feel his breath on your neck? Give me my glasses, I don't want to see him anymore! He's standing there now, right behind you!

> The Girl *screams and rushes out. A door creaks and slams shut. Then, very loudly, the "tick-tock" of crutches is heard.*

BECKMANN *(whispering)*: The giant!

ONE LEG *(in a flat, toneless voice)*: What are you doing here? You. In my clothes? In my place? With my wife?

BECKMANN *(weakly)*: Your clothes? Your place? Your wife?

ONE LEG *(tonelessly and apathetically)*: I'm asking you: what are you doing here?

Beckmann *(almost mumbling, and stumbling for words)*: That's what I asked the man who was with *my* wife last night. In my shirt. In my bed. What are you doing here? I asked. And he shrugged his shoulders and let them fall again and said: "Yes, what am I doing here?" That's what he answered. Then I shut the bedroom door again—no, first I put out the light again. And then I was outside.

ONE LEG: Let me see your face in the light. Come closer. *(in a hollow voice)* Beckmann!

BECKMANN: Yes. That's me. Beckmann. I didn't think you'd recognize me again.

ONE LEG *(quietly, but with immense reproach)*: Beckmann . . . Beckmann . . . Beckmann!!!

BECKMANN *(in agony)*: Shut up, you. Don't use that name to me! I won't have that name! Shut up!

ONE LEG *(tauntingly)*: Beckmann. Beckmann.

BECKMANN *(screaming)*: I'm not. I'm not that anymore. I won't be Beckmann anymore!

> *He runs out. A door creaks and slams shut. Then the wind is heard, and a man running through the silent streets.*

THE OTHER: Stop! Beckmann!

BECKMANN: Who's there?

THE OTHER: I. The other one.

BECKMANN: Are you here again?

THE OTHER: Still here, Beckmann. Always here.

BECKMANN: What do you want? Let me past.

THE OTHER: No, Beckmann. That path leads to the Elbe. Come, the road's up here.

BECKMANN: Let me by. I want the Elbe.

THE OTHER: No, Beckmann. Come. You want this road.

BECKMANN: Take this road? You mean I'm supposed to live? You mean I'm supposed to carry on? Supposed to eat, sleep, all the rest?

THE OTHER: Come, Beckmann.

BECKMANN (*more apathetic than actually angry*): Don't say that name. I won't be Beckmann anymore. I have no name anymore. So I'm to go ahead and live, when there's somebody—somebody with only one leg, somebody who's got only one leg, thanks to me? Who's got only one leg because there was once a Sergeant Beckmann who said: "Corporal Bauer, you'll hold your ground to the very last." I'm supposed to go on living, when there's this one-legged man who keeps repeating the name, Beckmann? Always, always—Beckmann! Spoken as if he were pronouncing the word *grave*, or the word *dog*, or the word *murder*. Who speaks my name the way you might say the word *doom*! Desperately, threateningly and hopelessly. And you say I ought to go on living? I'm outside, outside again. Last night I was outside. Today I've been outside. I'm outside forever. The doors are permanently shut. And yet I'm a man with legs that are tired and heavy. With a stomach that yells with hunger. With blood that's freezing out here in the night. And the one-legged man keeps saying my name. And at night I can't even sleep anymore. So where am I supposed to go, you? Where? Let me by!

THE OTHER: Come, Beckmann. We'll take the road. We'll pay a certain somebody a visit. And you'll give it back to him.

BECKMANN: Give what back?

THE OTHER: The responsibility.

BECKMANN: We'll pay somebody a visit? Yes, let's do that. And I'll give the responsibility back to him. Yes, we'll do that. I want a night's sleep without cripples. I'll give it back to him. Yes! I'll take the responsibility right back to him. I'll bring his own dead right back to him. To him! Yes, come, we'll pay somebody a visit, a certain somebody who lives in a nice warm house. In this town, in every town. We'll pay a man a visit, we want to give him a present—a dear, sweet, brave man, who his whole life long has only done his duty, always his duty! But it was a cruel duty! It was a frightful duty! A cursed—cursed—cursed duty! Come on now! Come on!

Scene 3

A room. Evening. A door creaks and slams shut. The Colonel *and his family.* Beckmann.

BECKMANN: *Bon apetit,* Colonel.
COLONEL *(chewing)*: Pardon?
BECKMANN: *Bon appetit,* Colonel.
COLONEL: You're interrupting supper. Is your business here that important?
BECKMANN: No. I only wanted to decide whether to drown myself tonight, or go on living. And if I am to go on living, just how to go about doing it. Days, I'd like a little something to eat now and then, perhaps. Nights, I'd like to sleep. That's all.
COLONEL: Come, come, come! Don't talk such unmanly nonsense. After all you were a soldier, weren't you?
BECKMANN: No, sir.
SON-IN-LAW: What do you mean, no? You're wearing a uniform, aren't you?
BECKMANN *(in a flat voice)*: Yes, that's right. For the last six years. But I always thought that even if I went around wearing a postman's uniform for ten years, I'd still be far from being a postman.
DAUGHTER: Daddy, do ask him what he really wants. He keeps on staring at my plate.
BECKMANN *(not unkindly)*: Your windows look so warm from outside there. I just wanted to remember again what it's like to look through windows like that. But from inside, from inside. Do you know what it's like to see such bright, glowing windows in the evening, and to be standing out there?
MOTHER *(without malice, but full of horror)*: Father, tell him to take off those glasses. It makes me shiver all over just looking at them.
COLONEL: Those are so-called special gas-mask glasses, my dear. Introduced into the armed forces in 1934 for personnel with bad eyesight, designed to be worn beneath one's gas mask. Why don't you throw those things away? The war's over.
BECKMANN: Yes, yes; it's over. That's what they all say. But I still need the glasses. I'm nearsighted; everything looks completely blurry

without them. But with them on, I don't miss a thing. From here for example I can see quite clearly what you've got on that table. . . .

COLONEL *(interrupting)*: Tell me now, just how did you get that remarkable haircut? You've been in jail, right? Been in a bit of a jam, right? Come on now, confess, you broke in someplace, right? And they caught you, right?

BECKMANN: Quite right, sir. Helped break in somewhere. Into Stalingrad, sir. But the job got bungled, and they nabbed us. We were sent up for three years, the whole hundred thousand of us. And our head man put on civvies and ate caviar. Three years of caviar! And the others lay under the snow with the sand of the steppes in their mouths. And we just went on spooning hot water from our soup bowls. But our head man had to eat caviar. For three years! And they shaved our heads. Either right down to the throat, or else just the hair, there was no definite ruling on that particular point. The ones with the amputated heads were the luckiest. At least they didn't have to go around eating caviar all the time.

SON-IN-LAW *(very annoyed)*: What do you think of that, Father! Did you hear? Well? What do you think of that?

COLONEL: My dear young friend, you're completely distorting the whole business, you know. We're all Germans—after all! Let's stick to good old German truth, my dear fellow. He who believes in the truth fights best—that's what General Clausewitz says.

BECKMANN: Right, sir. That's just fine, sir. I'm willing to play this game of truth. We eat until we're full, sir, really full. We put on a new shirt and a new suit with none of its buttons missing, and with no holes in it. And then we light the stove, sir, for indeed we do have a stove, sir. And we put on the teakettle so as to make some nice hot rum. And then we lower the blinds and drop into an armchair, for we have an armchair too, after all. We can smell our wife's fine perfume—but not blood, isn't that right sir, no blood—and we think about the clean white bed we have, just we two, sir, the bed that's waiting for us upstairs in the bedroom, so soft, so white, so warm. And then we believe in the truth, sir, our good, old German truth.

DAUGHTER: He's mad.

SON-IN-LAW: Nonsense, he's just drunk.

MOTHER: Please put a stop to it, Father. This person's giving me the chills.

COLONEL *(still mildly)*: You know I definitely get the impression that you're one of these people whose sense of things has been somewhat confused by that little touch of warfare. Why didn't you become an officer? You'd have traveled in different circles then—had a decent wife and a decent house by now, too. You'd have been quite a different person. Yes—why didn't you become an officer?

BECKMANN: My voice was too quiet, sir. My voice was just too quiet.

COLONEL: There you are: you're too quiet. Tell the truth: you're one of those kind of tired, run-down types, right?

BECKMANN: That's right, sir. That's it. Kind of quiet. Kind of run-down. And tired, sir, tired, so tired! You know I can't sleep, sir, same thing every night. And that's why I'm here, why I've come to see you, sir. I know you can help me. I want to be able to sleep again at last! That's all I want. Just sleep. Deep, deep sleep.

MOTHER: Father, protect us! I'm afraid. He gives me the chills.

DAUGHTER: Nonsense, Mother. He's just one of those people who haven't got all their marbles anymore—you know. Perfectly harmless.

SON-IN-LAW: I think the "gentleman's" quite uppity, myself.

COLONEL *(in a superior sort of way)*: Just leave everything to me, children, I've met this type before among the troops.

MOTHER: My God, he's half-asleep on his feet.

COLONEL *(almost paternally)*: They have to be dealt with a little sharply, that's all. I'll settle this, just leave it to me.

BECKMANN *(far away)*: Sir?

COLONEL: Well, what is it you want?

BECKMANN *(far away)*: Sir?

COLONEL: I'm listening, I'm listening.

BECKMANN *(drunk with sleep, dreamily)*: You're listening, sir? That's fine then, if you're able to listen, sir. I'd like to tell you about my dream. The dream I dream every night. Then I wake up, because somebody's screaming so horribly. And do you know who's screaming? It's me, sir, I am. Funny, isn't it, sir? And then I can't fall asleep again. Every night, sir, just think of it, lying awake every night. That's why I'm tired, sir, so horribly tired.

MOTHER: Protect us, Father. I feel cold.

COLONEL (*interested*): And your dream wakes you up, you say?

BECKMANN: No, it's when I scream. It's not the dream but the scream.

COLONEL (*interested*): But the dream is the cause of the scream, right?

BECKMANN: There you are—you've got it. Dream causes scream. And it's a most unusual dream, I ought to tell you, too. I'll just describe it a little to you. You're listening, sir, aren't you? A man stands there playing the xylophone. He plays the most wild, abandoned rhythm. And he sweats, this man, because he's extraordinarily fat. And he's playing on a gigantic xylophone. And because he's so fat he has to lunge about wildly to reach all the notes. And he sweats, because he's really very fat. But it's not sweat that he sweats, that's the odd thing. He sweats blood, steaming, dark blood. And the blood runs down his trousers in two broad red stripes, so that from far away he looks like a general. Like a general! A fat, bloodstained general. He must be quite a seasoned old campaigner of a general, too, for he's lost both arms. Yes, he plays with long artificial arms that look like mechanical grenade launchers, wooden, with two metal rings. He must be quite an odd old musician too, this general, because the keys of his xylophone aren't made of wood. No, believe me, sir, believe me, they're made of bones. Believe me, sir, bones!

COLONEL (*quietly*): Yes, I believe you. They're made of bones.

BECKMANN (*still in a trance, in a haunted voice*): Yes, not wood, bones. Wonderful white bones. He's got skull bones, shoulder blades, pelvises. And for the high notes, arms and leg bones. And then ribs—thousands of ribs. And finally, right at the end of the xylophone, where the very highest notes are, he's got little finger-bones, toes, teeth. Yes, right at the end come the teeth. And that's the xylophone played by the fat man with the general's stripes. Isn't he a joke of a musician, this general?

COLONEL (*uncertainly*): Yes, that's right, a joke. A great big joke!

BECKMANN: Yes, and now it really gets going. Now the dream really begins. Now: the general stands in front of his gigantic xylophone of human bones, and with his artificial arms beats out a march. "Glory be to Prussia" or "The Badenweiler." But mostly he plays "The Entry of the Gladiators" and "The Old Comrades." Mostly he plays those. You know that one, sir, don't you, "The Old Comrades"? *(hums)*

COLONEL: Yes, yes. Of course. *(also hums)*

BECKMAN: And then they come. Then they advance, the Gladiators, the Old Comrades. Then they rise up from their mass military graves, and their bloody moaning and groaning stinks to the high white moon. And that's what makes the nights the way they are. As piercing as cat pee. As red, as red as raspberry juice on a white shirt. That's when the nights become so close that we can't even breathe. That's when we smother if we have no mouth to kiss and no liquor to drink. That bloody moaning and groaning stinks to the moon, sir, to the high white moon, when the dead come, the lemonade-spotted dead.

DAUGHTER: I told you—he's crazy! He says the moon is supposed to be white! White!—The moon!

COLONEL *(soberly)*: Nonsense. The moon is quite obviously yellow, and always has been yellow. Like honey bread. Like an omelette. The moon's always been yellow.

BECKMANN: Oh no, sir. Oh no! These nights when the dead go walking around she's white and sick. Like the belly of a pregnant girl drowned in a stream. So white, so sick, so round! No, sir, the moon is white on these nights when the dead go walking around and the bloody moaning and groaning stinks to the moon, as cutting as cat pee against the white sick moon. Blood. Blood. Then they rise up from their mass graves with rotting bandages and bloodstained uniforms. They materialize from forests, from streets and ruins, they desubmerge from the oceans, from the steppes and the marshes, frozen black, green, moldering. They come up out of the steppes, one-eyed, one-armed, toothless, legless, and with their insides torn to shreds, without skulls, without hands, shot through, stinking, blind. They come together in a fearful flood, immeasurable in numbers, immeasurable in agony! The fearful immeasurable flood of the dead overflows the banks of its graves and rolls thick, pulpy, diseased and bloody over the earth. And then the general with his stripes of blood says to me: "Sergeant Beckmann, assume command—it's your responsibility. Count off!" And then I stand there, before the millions of grinning skeletons, before all those bits and pieces of bone, stand there with my responsibility, and order them to count off. But the company won't count off. Their jaws twitch horribly—but they won't count off for me. The general orders fifty deep knee bends for punishment. The rotting bones rattle, lungs hiss and wheeze, but they won't count off. Is that not mutiny, sir? Outright mutiny?

COLONEL *(whispers)*: Yes, outright mutiny.

BECKMANN: They'll all be damned if they'll count off. But then these ghosts do line up, get into formation—and form choruses. Thundering, droning, hollow-voiced choruses. And do you know what they roar, Colonel?

COLONEL *(whispers)*: No.

BECKMANN: Beckmann, they roar. Sergeant Beckmann. Always Sergeant Beckmann. And the roaring grows. The roaring rises, brutal as the cry of some God, strange, cold, gigantic. And the roaring grows and rolls, grows and rolls!—It grows so huge, so smothering and huge that I can't breathe anymore. And then I scream, then I scream out in the night. Then I have to scream, scream so terribly, so terribly. And it always wakes me up. Every night. Every night the concert on the bone xylophone, every night the choruses, and every night the terrible screaming. And then I can't go back to sleep again, because I had assumed command, because I had assumed the responsibility. Yes, the responsibility was mine. And that's why I've come to you, sir, because I want at last to be able to sleep again. I want to sleep once more, and that's why I've come: just to be able to sleep, just sleep.

COLONEL: What do you want of me?

BECKMANN: I'm bringing it back to you.

COLONEL: What?

BECKMANN *(in a naïve voice)*: Why, the responsibility. I'm bringing you back the responsibility. Have you completely forgotten, sir? The fourteenth of February? At Gorodok. It was forty-two below zero. You came to our post, sir, and said: "Sergeant Beckmann." "Here," I shouted. Then you said, and your breath hung like ice on your fur collar—I remember that quite distinctly because you had a very beautiful fur collar—then you said: "Sergeant Beckmann, I'm giving you responsibility for these twenty men. You'll patrol the forest to the east of Gorodok and if possible take a few prisoners, is that clear?" "Very good, sir," I answered you. And then we set off and patrolled. And I—I had the responsibility. We were on patrol all night, and there was some shooting, and when we got back to our post, eleven men were missing. And I had the responsibility. And that's all, sir. But now the war's over, now I want to sleep, now I'm giving you back the responsibility, sir, I don't want it any more, I'm giving it back to you, Colonel.

COLONEL: But, my dear Beckmann, you're exciting yourself unnecessarily. It wasn't meant like that at all.

BECKMANN (*without excitement, but earnestly indeed*): It was. It was, Colonel. It must have been meant like that. Responsibility is not simply a word, a chemical formula for transforming warm human flesh into dark cold earth. You just can't let men die for the sake of an empty word. Somewhere along the line we've got to take our responsibility. The dead don't answer. God doesn't answer. But the living go on asking. They go on asking every night, sir. While I lie there awake, they come and they ask. Women, sir, sad, lamenting women. Old women with gray hair and hard, cracked hands—young women with lonely, longing eyes; children, sir, children, a *very* great number of little children. And out of the darkness they whisper: Sergeant Beckmann, where is my father, Sergeant Beckmann? Sergeant Beckmann, what did you do with my husband? Sergeant Beckmann, where is my son, where is my brother, Sergeant Beckmann, where is my fiancé, Sergeant Beckmann? Sergeant Beckmann, where? Where? Where? And so they whisper, until it gets light. There are only eleven women, sir, only eleven women who come to me. How many come to you, sir? A thousand? Two thousand? Do you sleep well, sir? Then I suppose it won't make any difference to you if I add to your two thousand the responsibility for my eleven. Can you sleep, sir? With two thousand ghosts every night? Can you even live, sir, can you live a single minute without screaming? Sir, sir, do you sleep well at night? If you can, this won't bother you, and I'll be able to sleep again at last—if you'll only be so kind as to take it back from me, this responsibility. Then finally my soul will be able to sleep in peace. Peace in my soul, yes, that's what I want—just a little peace in my soul, sir!

And then: sleep! Oh my God, sleep!

COLONEL (*he finally seems a bit affected by all this. But then he laughs aloud, not disagreeably—with rough joviality, quite good-naturedly; then he says, rather uncertainly*): Young man, young man! I just don't know about you—I really just don't know. You aren't deep down one of these pacifists, are you? Just a soupçon of the nihilist in you, perhaps? But—*(He begins to laugh quietly to himself; then his hearty old Prussianism taking over, he bellows at the top of his lungs:)* My dear boy, my dear boy! I'd almost suspect you of being a bit of a wag, you know that? Am I right? Well? You're a joker, isn't that it? *(he laughs)* Delicious, you're absolutely delicious! You're a regular pro at it! That good old basic humor! You know *(he is again overcome with laughter)*, you know, with that material, with those gags, you should really be on the stage! (The Colonel *actually doesn't wish to offend* Beckmann, *but he is so hearty, so naïve and so much the old soldier that he can only grasp* Beckmann's *dream as a joke, a prank.*) Those absurd glasses, that silly mess of a haircut! You should be set to music. *(laughs)* My God, that priceless dream of yours! The deep knee bends, those deep knee bends to that xylophone music! My dear boy, you'd be a smash hit on the stage with all that! The whole world will laugh itself half to death over it! Oh my God! *(laughs wheezingly, with tears in his eyes)* I honestly didn't realize at first that it was all a comic routine. I figured you didn't have all your marbles or something. I never would have taken you for such a comedian at first. Now, my dear young man, you've given us a delightful evening, and that's worth something in return. You know what! Go down to see my chauffeur, get some hot water, wash yourself, get rid of that stubble on your chin. Make yourself human. And then have my chauffeur give you one of my old suits. Yes, I'm absolutely serious! Throw those rags of yours away and put on one of my old suits. Go on, you can accept in all good conscience, my boy! And then you'll feel yourself becoming human again at least!

BECKMANN *(coming to; also coming out of his apathy for the first time)*: Human? Become? I'm supposed to become human again at least? *(yells)* I'm supposed to become human at least you say? What are you supposed to be then? Human? Well? Human? Are you supposed to be human? Are you?

MOTHER *(screams shrilly and jumps up; something is knocked over)*: Oh no! He'll kill us all! Oh no, no!

> Great tumult; the voices of the family are heard shrieking at one another:

SON-IN-LAW: Somebody grab the lamp!

DAUGHTER: Help! The light's out! Mother upset the lamp!

COLONEL: Quiet, children, quiet!

MOTHER: Put the light on!

SON-IN-LAW: Where did the lamp go?

COLONEL: Look—it's right over there.

MOTHER: Thank God we've got our light back.

SON-IN-LAW: And that character's gone. I suspected right off there was something the matter with that guy.

DAUGHTER: One, two, three—four. No, everything's still here. But the serving dish is broken.

COLONEL: Damn it, it is. What on earth could he have been after?

SON-IN-LAW: Perhaps he really was just plain crazy.

DAUGHTER: No—look! Our bottle of rum's missing!

MOTHER: Oh my, Father, all your lovely rum.

DAUGHTER: And that half-loaf of bread—it's gone too!

COLONEL: What's that? Our bread?

MOTHER: He ran off with that loaf of bread? Whatever would he want with half a loaf of bread?

SON-IN-LAW: Perhaps he wants to eat it. Or sell it someplace. Those people stop at nothing!

DAUGHTER: Yes, that's right, perhaps he wants to eat it.

MOTHER: Yes, maybe—but just plain dry bread—?

A door creaks and slams shut.

BECKMANN (*out in the street again; a bottle gurgles*): Those people are right. (*gradually getting drunker and drunker*) Down the hatch! That warms you up, all right. No, those people are right. Are we all supposed to sit around and think about death, when he's right on our heels? Down the hatch! Those people are right. The dead are piling up over our heads. Ten million yesterday. Today—thirty million. Tomorrow somebody's going to come along and blow up an entire continent. By next week they'll be able to manage the murder of everyone on earth with ten grams of poison, all in about seven seconds. And we're supposed to just sit around and mourn? Down the hatch! I've got a deep dark suspicion that pretty soon we should start looking around for another planet for ourselves. Down the hatch! Those people are right. I'm off to the circus. They're right all right. The Colonel laughed himself silly. He says I should go on the stage. Limping, with this coat, with my face and with these glasses on it, with my brush-bristle hairdo on my head—the Colonel's right, humanity's going to laugh itself to death. Down the hatch! Long live the Colonel! He's saved my life. Hail, hail, the Colonel. Down the hatch! Long live bloodshed! Long live laughter at the expense of the dead! Yes, I'll go to the circus, people will laugh themselves silly when it gets really gruesome, with blood and bodies lying all over the place. Come on, let's toast it all again! This booze has saved my life, my brains are submerged, I'm soused. Down the hatch! *(grandiosely and drunkenly)* Whoever has booze or a bed or a broad, let him dream his last! Tomorrow may be too late! Let him build a Noah's Ark of his dream and sail sousing and singing over all the horror and into eternal darkness. Let the others drown in dread and despair! Whoever has booze shall be saved! Down the hatch! Long live the bloodstained Colonel! Long live responsibility! All hail, all hail! I'm off to the circus. Long live the circus! The whole damned circus!

Scene 4

A room. A Cabaret Producer. Beckmann, *still slightly tipsy.*

PRODUCER *(with great conviction)*: So you see, it's precisely here in the field of art that we really need youth most again, a youth which will take a fresh, active stand on all our problems today. A courageous, sober—

BECKMANN *(to himself)*: Yes, it absolutely must be sober.

PRODUCER: —and revolutionary youth. We need the spirit of a Schiller, who wrote his play *The Robbers* at the age of twenty. We need a Grabbe, a Heinrich Heine! That's the kind of aggressive genius we need today! An unromantic, realistic, sturdy youth which looks the dark side of life straight in the eye, unsentimentally, objectively, with detachment. We need a *true* youth, a generation that understands the world as it is, and loves it the way it is. Which prizes truth, which has plans, projects. They needn't be the most profound truths in the world, of course—for heaven's sake, we want nothing finished, mature, serene. It should all be like a cry, a cry from the heart. Questions, hopes, longings, hungers!

BECKMANN *(to himself)*: Hunger, ah, yes, that we have.

PRODUCER: But this youth must be young, passionate, courageous.

Particularly in art! Now look at me: when I was seventeen years old I stood there on the cabaret stage and showed all those petty bourgeoisie in the audience my teeth—*I* spoiled the taste of their cigars, believe me. What we lack is an avant-garde, the kind perpetually poised to present the living gray suffering face of our times!

BECKMANN *(to himself)*: Yes, yes: "present," and then "present" again. They "present" faces. They "present" arms. They "present" ghosts. They've always got to "present" something.

PRODUCER: Did you say face? That reminds me: why do you run around in those grotesque glasses? Where did you ever find such weird things, anyway? Just looking at you gives me the hiccups. That's really quite a bizarre piece of mechanism you've got sitting on your nose there.

BECKMANN *(automatically)*: These are my gas-mask glasses. We got them in the army—at least those of us who needed them did—so that even in gas masks we could recognize the enemy and strike him down.

PRODUCER: But the war has been over for months now! We've been lolling around in the lap of civilian luxury for ages! How can you possibly still show up in that military regalia?

BECKMANN: You mustn't hold it against me—I just arrived from Siberia the day before yesterday. *(half to himself)* The day before yesterday? Yes, the day before yesterday.

PRODUCER: Siberia? Dreadful—just dreadful! Oh, that terrible war! But those glasses—don't you have another pair?

BECKMANN: I'm lucky to have these at least. They've been my salvation. It's the only salvation there is—the only pair of glasses I have, I mean.

PRODUCER: My dear fellow, why didn't you just put aside a spare pair somewhere?

BECKMANN: Where? In Siberia?

PRODUCER: Oh. Of course. That silly Siberia! Look here—observe how I've covered myself on this matter of glasses. *(he digs in his pocket)* Yes, my boy! I am the proud possessor of three pairs of first-class horn-rimmed glasses. *(he holds up three pair)* Genuine horn, my friend! A yellow pair for work. An unobtrusive pair for going out. And in the evening—for stage purposes, you understand—a heavy black pair. And the result, my friend: class!

BECKMANN: And I don't even have anything I could give you in exchange for one. I know I look all thrown together and patched up. *(pointing at glasses)* I know how preposterous these things seem, but what can I do? Couldn't you perhaps—

PRODUCER: My dear man, whatever are you thinking of? I can't spare a single one. All my inspirations, my moods, my whole *effect* depend on them.

BECKMANN: That's the problem: all mine do too. And it's hard to get a drink every day these days, too. And when that's gone, life is like lead: rough, gray, and worthless. But just think—on stage these fantastically hideous glasses would probably be quiet effective.

PRODUCER: What? How do you mean?

BECKMANN: I mean: they'd seem humorous. People laugh themselves sick when they see me in these glasses, right? And then there's the haircut and the coat. And my face, just think, my face! It's all terribly funny, don't you think?

PRODUCER *(gradually contracting a slight case of the creeps)*: Funny? Funny? The laughter will probably stick in their throats, my dear man. Just looking at you will send cold horror creeping up their necks: naked fear in the face of a ghost from the underworld. You know, really, people want to use art for pleasure, to be elevated, edified by—they can do without looking at visions of ice-cold ghosts. No, we can't just let you loose on them like that. The approach has to be more genial, more self-assured—cheerier. Positive! Yes, my dear man, positive! Consider Goethe! Think of Mozart! The Maid of Orleans! Richard Wagner! Max Schmeling! Shirley Temple!

BECKMANN: Well, I can't really compete with names like that, I'll admit. I'm just Beckmann. Begins with *B*—ends with eckmann.

PRODUCER: Beckmann? Beckmann? At the moment it doesn't ring a bell with me in cabaret. Have you been working under a stage name?

BECKMANN: No, I'm sort of new. I'm a beginner, in fact.

PRODUCER: *(complete about-face)*: A beginner? Now look—things in this life aren't quite that easy. Not quite that easy in the least! You can't walk into a career just like that! You underestimate the promoter's responsibility! Presenting a beginner can mean absolute ruin. The public wants names!

BECKMANN: Goethe, Schmeling. Shirley Temple and so on, eh?

PRODUCER: Precisely. Not beginners, newcomers, complete un-
knowns! How old are you?

BECKMANN: Twenty-five.

PRODUCER: There, you see. Let the wind blow past your nose a little,
young man. Inhale the fragrance of life. What sort of thing have
you been doing up till now?

BECKMANN: Not much. War. Been starved, frozen; used a rifle: war.
That's all.

PRODUCER: Is that all? Well what's that supposed to amount to? Let
yourself mature on the battlefield of life, my dear boy. Work!
Make a name for yourself, then we'll make you a star. Learn to
know the world, then come back again. Become somebody!

BECKMANN (*who has thus far been subdued, now gradually becomes more and more excited*): And where shall I start? Where?
A man has to be given a chance someplace. Somewhere or other a
beginner must begin. The wind didn't go blowing past our noses
too much in Russia, did it; but then metal did, a great deal of
metal. Hot, hard, heartless metal. Where are we to begin then,
anyway? Tell me, exactly where? Yes, we want to get the show on
the road, damn it!

PRODUCER: Take it easy. After all, I didn't send anybody off to
Siberia—that had nothing to do with me.

BECKMANN: That's right: nobody sent us to Siberia. We went on our
own. All of us, on our own. And some decided to stay out there,
all on their own. Under the snow, under the sand. The ones who
stayed out there had a chance, the dead ones. But as for us—we
can't get a start anywhere. Nowhere.

PRODUCER (*resigned*): All right, all right. Start, then. Please. Just
stand there and start. But don't take too long. Time is money.
Please, now: be so kind as to proceed. Begin. I'm giving you your
big chance, a real opportunity. You're a very lucky man: I'm
lending you my ear now. You should appreciate that, young man,
you should appreciate that—believe me! So in God's name, start.
Please. Ah. Here we go now—

> Soft xylophone music. The tune of "Tapferen kleinen Sol-
> datenfrau" may be recognized.

BECKMANN (*sings, almost speaking, softly, apathetically and mo-
notonously*):

> Brave little soldier's wife

That old song haunts my life
Oh that sweet, that charming song
But really: everything went wrong.
Refrain:
   I hear the whole world's laughter
   At the things I suffer.
   And the mists of a long, long evening
   Cloud over everything.
   Only a grinning moon
   May be seen
   Through one of the holes in my curtain.

Coming home just now I saw
My bed was far from empty.
If I cared about anything anymore
I'd find some way to end this misery.
Refrain:
   I hear the whole world's laughter
   At the things I suffer.
   And the mists of a long, long evening
   Cloud over everything.
   Only a grinning moon
   May be seen
   Through one of the holes in my curtain.

By the time that midnight came
I'd had myself another woman.
About Germany we made very little fuss,
And Germany didn't bother us.
The night was short, morning came,
I saw him standing there in the door:
Mr. One-Leg, her husband,
And that was in the morning—around four.
Refrain:
   I hear the whole world's laughter
   At the things I suffer.
   And the mists of a long, long evening
   Cloud over everything.
   Only a grinning moon

May be seen
Through one of the holes in my curtain.

Now I run around outside again
Remembering, remembering the old refrain:
The song of the fast—
The song of the fast—
The song of the fastidious little soldier's wife.
  The xylophone dies away.

PRODUCER *(cowed)*: Well—that wasn't so bad at all, no, not so bad.
A good try—and for a beginner, very good. But of course, my dear
boy, the whole thing could use a little more spirit! It doesn't
sparkle enough. It lacks a certain polish. And of course it's not
really a true lyric yet. It lacks the delicate tone, the discreet,
piquant erotic quality the infidelity theme demands. The public
wants to be tickled, not *pinched* like that. But still, it's a very good
try, considering your youth. The moral, the sense of a deeper
wisdom, are lacking, but still, as I say, not at all bad for a
beginner. It is, though, a bit too explicit, too obvious—

BECKMANN *(to himself)*: Too obvious. . . .

PRODUCER:—yes, too loud. Too direct, if you follow me. Of course,
with your youth you lack that genial—

BECKMANN *(slowly, to himself)*: Genial. . . .

PRODUCER: —sense of serenity, of assurance. Think of that great old
master, Goethe. Goethe! who accompanied his duke to the battlefield, and there, around the old campfire, wrote an operetta.

BECKMANN *(softly, to himself)*: An operetta. . . .

PRODUCER: That's genius for you! That's what makes all the difference!

BECKMANN: Yes, one must admit, there's quite a difference there.

PRODUCER: My friend, tell you what—let's wait a couple of years, all
right?

BECKMANN: Wait? I'm hungry! I've got to work!

PRODUCER: Yes, but your art needs time to mature. So far your
delivery lacks elegance, lacks experience. It's too bleak, too naked.
You'll upset my public! No, we can't force black bread on people
when—

BECKMANN *(softly, to himself)*: Black bread. . . .

PRODUCER: —when what they want is cake. Have a little patience.

Work on yourself, become slicker, smoother—mature! Yes; nice try, as I say, a very nice try; but still—it's not art.

BECKMANN: Art! Art! But it's the truth!

PRODUCER: Truth! Truth has nothing to do with art!

BECKMANN (*softly, to himself*): No. . . .

PRODUCER: Truth won't get you anyplace!

BECKMANN (*softly, to himself*): No. . . .

PRODUCER: No—it'll only make you unpopular! Where would we all be if everybody suddenly started telling the truth? Who wants to know anything about things like truth these days? Well? Who? Never let yourself forget that fact.

BECKMANN (*bitterly*): Yes, yes. I understand now. And I thank you. Slowly I'm beginning to understand. It's a fact you can't forget. (*his voice gets harsher and harsher; by the time he opens the door he is almost shouting*) You musn't ever forget: truth won't get you anywhere. Truth will only make you unpopular. And who wants to hear anything about truth these days? (*very loud now*) Yes, slowly I'm beginning to understand, these are the facts—

> Beckmann *goes out without any leave-taking. A door creaks and slams shut.*

PRODUCER: Hey—hey, young man! Why did you suddenly get so touchy!?

BECKMANN (*outside, despairingly*):

> The booze was finished
> The world turned hard
> As the skin of some savage beast—
> Armored.

And this road heads straight down to the Elbe.

THE OTHER: Stay here, Beckmann. This is the road! Here! Up here!

BECKMANN: That road smells of blood. They massacred truth there. My road goes to the Elbe. And that's the one down here.

THE OTHER: Come, Beckmann. Don't give in! Truth lives!

BECKMANN: Truth is like the town whore. Everybody knows her, but nonetheless, it's embarrassing to meet her in the street. Therefore one must try it out at night, and in secret. In the daylight they're gray, raw, and ugly—both the whore and the truth. And some never stomach either of them as long as they live.

THE OTHER: Come, Beckmann. There's always a door open somewhere.

BECKMANN: Yes, for Goethe. For Shirley Temple or Schmeling. But I'm just Beckmann. Beckmann with the funny glasses and the funny haircut. Beckmann with the game leg and the old Santa Claus suit. I'm just a bad joke made by the war, a ghost of yesterday. And because I'm just Beckmann and not Mozart, every door is shut tight. Bang. That's why I stand outside. Bang. And again: Bang. Always, always: Bang. Here I am outside again: Bang. And because I'm a beginner I can't begin anywhere. And because I'm too quiet I wasn't commissioned. And because I'm too loud I frighten the public. And because I've a heart that cries at night for the dead I'm told that I have to become "a little human again." And in the Colonel's old suit!

 The booze is finished
 The world turns hard
 As the skin of same savage beast—
 Armored.

That road stinks of blood, because they massacred truth there, and every door is shut. I want to go home, but all the streets are dark. Only the path to the Elbe is light. Oh, how light!

THE OTHER: Stay here, Beckmann. This is your road up here. This is the way home. You must go home, Beckmann. Your father is sitting in the living room and waiting. And already your mother's standing at the door. She recognized your footsteps.

BECKMANN: My God! Home! Yes, I'll go back home. I'll go to my mother. I'll go at last to my mother!!! To my—

THE OTHER: Come. This is your way, straight home. It's true: the place one should go first is always the last one thinks of.

BECKMANN: Home, where my mother is, my mother—

Scene 5

A house. A door. Beckmann.

BECKMANN: Our house is still standing! And it has a door—and that door is open just for me. My mother is there and my mother will open the door and I'll enter. To think that our house is still standing! And listen—the steps still creak, too. And there—our door. My father comes out of it every day at eight in the morning. And every evening at six he enters it again. Except for Sundays. He fumbles with his bunch of keys and mumbles a little to himself. Every single day. A whole lifetime. And there my mother goes in and out—three, seven, perhaps ten times a day. Every single day. Her whole life long. That, *that* is our door. Behind it the kitchen door squeaks, behind it the clock with its deep, deep tones ticks away the irrecoverable hours. Behind it I used to sit on a chair turned around backwards and pretend it was the seat of a racing car. And behind it my father coughs. Behind it the running faucets gurgle and the kitchen tiles click as my mother fusses about. That's our door. Behind it a life is unwound from an inexhaustible reel. A life which has gone on, unchanged, for thirty years. And which will always go on. War has passed this door by. It hasn't broken it down, it hasn't ripped it off its hinges. It has left our door standing, purely by chance; an oversight. And now the door's there for me. It will open for me; it will close behind me, and I won't be outside anymore. Then I'll be home—*home*. That's our old door with the paint peeling off and the dented letterbox. With the wobbly white bell push and the shining brass plate, which my mother polishes every morning and which bears our name: Beckmann—

No! the brass plate's missing! Why isn't the brass plate there? Who's taken our name away? What's this dirty card on the door? With this strange name? Nobody named Kramer lives here! Why isn't our name still on the door? It's been there for thirty years. It can't simply be removed and another just stuck in its place! Where's our brass plate? The other names in the house are still on their doors. As always. Why isn't Beckmann there too? You can't simply nail on a new name when Beckmann's been there for thirty years! Who's this Kramer, anyway?

> *He rings. The door opens.*

MRS. KRAMER (*with an indifferent, chilling, cheery amiability, more terrible than any outright rudeness or outright brutality*): What can I do for you?

BECKMANN: Oh, good morning, I was just—

MRS. KRAMER: Yes?

BECKMANN: Do you know where our brass plate's gone?

MRS. KRAMER: What do you mean, "our brass plate"?

BECKMANN: The nameplate that's always been here—thirty years!

MRS. KRAMER: How should I know?

BECKMANN: Then you don't know where my parents are?

MRS. KRAMER: Who are they? And who are you?

BECKMANN: My name's Beckmann. I was born here. This is our apartment.

MRS. KRAMER *(still chatty and mildly snotty, rather than deliberately nasty)*: No, you're wrong there, it's our apartment. For all I care, you *were* born here, but this isn't your apartment. It's ours.

BECKMANN: Yes, yes, I see—but what's happened to my parents then? They must be living somewhere.

MRS. KRAMER: You're the son of those people, the Beckmanns, is that it? Your name is Beckmann?

BECKMANN: Yes, of course, Beckmann. I was born here in this very house.

MRS. KRAMER: That's fine—I really couldn't care less one way or the other, though. You see, the apartment's *ours* now.

BECKMANN: But my parents! Where are my parents staying? Can't you tell me where I can find them?

MRS. KRAMER: You mean you actually don't know? Well, you're a fine son, you are. You actually don't know?

BECKMANN: For God's sake, where could those old people have gone!? They've lived here thirty years, and now they're simply not here any more? Tell me—they must be someplace!

MRS. KRAMER: They are. As far as I know: Plot Five.

BECKMANN: Plot Five. What's Plot Five mean?

MRS. KRAMER *(resigned to the effort of explanation; still casual, rather than simply brutal)*: Plot Five at Ohlsdorf. Do you know what Ohlsdorf is? It's a cemetery. Do you know where Ohlsdorf is? It's near Fuhlsbüttel. Three city train lines have last stops out there. In Fuhlsbüttel the prison, in Alsterdorf the insane asylum. And in Ohlsdorf the cemetery. Do you see—that's where they stay now, those old people of yours. That's where they live now. Moved away, left, departed. And you really didn't know?

BECKMANN *(dazed; half to himself, half to Mrs. Kramer)*: What are they doing out there? Can they really be dead? But they were alive just now. How could I know anything about this? I've been in Siberia three years—more than a thousand days. They're dead? But they were here just now. Why did they have to die before I could get home? There wasn't anything wrong with them. My father had a cough—but he'd always had it. And my mother used to say that the tiles on the kitchen floor gave her cold feet all the time. You don't die of things like that. They had no reason to die. They can't just have suddenly, mysteriously died like that.

MRS. KRAMER *(vulgar, familiar; and with a sudden touch of coarse sentimentality)*: You're really too much—just too much, you silly son you! Oh well, all right, skip it. A thousand days in Siberia is certainly no joke at that—I guess it really can knock your feet out from under you. Well, what happened was that the old Beckmanns just couldn't take it anymore. You know. They were just a wee bit overboard during the Third Reich—if you follow. Why should an old man like him want to go around wearing a uniform, anyway? And he was a bit nutty about the Jews, as his son you know that, don't you? Your old man couldn't stand them—in fact, they gave him fits. He was always announcing that he'd like to chase them all back to Palestine, single-handed. In the air-raid shelter, you know, every single time a bomb went off he'd let loose about the Jews. He was a bit too active, your old man. He gave a bit too much of himself to the Nazis. Then, when the Brownshirts disappeared, he found himself high and dry, your father did. And all just over the Jews. He really did overdo it. Why couldn't he keep his mouth shut, anyway? He was just too involved, old Beckmann was. And when it was over with those brown-shirted boys, the authorities came around and touched him on his sore spot. Yes, and a very sensitive sore spot it was, too, believe me, very sensitive by that time. And—you know, I have to tell you: you're really killing me with those ridiculous things you've got on your nose for glasses. You're an absolute holy terror in them. You can't tell me those are sensible glasses. Haven't you got a regular pair, young man?

BECKMANN *(automatically)*: No. These are the gas-mask glasses which soldiers were issued who—

MRS. KRAMER: I know that all right—but you wouldn't catch me going around with those things on. I'd stay at home first. You know what my dear better half would say to you if he saw you? He'd say: *achtung,* young man, off with that bridgework!

BECKMANN: Yes—go on: what happened to my father? You're confusing me—go on, Mrs. Kramer, go on!

MRS. KRAMER: Well, there's really nothing else to say. They gave your dad the sack, without benefit of pension, of course. And then they had to get out of the house, too—and all they could keep were the shirts on their backs. It was a sad, sad situation, of course, I guess that pretty much finished them off. The old people just couldn't cope with it all. They didn't even want to, I guess. So—they denazified themselves once and for all. That was very consistent of your old man, I'll say that about him.

BECKMANN: What was that? You say they—

MRS. KRAMER *(chattily; still not consciously being mean)*: Denazified themselves. Just an expression, you know. Sort of a little private joke with us. Yes, those parents of yours had had it. They were found one morning stretched out stiff and blue in the kitchen. Pretty stupid, my better half said; with all that gas we could have done a month's cooking!

BECKMANN *(softly, but with enormous menace)*: I think it would be a very good idea if you shut that door now, and shut it fast. Fast! And you'd better lock it! I'm warning you to shut that door!

Mrs. Kramer *screams; the door slams shut.*

BECKMANN *(softly)*: I can't stand it! I can't stand it! I can't stand it!

THE OTHER: Yes, Beckmann, yes. One can stand it.

BECKMANN: No! I can't—I can't anymore! Go away! You soft-headed optimistic idiot! Go away!

THE OTHER: No, Beckmann. Your road's up here. Keep going, Beckmann, keep going—you've still a long way to go. Come!

BECKMANN: You filthy swine! Oh, sure, "one can stand it," oh, sure. You can stand it, *you* can stand going on this way. Sometimes it takes your breath away—other times you want to kill someone. But you go on breathing anyway and the murder doesn't happen. And you don't scream anymore and you don't sob anymore. You stand it. You stick it out. Two corpses! Who bothers these days about two little corpses.

THE OTHER: Quiet, Beckmann. Come!

BECKMANN: Naturally it's rather vexing when they happen to be your parents, these two little corpses. But then, two corpses, two old people? Too bad about the gas, though! We might have done a month's cooking with it!

THE OTHER: Never mind, Beckmann. Come. The road's waiting for you.

BECKMANN: Yes, never mind. When one has a heart that's screaming, a heart that'd commit murder in a minute. A poor idiot of a heart that would murder these mourners who regret only the passing away of—gas! A heart that wants to sleep, deep in the Elbe—do you understand me! A heart that has screamed itself hoarse; and no one has even heard it. No one below. No one above. Two old people have wandered off to Ohlsdorf cemetery. Yesterday it was perhaps two thousand, the day before yesterday perhaps seventy thousand. Tomorrow it'll be four hundred thousand or six million—all just wandered off into the world's mass graves. Who cares? No one. Not a soul below—not a God above. God sleeps, and we just go on living.

THE OTHER: Beckmann! Beckmann! Don't think about it, Beckmann. You see everything through your gas-mask glasses. You see everything distortedly, Beckmann. Pay no attention. There was *once* a time, Beckmann, when people reading the evening newspapers under the greenish lights of Capetown would sigh, sigh deeply for two little girls frozen to death in the ice of Alaska. There was *once* a time when they couldn't sleep in Hamburg because a child had been kidnapped in Boston. There was *once* a time when it could happen that they mourned in San Francisco if a balloonist crashed in Paris.

BECKMANN: There was once a time, once, once! When was it? Ten thousand years ago? It takes casualty lists running to seven digits to get any kind of reaction now. And people don't even sigh in the lamplight any more, they sleep deeply and peacefully—at least when they still have a bed to sleep in. People stare right past each other, stunned by so much agony: hollow-cheeked, hard, bitter, warped, and lonely. They're fed with numbers, numbers that are so long they can hardly pronounce them. And what the numbers stand for—

THE OTHER: Don't think about it, don't think about it.

BECKMANN: No, *do* think about it, think about it until you go to pieces! The numbers are so long you can hardly pronounce them. And what the numbers stand for are—

THE OTHER: Don't think about it!

BECKMANN: Yes, think about it! They stand for the dead, the half-dead, men killed by grenades, by shrapnel, starvation, bombs, freezing, drowning, despair, the lost, the bewildered, the lifeless. And those numbers have more digits than we have fingers!

THE OTHER: Never mind, never mind—the road is waiting for you, Beckmann, come!

BECKMANN: Tell me, tell me for the love of God, where does it lead? Where are we now? Are we still here? Is this still the old earth? Haven't we grown fur yet? Or tails? Or fangs? Or claws? Do we really still go around on two legs? Man! Man! What kind of road are you? Where do you lead? Answer me that, you other one, you great optimist! You eternal Answerer—answer me that!

THE OTHER: You're losing the way, Beckmann; come, stay up here, your road is here! Don't think, don't. The road goes both up and down. Don't cry out when it goes down, and everything falls into darkness—the road goes on, and everywhere there are lamps and lights: the sun, stars, women, windows, light bulbs and opened doors. Don't cry out if you have to stand alone at night for half an hour in the fog. You'll come across others eventually. Come on, boy, don't get tired! Don't listen to that sweet xylophone player's sentimental tripe, don't listen.

BECKMANN: Don't listen? And that's your answer? Millions of the dead, half-dead, unaccounted for—and that just doesn't matter? And you tell me: just don't listen! I've lost my way, you say? Yes, this road's gray, terrible, abysmal. But we're out here on it just the same—limping, weeping, and starving; poor, cold, and tired! And the Elbe threw me up again like rotten meat. The Elbe won't let me sleep. I'm supposed to live, you say! Live *this* life? Tell me exactly why: for whom? For what?

THE OTHER: For yourself! For life itself! Your road is waiting. And every so often there are lights. Are you such a coward that you're afraid of the darkness between them? Do you want only lights? Come, then, Beckmann, go now to the next light.

BECKMANN: Listen to me now: I'm hungry and it's cold—understand? I can't stand up anymore, I'm exhausted. Open a door somewhere. I'm hungry. The road's dark and all the doors are shut. Optimist, save your breath for somebody else: I'm homesick. Yes—even for my own mother, for black bread. It doesn't even have to be those old special dinner biscuits—that's not necessary now. My mother would have had a piece of black bread for me, and warm socks. And then I would have sat myself down, cozy and full, right next to the Colonel—and I would have sat there and read Dostoyevsky. Or Gorky. It's wonderful when one's warm and full to read about the misery of other people, and sit there so sympathetically, sighing. But unfortunately my eyes keep shutting on me; I'm dog-tired. And I want to yawn like a dog—yawn my whole head off. And I can't go on. I'm tired, I'm tired. There's no going on—do you understand me? I won't and I can't. Not even an inch. Not even—

THE OTHER: Beckmann, don't give up. Come, Beckmann, life's waiting, Beckmann, come!

BECKMANN: I don't want to read Dostoyevsky, I'm afraid enough as it is, all by myself. I'm not coming. No. I'm tired. No, I'm not, I'm *not* coming. I want to sleep. Here in front of my door. I'll sit down on the steps in front of my door, and then I'll sleep. I'll sleep—sleep until someday the walls of the house begin to collapse from old age. Or until the next mobilization. I'm as tired as the rest of this whole yawning world!

THE OTHER: Don't tire, Beckmann. Come. Live!

BECKMANN: This life? No, this life is less than no life at all. I won't do it. Don't you know what you're saying? "Come on, everybody; the show has to keep going until it's over. Who knows in what dark corner we shall lie or on which sweet bosom by the time the curtain finally, finally falls?" Five gray, rain-drenched acts.

THE OTHER: Get on with it, then, Beckmann, be alive with life!

BECKMANN: Be quiet. Life is as follows:

Act I: Gray skies. Somebody is hurt.

Act II: Gray skies. Somebody hurts back.

Act III: It gets a little darker and it rains.

Act IV: It gets much darker. Somebody sees a door.

Act V: It is night, the dead of night, and the door is shut. A man stands outside—outside that door. He stands by the Elbe, by the Seine, by the Volga, by the Mississippi. He stands there thinking, cold, hungry and damned, damned tired. And then suddenly there's a splash, and the waves make neat little round circles, and the curtain falls. Worms and fishes burst into noiseless applause.—And that's the way it goes. Is that really anything more than nothing at all? I—I, at any rate, won't go on with the show anymore. My yawns are as enormous as the whole wide world.

THE OTHER: Stay awake, Beckmann! You must go on.

BECKMANN: What was that?—You suddenly sound so muted to me. . . .

THE OTHER: Get up. Beckmann, the road is waiting.

BECKMANN: The road will have to survive without my weary tread. But why are you so far away suddenly? I can hardly—hardly—under—stand. . . . *(he yawns)*

THE OTHER: Beckmann! Beckmann!

BECKMANN: Hmmmmm. . . . *(he falls asleep)*

THE OTHER: Beckmann, you're asleep!

BECKMANN *(in sleep)*: Right—I'm asleep.

THE OTHER: Stop that right now—you have to live!

BECKMANN: No thanks—I wouldn't think of waking up. I'm dreaming now. I'm dreaming a wonderful dream.

THE OTHER: No more dreaming, Beckmann—you have to live.

BECKMANN: Live? No, never; I'm dreaming right now that I'm dying.

THE OTHER: Stand up, I'm telling you—live!

BECKMANN: No. I don't ever want to get up again. I'm having such a wonderful dream. I'm lying in the road and I'm dying. My lungs won't go on, my heart won't go on, and my legs won't go on, either. The entire Beckmann won't go on, in fact, do you hear? Rank disobedience, that's what it is. Sergeant Beckmann says he won't go on—now isn't that just wonderful?

THE OTHER: Come, Beckmann, you must keep on going.

BECKMANN: Keep on going? Keep on going, you mean, keep on going downward! *À bas,* as the French say. It's really quite delightful to die, you know, I'd never have thought it. I'm getting the idea that death must be quite tolerable after all. After all, nobody's come back because he couldn't stand death, has he? Perhaps death's quite nice, perhaps much nicer than life. Perhaps— Do you know, I actually believe I'm already in heaven. I can't feel anything anymore—and isn't that just like being in heaven, not to feel anything anymore? And here comes an old man looking rather like God. Yes, almost like God himself. Except that he looks a little too theological, come to think of it. And he's in tears. Can that possibly be God? Good evening, old man. You're not God, are you?

GOD *(tearfully)*: I'm God all right, my poor dear boy.

BECKMANN: Oh, so you're God, are you. Who actually called you that, God? Mankind? Well? Or is that what you call yourself?

GOD: Mankind calls me God, "dear God," in fact, usually.

BECKMANN: Odd, they must be very unusual men to go around calling you that. They must be the Contented, the Satisfied, the Very Lucky Ones—or, of course, those who are afraid of you. Those who walk in the sunshine of life, those in love, or satisfied or contented in general—or else those who are frightened at night. Yes, they say: God! Dear God! But I don't say dear God, understand, because I don't happen to be acquainted with any "dear God."

GOD: My child, my poor—

BECKMANN: When exactly are you dear, dear God, anyway? Were you dear when you let my little son, my little son who was exactly one year old, get torn to pieces by a screaming bomb? Were you dear when you let him get murdered that way, dear God?

GOD: I didn't have him murdered.

BECKMANN: Right, exactly right. You only *let* him get murdered. You didn't bother yourself when he started screaming and those bombs started exploding. Where were you actually, when those bombs were exploding, dear God? And were you dear, when one night eleven men from my patrol were missing? Eleven men shot, dear God, and you weren't there either, dear God. Those eleven men must have screamed awfully loudly in that lonely wood, but you weren't there, dear God, you simply weren't there. Were you dear in Stalingrad, dear God, were you dear there? Well? Well? When in fact were you dear, then, God, when? When have you ever bothered yourself about us, God?

GOD: No one believes in me anymore. Neither you nor anyone else. I am the God no one believes in anymore. No one bothers himself about me anymore. No—not a single one of you cares about me anymore.

BECKMANN: Has God been studying theology too? Who's supposed to care for whom, you want to know? Oh, you're old, God, all right, you're old-fashioned; you can't just cope with our long lists of the dead, with our agonies now. We really don't know you anymore, you're a fairy-tale God. Today we need a new one. One for our own misery and our own particular fear. A completely new one. Oh, we've searched for you, God, believe me, in every shell hole, during every passing night. We've called for you, God! We've roared for you, wept for you, cursed for you. And where were you then, dear God? Where are you this very evening? Have you turned away from us? Have you completely walled yourself up in those picturesque, lovely old churches of yours? Can't you hear our cries through the shattered windows, God? Where are you?

GOD: My children have turned away from me, not I from them. You from me, you from me. I am the God whom nobody believes in anymore. You have turned away from me.

BECKMANN: Go away, old man—you're spoiling my death. Go away, you're just one more tired, pitiful old theologian. You play around with phrases: who cares for whom? Who's turned away from whom? You from me? We from you? You are dead, God. Live—live with us, live with us at night when it's cold and lonely and when we can hear our stomachs in the silence—live with us then, God. Oh, go away, you ink-blooded theologian, just go away. You pitiful, pitiful old man.

GOD: My boy, my poor, poor boy. I can't help it! I just cannot, cannot help it.

BECKMANN: Yes, that's it, God. You just can't help it. And we're not afraid of you anymore. And we don't love you anymore. And you're too old-fashioned. The theologians have let you grow old. Your pants have patches in them, your shoes are worn through and your voice has become a squeak—a squeak against the thundering of our time. We just can't hear you anymore.

GOD: No, no one hears me anymore, ever. You're all too loud!

BECKMANN: Or are you too quiet, God? Have you too much ink in your blood, God, too much thin theologian's ink? Go away now, old man, you've walled yourself up there inside your fine old churches, we can't hear each other anymore. Go—and before total darkness falls make sure that you find yourself a little out-of-the-way hole somewhere, or a fine new suit, or dark forest to hide in; otherwise they're sure to stick you with the blame when everything's finally fallen completely to pieces. And don't slip in the dark, old man, the road is steep, and strewn with skeletons. Hold your nose, God. And then sleep well, old man, which is only to say: sleep as well as you always do anyway. Good night!

GOD: A new suit or a dark forest? My poor, poor children. My dear, dear boy—

BECKMANN: Just go! Good night now!

GOD: My poor, poor. . . . *(he goes off)*

BECKMANN: Old people have it the hardest of all these days; they have difficulty adjusting to new conditions. We're all outside. Even God's outside here, and no one opens any doors, even for him. Only death, only death has a door left for us. And that's exactly where I'm headed.

THE OTHER: You mustn't just wait for the door death opens. Life has a thousand doors. Who promised you that behind death's door anything exists but emptiness?

BECKMANN: And what's behind the doors that life opens for us?

THE OTHER: Life! Life itself! Come, you must go on.

BECKMANN: I can't, I can't. Just listen to the way these lungs of mine are wheezing—*(he coughs unconvincingly)*—wheeze—wheeze— wheeze! See? I just can't.

THE OTHER: You can. Your lungs are *not* wheezing.

BECKMANN: My lungs are *so* wheezing. What could be wheezing if not my lungs? Listen: wheeze—wheeze—wheeze! What else?

THE OTHER: A street cleaner's push broom! Look, there's one coming now. He's coming past us, and his push broom's scratching down the street like asthmatic lungs. See—your lungs weren't wheezing at all. It was just the push broom—see? Hear it: whisk—whisk—whisk!

BECKMANN *(bitterly)*: Yes, that's right, the sounds of the lungs of a man in his death rattle sound like a street cleaner's broom. And look—that street cleaner has red stripes down his trouser legs. He's a street cleaner general. A member of the High Command of the street cleaners. And when he pushes that broom of his, lungs in their death rattlings go wheeze—wheeze—wheeze. Hey, street cleaner!

STREET CLEANER: I am *not* a street cleaner.

BECKMANN: You aren't a street cleaner? What are you then?

STREET CLEANER: I'm an employee of the Rubbish, Refuse, and Remains Interment Institute.

BECKMANN: You're Death? And you work as a street cleaner?

STREET CLEANER: Today a street cleaner; yesterday a general. Death isn't particularly choosy, you know. The dead are everywhere, right? And lately they actually lie all over the sidewalks and streets. Yesterday they lay on the battlefield—then Death was a general and the accompaniment a xylophone. Today they lie all over the streets and the push broom of Death goes wheeze— wheeze.

BECKMANN: And the push broom goes wheeze—wheeze? From general to street cleaner. Are the dead so devaluated?

STREET CLEANER: They're going down all right, they're going down. No salute. No tolling bell. No funeral oration. No war memorial. They're going down. And the push broom goes wheeze—wheeze!

BECKMANN: Must you go so soon? Stay here a moment, won't you? I mean—take me with you. Death, Death, you're forgetting me—Death!

STREET CLEANER: I forget no one. My xylophone plays "The Old Comrades," and my push broom goes wheeze—wheeze—wheeze! I forget no one.

BECKMANN: Death, Death, leave the door open for me. Death, don't shut your door. Death—

STREET CLEANER: My door is always open. Always. Morning, afternoon, and night. In light and in darkness. My door is always open. Always and everywhere. And my push broom goes wheeze—wheeze.

The noise grows softer as Death *moves off.*

BECKMANN: Wheeze—wheeze. Do you hear how my lungs are wheezing? Like a street cleaner's broom. And the street cleaner leaves his door wide open. And the street cleaner's name is Death. And his push broom sounds just like my lungs, or like a tired, rusty old clock: wheeze—wheeze. . . .

THE OTHER: Beckmann, stand up now, there's still time. Come, breathe, breathe yourself well again.

BECKMANN: But my lungs sound just like—

THE OTHER: Not your lungs, not your lungs. Just an old broom, Beckmann, a civil servant's push broom.

BECKMANN: A civil servant?

THE OTHER: Yes, and now he's far, far away. Come, stand up again, breathe. Life is waiting with a thousand lights and a thousand open doors.

BECKMANN: Just one door, just that one would be enough. And he's leaving it open for me, he said, always and anytime. One door.

THE OTHER: Stand up, you're dreaming a deadly dream. You'll die of your dream. Stand up.

BECKMANN: No, I'll stay here. Here in front of the door. And the door is open—that's what he said. Here I'll stay. Am I really supposed to stand up—when I'm having such a wonderful dream? I'm dreaming, dreaming that it's all over. A street cleaner came by and identified himself as Death. And his broom whisked along just like my lungs. A dead ringer for them. And he promised me a door, an open door. Street cleaners can be really delightful people. Delightful as death. Yes, he was really quite, quite delightful.

THE OTHER: You're dreaming, Beckmann, you're dreaming an evil dream. Wake up, live!

BECKMANN: Live? I'm lying here in this street and it's all over now, all, all over. I'm unquestionably, indisputably dead. It's all over and I'm dead, beautifully dead.

THE OTHER: Beckmann, Beckmann, you must live. Look—everyone's alive. Beside you. To the left, to the right, in front of you: all the others. And you? Where are you? Live, Beckmann, everyone's alive.

BECKMANN: Everyone? Who's everyone? The Colonel? The producer? Mrs. Kramer? Live along with them, you mean? Oh, I'm so wonderfully, wonderfully dead! All those people are far, far away, and I never want to have to see them again. Those people are murderers.

THE OTHER: Beckmann, you're lying.

BECKMANN: I'm lying? Aren't they all evil? You mean they're good?

THE OTHER: You don't know people. They're good.

BECKMANN: Oh, they're good, all right. And in all goodness they've killed me. Laughed me to death. Shown me the door. Chased me away. In all human goodness. They are hardened even when they dream. Hardened even in the depths of their deepest dreams. And they casually pass by my corpse—hardened even in sleep. They laugh and chew and sing and sleep and digest their way casually past my corpse. My death is nothing.

THE OTHER: You're wrong, Beckmann.

BECKMANN: No! Optimist, face it: these people do, quite casually, pass by my corpse. Corpses are, after all, unpleasant and boring.

THE OTHER: Mankind does not casually pass by your death, Beckmann. Mankind has a heart. Mankind mourns your death, Beckmann, and your corpse lies in their way when they want to fall asleep at night. They don't pass casually by.

BECKMANN: Oh yes they do, optimist. Corpses are most unsightly, most unpleasant. They just go by as fast as possible holding their noses and shutting their eyes.

THE OTHER: They do not! Their hearts contract at every corpse!

BECKMANN: Look—here comes somebody now. Do you remember him? It's the Colonel who wanted to make a new man out of me by letting me have his old suit. Colonel! Colonel!

COLONEL: Merciful heavens—beggars again! It's just like old times.

BECKMANN: Exactly, sir, exactly. Just like old times. From the same background, the same beggars. But I'm not actually a beggar, sir, to tell the truth. I'm a drowned corpse. I'm a deserter, sir. I was a very tired trooper, sir. Yesterday I was Sergeant Beckmann, sir, do you remember? Beckmann. I was rather on the soft side, wasn't I, sir, remember? Yes, and tomorrow evening I shall drift dumb and numb and bloated onto the beach at Blankenese. Awful, isn't it, sir. And you'll have me on your account then, Colonel. Just awful, right? Two thousand and eleven plus Beckmann makes two thousand and twelve. Two thousand and twelve ghosts a night, brr!

COLONEL: Never seen you before in my life, my good man. Never heard of any Beckmann. What rank did you hold?

BECKMANN: But, sir! Surely you must still remember your last murder! The one with the gas-mask glasses and the convict's haircut and the game leg?! Sergeant Beckmann, Colonel!

COLONEL: Yes—of course! *That* character! Just goes to show: you can't depend in the least on these lower ranks. Imbeciles, guardhouse lawyers, pacifists, hari-kari candidates. So you finally drowned yourself, eh? Yes, that's right, you were the type that got a little tangled up, a little overly upset during the war; yes indeed, utterly lacking in military qualities. A truly unfortunate sight, a thing like that.

BECKMANN: Yes, isn't it, Colonel, a truly unfortunate sight indeed, all these soft, white corpses in the water nowadays. And you're the murderer, sir, you! Can you really stand it, Colonel, being a murderer? How does it feel to be a murderer, sir?

COLONEL: What's that? What do you mean? Me?

BECKMANN: Yes, Colonel, you laughed me to death. Your laughter sounded more dreadful to me than all the deaths in the world, Colonel. You actually laughed me to death, sir, you actually did!

COLONEL (*completely uncomprehending*): Really? Oh well. You were the type that would have ended up by going to the dogs, anyway. And now, good evening.

BECKMANN: Pleasant dreams, Colonel. And many thanks for the obituary! Well, did you hear, optimist, you great friend of man? Obituary for a drowned soldier. Epitaph of a man for a man.

THE OTHER: You're dreaming, Beckmann, you're dreaming. Mankind is good.

BECKMANN: You're beginning to sound a little hoarse, you with that optimistic obbligato of yours! Has all this begun to ruin your voice? Oh, yes, mankind is good. However, there *do* seem to be days when you keep on incessantly running into the few bad ones there are. But mankind's not really all that bad. Oh, no. And I'm only dreaming. I don't want to be unjust. Mankind is good. It's only that they're all so terribly different, right?—so incredibly, incredibly different. This man's a colonel, that man's just some lower rank or other. The Colonel's content, healthy, and goes around in nice, snug woolen underwear. And at night he has a bed and a wife.

THE OTHER: Beckmann, stop dreaming! Stand up now and live. You're dreaming everything wrong.

BECKMANN: And the other man—he starves, he limps and hasn't even a shirt any more. At night he has an old deck chair as a bed, and the squeaking of asthmatic rats from some cellar takes the place of his wife's whispering. No, mankind is good. Only their representatives *do* vary—they're really quite extraordinarily different and various.

THE OTHER: Mankind is good. Only they are so, so unaware. Perpetually unaware. But their hearts, look into their hearts— their hearts are good. Only life won't allow them to show their hearts. But don't disbelieve that at bottom they're good.

BECKMANN: Oh, naturally. At bottom. But the bottom is usually so deep, so very, very incredibly deep. Yes, at bottom they're good— just different. One is white and the other is gray. One has pants and the other hasn't. And that gray one there, without the pants—that's me. Had a run of bad luck: Corpse Beckmann, formerly Sergeant Beckmann (retired), fellow creature (retired).

THE OTHER: You're dreaming, Beckmann, get up. Life! Come, see, mankind is good.

BECKMANN: And they pass by my corpse and chew and laugh and

spit and digest. That's how they pass my death by, the very kindliest of your good ones.

THE OTHER: Wake up, dreamer! You're dreaming an evil dream, Beckmann. Wake up!

BECKMANN: Oh, yes, I'm dreaming a terribly evil dream, all right. And here comes our cabaret director now. Dare I engage him in a bit of conversation, answerer?

THE OTHER: Come, Beckmann! Live! The street is full of lamps. Everyone's alive! Live with them!

BECKMANN: Live with them? With whom? With the Colonel? No!

THE OTHER: With the others, Beckmann. Live with all the others.

BECKMANN: And with that producer?

THE OTHER: With him as well. With everyone.

BECKMANN: Fine. With the producer as well. Greetings to you, Mr. Producer!

PRODUCER: What's that? Yes—what's the matter?

BECKMANN: Do you recognize me?

PRODUCER: No—Oh yes, just a moment now. Gas-mask glasses, Russian haircut, soldier's overcoat. Yes—the beginner with the little chanson about marital infidelity, right? What was your name again?

BECKMANN: Beckmann.

PRODUCER: Of course. Well?

BECKMANN: You murdered me, Mr. Producer.

PRODUCER: But, my dear boy—

BECKMANN: Yes you did. Because you were a coward. Because you betrayed truth. You drove me straight into the River Elbe, because you wouldn't give that beginner a chance to begin. I wanted to work. I was starving. But you shut your door behind me. You chased me straight into the Elbe, Mr. Producer.

PRODUCER: Must have been quite a sensitive boy, running into the Elbe like that, into that damp. . . .

BECKMANN: Straight into that damp, deep Elbe, Mr. Producer. And there I let myself slowly fill up with Elbe water—I was full for once, Mr. Producer, but I unfortunately died of it. Tragic, isn't it? A real killer-diller for your revue, right? A little chanson for our time: full for once, but died of it.

PRODUCER (*sympathetic, but only superficially*): That's just terrible—terrible! You were one of those overly sensitive types, I suppose. Such a mistake today, completely out of step. You were completely possessed by truth, weren't you, you little fanatic! You'd have had whole audiences skipping out on me with that song of yours!

BECKMANN: And so you slammed the door on me, Mr. Producer. And just a little further on lay the Elbe.

PRODUCER *(as above)*: Yes, the Elbe. Drowned. Through. Kaput. Poor old thing. Run over by life. Overwhelmed and flattened. Finally filled up—and so finally finished off. Well, if we were all as "sensitive" as that. . . !

BECKMANN: Never fear, Mr. Producer; we're not all as sensitive as that.

PRODUCER *(as above)*: No; God knows we're not, no. You were merely one of those poor miserable millions of people who have to limp through life and who are actually happy when they fall. Into the Elbe, into the Spree, into the Thames—it doesn't matter where. Until then they don't know a single moment's peace.

BECKMANN: And so you just tripped me up a little, to help me fall.

PRODUCER: Nonsense! Who ever said that? Can't you see—you were cut out for tragic roles. Your material's a knockout! "The Ballad of a Beginner"! The Floating Body with the Gas-Mask Glasses! Tsk, tsk, too bad the public doesn't want that sort of thing, tsk tsk, just too, too bad. . . . *(he leaves)*

BECKMANN: Pleasant dreams, Mr. Producer! Well—did you hear? Shall I go on living with the Colonel? Go on living with the Producer?

THE OTHER: You're dreaming, Beckmann, wake up.

BECKMANN: Am I really dreaming? Is it possible that I do see everything twisted and distorted through these damned gas-mask glasses? Can they really all be puppets? Grotesque, caricatured, human puppets? Did you hear the obituary my murderer dedicated to me? Epitaph for a beginner: "Just one more of the infinitely many." Did you hear that, you Other—shall I go on living now? Shall I go limping along the road? With all those others? They've all got the identical dreadfully indifferent faces. They chatter and mutter endlessly as they go—but if anyone tries to get a single yes out of them they go numb and dumb, like—yes, like all humanity. And they're afraid. They've betrayed us. Betrayed us so terribly. Listen. When we were quite young they decided to make war. And as we grew older they told us stories about their war. Enthusiastically—about this they never failed to be enthusiastic. And so when we grew just a little bit older they thought they'd think up a war for us, too. And then they sent us off to fight it. They were enthusiastic, one thing they never failed to be was enthusiastic. But nobody told us exactly where we were going. Nobody happened to mention that we were going straight to hell. Not a living soul. They made up marching songs and held celebrations. They thought up heroes' songs and initiation ceremonies for us. And then court-martial proceedings and campaigns. They never failed to be enthusiastic. And finally came the actual war. And they enthusiastically shipped us off to it. And they told us just this one thing: "Do a good job, boys!" That was the sum of their advice. And that's how they betrayed us. So dreadfully betrayed us. And now they're all sitting there—behind their doors. The Professor, the Producer, the Judge, the Doctor. But no one's shipped us off anywhere this time. Oh no, far from it. They're all sitting there behind their doors—and the doors are shut tight, very tight. And we're here, outside. And from their pulpits and from their armchairs they point their fingers at us. That's how they've betrayed us. Betrayed us terribly. And now they ignore their murderings, simply ignore them. Or pass them by without looking.

THE OTHER: They don't ignore them, Beckmann. You exaggerate. You're dreaming. Look at their hearts, Beckmann. They have hearts. They're good!

BECKMANN: But Mrs. Kramer ignores my corpse.

THE OTHER: No! Even she has feelings!

BECKMANN: Mrs. Kramer!

MRS. KRAMER: Yes?

BECKMANN: Do you really have feelings, Mrs. Kramer? Where were you keeping them, Mrs. Kramer, when you murdered me? That's right, Mrs. Kramer, you murdered the old Beckmanns' son. And didn't you finish off his parents as well—now honestly, Mrs. Kramer, you did "assist" them a little, didn't you? Maybe made their life just a little sour for them somehow, perhaps? And then chased their son straight into the Elbe—but ah, your feelings, Mrs. Kramer, just what do your feelings say now?

MRS. KRAMER: You with the funny glasses—you threw yourself into the Elbe? I thought something was a little odd about you, right off. You looked so sad, too, poor little thing. Yes, I might have known it. Threw himself into the Elbe! Poor baby! Imagine!

BECKMANN: Yes, because you informed me so sympathetically and truly tactfully of the passing away of my parents. Your door was really the very last one for me. And you let me go on standing outside it. And for a thousand days and a thousand Siberian nights I'd looked forward to that particular door. You did commit a little murder there on the side, now didn't you?

MRS. KRAMER (very vigorously, so as not to cry): There are people who always have hard luck. You just happened to be one of them. Siberia—gas jet—Ohlsdorf. It was all just too much for you. It goes straight to my heart—but where would we be if we went around crying for everybody? You did look so gloomy, though, poor baby. Such a little boy! But we mustn't let it get at us—or even the little margarine we can afford to put on our bread these days might start tasting badly. (sighs) Well well, we certainly do see life. And people keep on throwing themselves in every day.

BECKMANN: Yes, that's right, that's right—and so farewell, Mrs. Kramer. Did you hear, Mr. Other One? Obituary for a young man by a good-hearted woman. Did you hear, Mr. Silent Answerer?

THE OTHER: Wake . . . up . . . Beckmann. . . .

BECKMANN: You suddenly sound so faint . . . you seem so far away suddenly. . . .

THE OTHER: You're dreaming a deadly dream, Beckmann. Wake up! Live! Don't take yourself so seriously. Death happens every single day. Should all eternity be filled with weeping? Live! Eat your bit of bread and margarine! Life has a thousand facets. Take it! Stand up!

BECKMANN: Fine—I'll stand up. For now I see my very own wife. My wife is good. No, she's got her friend with her. Still, once she was good. Why did I have to spend those three long years in Siberia? She did wait those three years, though, I'm sure of that. She was always good to me. It's my fault. Once she was good, but I don't know about her now.

THE OTHER: Try it! Live!

BECKMANN: Don't be afraid, dear, it's only me. Look at me! It's your husband—it's Beckmann. I've just taken my life. You shouldn't have gone and done all that, dear, with the other man. You were the only one I had. You're not listening! I know, dear, I know you had to wait too long. But don't be upset anymore, I'm fine now. I'm dead. Without you I couldn't go on. Look at me! Look at me!

The wife *goes slowly past, arm in arm with her lover, without even hearing* Beckmann.

But you were my wife! Look at me! You killed me; surely you can just look at me! You're not even listening to me! You murdered me—and now you just simply pass me by? Why don't you listen at least. . . ?

Wife *and* friend *exit.*

She didn't hear me. She doesn't even know me anymore. Have I really been dead that long? She's forgotten me and I've been dead only one day. So good, oh, mankind is so good! And you, Mr. Optimist, Mr. Cheerleader, Mr. Answerer!? You don't wish to make any comment? Oh, you're so far, far away. Shall I go on living? She was the reason that I came back from Siberia. And you say I'm supposed to go on living? Every single door, to the left as well as to the right of the roadway is now closed. All the lamps have gone out, all, to the very last one. And the only way a man can move at all forward is by falling. And you say I'm supposed to go on? Have you got another pratfall left for me to take for you? Is that it? Don't start hiding again, Mr. Silent One; haven't you got even one lamp left for me somewhere in this darkness? Tell me—you've always got so many wonderful ideas!

THE OTHER: Here comes the girl who pulled you out of the Elbe and who kept you warm a while. The girl who wanted to kiss your silly stupid head, Beckmann. She doesn't ignore your death; she hasn't passed by your corpse. She's been searching for you everywhere.

BECKMANN: No! She hasn't been searching for me! Nobody's been searching for me! I won't go on believing it time after time. I can't fall anymore, do you understand? Nobody's, nobody's been searching for me!

THE OTHER: This girl has been searching for you everywhere.

BECKMANN: Optimist, you're torturing me. Just go away.

GIRL *(without actually seeing him)*: Fish! Fish! Where are you? Little cold fish.

BECKMANN: I'm dead.

GIRL: Oh, you're dead? And I'm searching for you all over the world.

BECKMANN: Why are you searching for me?

GIRL: Why? Because I love you, poor ghost! And now you're dead? And I would so have loved to kiss you, poor cold Fish.

BECKMANN: Are we supposed to stand up and carry on just because a girl calls to us? Tell me, girl. . . .

GIRL: Yes, Fish?

BECKMANN: What if I weren't dead?

GIRL: Oh, then we'd go home together, to my house. Oh do be alive again, little cold Fish! If only for me. If only with me. Come, let's be alive together.

BECKMANN: Should I live? Have you really searched for me?

GIRL: Always. You and only you. On and on. Oh my, why are you dead, poor gray ghost? Won't you be alive with me?

BECKMANN: Yes, yes, yes. I'm coming with you. I want to be alive with you!

GIRL: Oh, my Fish!

BECKMANN: I'll stand up. You're the one light left burning for me. For me alone. We'll be alive together. And we'll walk pressed close together down the dark road. Come, let's be alive together and close together—

GIRL: Yes, yes, I'm burning for you alone on the dark road!

BECKMANN: You're burning? What's that—? It's getting dark suddenly—where are you?

The tick-tock of the one-legged man *is heard faintly again.*

GIRL: **Do** you hear? The death worm's knocking—I must go now, Fish, I must go, poor, cold ghost.

BECKMANN: Why? why? Stay here! Everything's suddenly so dark! Light, my little light! Shine for me! Who's that knocking now? Someone's knocking! Tick-tock-tick-tock! Who knocks like that? There—tick-tock-tick-tock! Louder! Nearer! Tick-tock-tick-tock! *(screams)* He's there! *(whispers)* The giant, the one-legged giant with his two crutches. Tick-tock—he's coming nearer. Tick-tock—he's coming toward me! Tick-tock-tick-tock!!! *(screams)*

ONE-LEGGED MAN *(quite matter-of-fact; almost detached)*: Beckmann?

BECKMANN *(softly)*: Here I am.

ONE-LEGGED MAN: You're still alive, Beckmann? You've committed a murder, Beckmann. And you're still alive.

BECKMANN: I've not committed any murder—

ONE-LEGGED MAN: Oh yes you have, Beckmann. We are murdered every day, and every day we commit a murder. And every day we ignore a murder. You murdered me, Beckmann. Have you forgotten already? I spent three years in Siberia, Beckmann, and yesterday I wanted to go home. But my place was taken—you were there, Beckmann, in my place. And so I went straight down to the Elbe, Beckmann, yesterday evening in fact. Where else was I supposed to go, Beckmann? That Elbe was amazingly cold and wet. But I've become used to it, since my death. How could you just forget that so quickly, Beckmann! You just can't forget murder as fast as that. It pursues you, Beckmann. Yes, I know, I made a mistake. I should not have come home. There was no place for me at home, Beckmann, because you were there. I don't blame you, Beckmann. We all commit murder, every day, every night. But we don't have to forget our victims so quickly! We shouldn't completely ignore our murders, not completely. Yes, Beckmann, you did take my place from me. On my own sofa, with my wife, my wife of whom I dreamt for three years, a thousand Siberian nights! But back home there was a man who had my clothes on, Beckmann; they were far too big for him, but he had them on, and he was very warm and doing quite well there in my clothes, with my wife. And you were that man, Beckmann; it was you. And so I withdrew. Straight into the Elbe. Quite cold down there, Beckmann, but one gets used to it quite quickly. Now I've been dead exactly one day—and you've forgotten your murder already. You mustn't do that, Beckmann, you shouldn't forget your murders right after you commit them: only bad people do that. You won't forget me, Beckmann, will you? You must promise me, Beckmann—you won't forget your murder!

BECKMANN: I won't forget you.

ONE-LEGGED MAN: That's good of you, Beckmann. Then I can be dead in peace, if at least one man is thinking of me, at least my murderer—just now and then perhaps—at night sometimes, Beckmann?—when you can't fall asleep! Then at least I can be dead in peace. . . .

    Exits.

BECKMANN *(waking up)*: Tick-tock-tick-tock!!! Where am I? Have I been dreaming? Aren't I dead? Aren't I still dead? Tick-tock-tick-tock through my whole life! Tick-tock—through my whole death! Tick-tock-tick-tock! Do you hear the death worm? And I'm supposed to live! And every night there will be a sentry by my bedside and I'll never be free from the sound of his steps: Tick-tock-tick-tock! No!

This is life, yes, *this*. There is a man, and the man comes home to Germany, and then the man freezes. He starves, and he limps! A man comes home to Germany! He comes home and his bed is taken. A door slams and he stands outside.

A man comes home to Germany! He finds a girl—but the girl has a husband, who has only one leg and who keeps on groaning a certain name. And that name is Beckmann. A door slams and he stands outside.

A man comes home to Germany! He searches for his fellow man—but a Colonel laughs himself half to death. A door slams and he stands outside again.

A man comes home to Germany! He searches for work—but a Producer is a coward and the door slams and he stands outside once more.

A man comes home to Germany! He searches for his parents—but an old woman is there, mourning the waste of gas, and the door slams and he stands outside.

A man comes home to Germany; and finally along comes a one-legged man—tick-tock-tick—as he comes—tick-tock, and the one-legged man says: Beckmann. Says again and again: Beckmann. He breathes Beckmann, he snores Beckmann, he groans Beckmann, he screams, he curses, he prays: Beckmann. And he walks through the life of his murderer—tick-tock-tick-tock! And I am his murderer. I?—I, the murdered, I whom they have all murdered, I am the murderer? What's to keep each and every one of us from becoming murderers then? We are all murdered each day, and each day we all commit murder! And murderer Beckmann can stand it no longer, murdering and being murdered. And he screams in the face of the world: *I die!* And then he lies down somewhere in the city streets, this man who came home to Germany, and he does indeed die. Once upon a time cigarette butts, orange peels, and old newspapers lay scattered around in our streets; more recently it's people, and about that most people care just as little. And then a street cleaner comes along, a German street cleaner in military regalia with bright red stripes, representative of the firm of Rubbish, Refuse, and Remains, and he finds the murdered murderer, Beckmann. Starved, frozen, abandoned. Here, in the middle decades of the twentieth century. In the street. In Germany. And people pass by his death distracted, resigned, bored, sickened, or indifferent, indifferent, oh so indifferent! And the dead man deep within his deadly dream realizes that his death was like his life: pointless, insignificant, and gray. And you—you say I'm supposed to live! Why? For exactly whom? For what particular purpose? Don't I even have any right to my death, my own suicide? Shall I go on murdering and being murdered? Where shall I finally go? How shall I live? With whom? For what? Where shall we go in this world! We've been betrayed. Terribly betrayed.

Where are you, you Other One? You've always been here before! Where are you now, Optimist? Answer me now! Suddenly you're just not available! Where are you, Answerer, where are you, you who begrudged me my own death? And where is the old man who went around calling himself God?

Why doesn't he speak now!!

Answer now!

Why are you all so silent? Why?

Will none of you answer?

Will no one answer?

Is there no answer at all?

Translated by Michael Benedikt

Günter Eich

Günter Eich was born in Lebus, a town in Mecklenburg, East Germany, in 1907. He studied sinology and economics in Berlin and Paris. Since 1932 he had worked as a free-lance writer until he was drafted into the German army. He fought as a soldier in World War II and was a US prisoner of war. After his return, he married the writer Ilse Aichinger. He lived the last years of his life with his family near Salzburg, Austria, and died there in 1972. He received various literary prizes, and his poems and radio plays were immensely popular in the postwar era. In the decades of the 1950s and 1960s, Günter Eich made major contributions to the genre of the radio drama, which had an initial success in the Weimar Republic through such writers as Brecht, Walter Benjamin, and Alfred Döblin. He almost single-handedly created a contemporary mode of the spoken word by structuring the play in a collage of realistic and dreamlike sequences.

He first became known as a lyric poet, a purist comparable to the Expressionist writer Gottfried Benn. At the beginning of his literary career, he insisted on the autonomy of art free from the appropriation of social or political issues. He defended the purposelessness of the poem against the intruding realities of the Weimar Republic and the emerging totalitarian ideology of the Third Reich. He set his artistic credo of an independent creative spirit and the autonomous self against the political realities. The poet Günter Eich may be charged for his early disengaged, elegiac position; after the war however, his conceptual and poetic convictions broadened. His texts are now characterized by a new social consciousness and his demand for a closer connection between the public realm and his literary production. The poetic, mystic dimension of his realism no longer conceals a critical and provocative voice. Although he was never as politically outspoken and actively involved in public affairs as Heinrich Böll and Günter Grass, he nevertheless responded critically to his environment. He never tired of pleading for the moral strength and integrity of the individual. The appeal to wake up and refuse to give in to pressure is heard at the end of his radio play *Dreams*, which concludes with the lines:

> Be troublesome, be sand,
> Not oil in the gears of the world!

In many of his plays the concrete experience in present-day society is frequently put into question by incorporating the surreal, the horrible and unexpected occurrences in life. The nocturnal, somnambulistic apparitions of the Romantics drift through his works. For him every word, every sentence was but an approximation of the original, unachievable text. As a writer he was convinced that no one will be able to articulate the essence of our experience. The radio play allowed Eich to embrace a more direct communicative discourse to represent existing conditions and fantastic hallucinatory dreams. He had begun to write for the public medium in the 1930s but his fame rests on his prolific production between the years 1950 and 1960. In 1952, he received the Prize of the War Blind for his radio play *The other Woman and I*.

The selection of plays included in our volume belong to the accepted canon in German literature. *Dreams* was broadcast in 1953 and created a public outcry. The reported dreams of five ordinary, pleasant people in the East and West infuriated the listeners. The narrative voice advises us that the characters in the play most probably have long forgotten their awful visions. The five episodes are structured in the Brechtian manner, with all five dreams connected by the ironic introductory comments of the narrator. His voice gives us to understand that sleep is not a cradle and bad dreams remind us that we are not our brother's keeper. Everybody is guilty of the atrocities committed in the name of mankind. In the first dream people are trapped in an ever faster moving train. They dimly remember days of comfort, beauty, and peace. A glimpse of the outside world reveals strange and unbearable faces. There is no help to be expected from them and no escape from the increasing speed of the train. In the following four dreams happiness is effervescent, gloom and terror reign supreme. In the name of profit and progress parents sacrifice their children (2), war rages, the enemy knocks at the gate, and neighbors close their doors to those who are in need (3). The white man, lost in the jungle, has long forgotten the purpose of the expedition (4) and in the final dream, mankind is attacked by termites, whose insatiable appetite reduces everybody to dust (5). In these dreams the horror is approaching, the roads lead nowhere, and the signposts have fallen apart. Only the narrator's voice speaks in the end to the listeners to admonish them to wake up and to be troublesome. The five texts of Günter Eich are learning plays about the human condition today.

Don't Go to Al-Kuwaid! was first published in 1953 as part of a collection that also included *The Tiger Jussuf* and *Sabeth*. It is an exemplary case of developing tension and surprise in order to undermine the illusionary reality of the literary text. The plot reveals Günter Eich's constant quest about the identity of the self and the unavoidable destiny of man's journey through life. The merchant Mahallab ignores the warning voice he has heard in a dream not to go to Al-Kuwaid. Recovering his consciousness, he is warned again but responds to his inner drive to meet his planned destiny. There is no chance of changing the life of the individual or the world, but what is still possible is to show courageous endurance. The ideological position of Günter Eich may be compared to the conviction of the well known playwright Friedrich Dürrenmatt who maintains that we face the end of tragedy but that "it might be an individual's decision to endure this world . . . . It is still possible to portray man as a courageous being." (*Problems of the Theater*, The German Library, volume 89, p. 225)

Another collection of radio plays apeared in 1964 under the title *In anderen Sprachen* (In other Tongues). The last play, called *Zeit und Kartoffeln* (Time and Potatoes), was finished in 1971. The poetic richness of his previous texts has given way to stoic observations about the increasing difficulty of human discourse. There is a deep cultural pessimism but also a mistrust of power and a genuine refusal to participate in the destruction of the planet.

M. H. S.

DREAMS

I envy all those who can forget,
who go to sleep unperturbed, and have no dreams.
I envy myself for my moments of blind contentment:
the vacation spot reached at last—North Sea beach or Notre Dame,
red burgundy in the glass, it's payday.
Yet I can't help thinking that even a good conscience is not
     enough,
and I doubt the quality of the sleep in which we all cradle
     ourselves.
Pure happiness no longer exists (did it ever?),
and I wish I could wake up one or the other sleeper
and tell him, it is better this way.

Did you, too, once wake up with a start in your love's arms
because a cry reached your ear, earth's ceaseless cry,
mostly just heard as the sound of rain, the soughing of wind.
See what goes on: imprisonment, torture, blindness,
paralysis, death in many guises,
disembodied pain, and the dread that life brings.
Earth gathers the sighs that rise out of many mouths,
dismay haunts the eyes of the people you love.
Everything that happens
concerns you.

The First Dream

CHARACTERS

Old Man   Old Woman   Grandson   Woman   Girl

In the night between the first and second of August 1948 master fitter Wilhelm Schulz, a native of Rügenwalde in Hinterpommem, now resident in Gütersloh, Westfalen, had a dream of a not particularly pleasant nature. It probably should not be taken too seriously, considering that Herr Schulz (meanwhile deceased) was found to have been suffering from digestive problems. Bad dreams arise from the stomach, which is always either too full or too empty.

Slow-moving train. Voices in a freight car.

OLD MAN: It was four o'clock in the morning, when they got us out of bed. The grandfather clock struck four.

GRANDSON: You're always telling us the same story. It's boring, Grandpa.

OLD MAN: But who was it that came to get us?

GRANDSON: Four stony-faced men. We know. You just keep on rehashing your past for us, day after day. Be quiet now. Get some sleep.

OLD MAN: But who were those men? Police? They wore uniforms I had never seen before. Not even uniforms, they just wore identical suits.

OLD WOMAN: *I* say they were from the fire brigade.

OLD MAN: You always say that. But why would the fire brigade come and get you out of bed, and take you to a train, and lock you in a freight car?

OLD WOMAN: Well, it's no stranger than if the police had done it.

OLD MAN: You get used to it after a while. The life we led up to that day was actually much stranger.

WOMAN: God knows it must have been pretty strange.

OLD MAN: In the end, is life in a freight car the normal thing?

OLD WOMAN: Shush! You mustn't say that.

WOMAN: Yes, just quiet down over there. So much idle talk! *(softly)* Come closer, Gustav, help me get warm.

GRANDSON: All right.

OLD MAN: It's cold. Come on, Ma, let's snuggle up too.

OLD WOMAN: I don't give off much warmth anymore.

OLD MAN: How long has it been since we had to leave our house? How long have we been riding in this car?

OLD WOMAN: No clock, no calendar. But the children have grown up, and the grandchildren, too, and when there's a little more light. . . .

OLD MAN: You mean, when it's day outside.

OLD WOMAN: When there's a little more light and I can see your face, then I can see the wrinkles that say you're an old man, and I'm an old woman.

OLD MAN: It must be at least forty years.

OLD WOMAN: Yes, it must be, I should think. Here, rest your head on my arm. The floor's so hard.

OLD MAN: Yes, thank you.

OLD WOMAN: Can you remember?—There was something we called sky and something we called trees.

OLD MAN: Behind our house, the road rose gently to the edge of the woods. In April, the meadows were full of flowering dandelions.

OLD WOMAN: Dandelions. . . . You use such strange words!

OLD MAN: Come on, you remember the dandelion—a yellow flower, the meadows were yellow with it. It had a milky white juice in its stem. And when it had flowered, there were these fluffy white balls on the stems, and when you blew on them, the feathery seeds flew away.

OLD WOMAN: I had forgotten that, completely. I remember now. . . .

OLD MAN: And do you remember the goat we kept in the stable?

OLD WOMAN: Yes, yes I do. I milked it, every morning.

OLD MAN: In the bedroom there was a wardrobe, and I kept my good suit in it, a dark blue one. Why do I think of that? As if that dark blue suit had been the most important, the best thing of all!

OLD WOMAN: What *was* the best thing?

OLD MAN: It was all good. The acacia in front of the house, the raspberries by the fence.

OLD WOMAN: The best thing was that we were happy.

OLD MAN: But we didn't know it.

OLD WOMAN: What was the name of that flower you were talking about, the yellow one?

OLD MAN: Dandelion.

OLD WOMAN: Dandelion, yes, I remember.

A child starts crying.

OLD WOMAN: What's the matter with the little one?

WOMAN: What's the matter, Frieda?

GIRL: They're always talking about yellow flowers.

GRANDSON: They're always talking about things that don't exist.

GIRL: I want a yellow flower!

GRANDSON: See there, Grandpa, it's all that silly talk of yours. Now the child wants a yellow flower. None of us knows what that is.

WOMAN: Sweetheart, there are no yellow flowers.

GIRL: But they're always talking about them.

WOMAN: Sweetheart, those are fairy tales.

GIRL: Fairy tales?

WOMAN: Fairy tales aren't true.

OLD MAN: You shouldn't say that to the child. It's not a fairy tale, it's true.

GRANDSON: Well, let's see it then, your yellow flower.

OLD MAN: You know I can't show it to you.

GRANDSON: Then it's a lie.

OLD MAN: Just because you can't see it, it has to be a lie?

GRANDSON: It's not just the kids. You're driving all of us crazy with your stories. We don't want to know those fairy tales. We don't want to hear the stuff you're dreaming up, day and night.

OLD MAN: But it isn't dream stuff. It's how life used to be.

OLD WOMAN: Yes, that's right.

GRANDSON: Who cares if it's right or not?—Do you think it makes us feel happier when you tell us that things used to be better and that there are nicer places than where we are? That there is something you call a yellow flower, that there are creatures you call animals, and that you used to sleep on something you call a bed, and that you drank something you called wine? It's all words, words—what use are they to us?

OLD MAN: One has to know these things. One can't go through life without knowing the real world.

GRANDSON: This is the only world there is.

OLD MAN: No world except this cage we're living in? Except this freight car rolling on forever?

GRANDSON: It gets a little lighter for a while, then it gets dark again. That's all.

OLD MAN: And that dim light, where does it come from?

GRANDSON: Through the hatch. Where our bread comes from.

OLD MAN: Moldy bread.

GRANDSON: Bread is always moldy.

OLD MAN: That's what you think because you've never seen any other kind.

OLD WOMAN: Listen, Grandson: who pushes the bread through that hatch?

GRANDSON: I don't know.

OLD WOMAN: But—so, there is something else besides this space we're in.

GRANDSON: Sure there is. But it can't be any better than here.

OLD MAN: It is better.

GRANDSON: We don't know anything about it, and we don't want to hear your fantasies about it. This, here, is our world, the one we live in. It consists of four walls, and darkness, and it is moving somewhere. I'm positive there's nothing out there except for other dark rooms moving through the darkness.

WOMAN: He's right.

VOICES: Yes, he's right.

WOMAN: We don't believe in the world you're always talking about. You've just dreamed it.

OLD MAN: Did we just dream it, Ma?

OLD WOMAN: I don't know.

WOMAN: Look around you—not a trace of your world.

OLD MAN: Suppose they're right? God, it's so long ago. Maybe I did just dream all of that, the blue suit, the goat, the dandelion. . . .

OLD WOMAN: . . . and I know it only from what you've told me. . . .

OLD MAN: But how did we get into this car? Wasn't it four in the morning when they got us out of bed? Yes, the grandfather clock struck four.

GRANDSON: Grandpa, there you go again.

The child starts crying again.

WOMAN: What's wrong, sweetie?

GIRL: There—look, there, on the floor!

GRANDSON: A glowing, shining bar. But—you can't touch it. It consists of—nothing.

OLD MAN: A ray of light. The wall must have got a hole in it somewhere, and a ray of sunlight is coming in.

WOMAN: Ray of sunlight? What's that?

OLD MAN: *Now* do you believe there's something out there that's different from what's in here?

OLD WOMAN: If there's a hole in the wall, we ought to be able to look outside.

GRANDSON: All right, I'll take a look.

OLD MAN: What do you see?

GRANDSON: I see things I don't understand.

WOMAN: Describe them.

GRANDSON: I don't know what words belong with them.

WOMAN: Why don't you keep looking?

GRANDSON: No. I'm afraid.

WOMAN: It isn't good, what you see out there?

GRANDSON: It is terrifying.

OLD MAN: Because it is new.

GRANDSON: Let's stop up that hole.

OLD MAN: What? You don't want to see the world the way it really is?

GRANDSON: No. I'm afraid.

OLD MAN: Let me take a look.

GRANDSON: Go ahead. See if it is the world that you're always talking about.

    Pause.

OLD WOMAN: What do you see?

OLD MAN: That's the world, all right. It's going by.

OLD WOMAN: Do you see the sky, do you see the trees?

OLD MAN: I see the dandelions—the meadows are yellow with them. And there are mountains, and forests and—oh my God!

GRANDSON: Can you stand to look at it?

OLD MAN: But *(hesitates)* something is different.

WOMAN: Why don't you keep looking?

OLD MAN: The people are different.

OLD WOMAN: What's with the people?

OLD MAN: Maybe I'm wrong. You look!

OLD WOMAN: All right.
  Pause.
OLD MAN: What do you see?
OLD WOMAN *(frightened)*: They're not people anymore—the way they used to be.
OLD MAN: So you see it, too.
OLD WOMAN: No, I don't want to look out any more. *(whispers)* They're giants. They're as tall as the trees. I'm afraid.
OLD MAN: Let's close the hole.
GRANDSON: Yes, let's close it. *(pause)* There.
WOMAN: Thank God. Things are back to normal. Like they were.
OLD MAN: Things are not like they were.
OLD WOMAN: I get the shivers when I think about those yellow flowers.
OLD MAN: What's left to think about, now?
OLD WOMAN: Memories frighten me.
GRANDSON: Shush! Haven't you noticed?
  Pause.
WOMAN: What?
  The girl starts crying again.
WOMAN: What's the matter, Frieda?
GRANDSON: Can't you tell? Something has changed.
OLD MAN: Yes. The world outside has changed.
GRANDSON: No, in here, where we are.
  Pause during which the sound of the train wheels can be heard clearly.
WOMAN: What made you cry, my sweet?
GIRL: I don't know.
GRANDSON: Something has changed. The child noticed.
OLD MAN: I know what it is. Can't you feel it?
WOMAN *(whispers)*: We're going faster.
OLD WOMAN: Yes, we're going faster.
  Pause. The sound of the wheels speeds up slightly.
OLD MAN: I wonder what it means?
WOMAN: I don't know, but I'm sure it isn't good.
OLD MAN: We have to see if the speed remains constant now.
GRANDSON: Or?
OLD MAN: Or if it keeps on speeding up.

OLD WOMAN: Listen!
>   *Pause. The sound of the wheels indicates increased speed.*
OLD MAN *(whispers)*: It keeps going faster.
WOMAN: Yes, it keeps going faster.
>   *The sound of the wheels accelerates and becomes louder.*
OLD MAN: We'll have a wreck! Can't someone help us?
GRANDSON: Who?
>   *Train noise reaches maximal volume, then recedes at great speed and fades away in the distance.*

Bear in mind that man is the enemy of man
and that he plots devastation.
Always bear that in mind, bear it in mind now
during a moment in April
under this overcast sky
while you believe you can hear the delicate rustling of growth,
while the maids are cutting thistles
under the lark's song,
even at this moment, bear it in mind!

While you're tasting the wine in the cellars of Randersacker
or picking oranges in the gardens of Alicante,
while you fall asleep in the Hotel Miramar by the beach, at Taormina
or light a candle on All Souls' Day in the cemetery at Feuchtwangen,
while you, a fisherman, raise your nets above the Doggerbank
or pluck, in Detroit, a screw off the assembly line,
while you plant seedlings in the rice terraces of Szechwan or cross
    the Andes on mule-back—
bear it in mind!

Bear it in mind when a hand touches you gently,
bear it in mind when your wife embraces you,
when your child laughs, bear it in mind!

Bear in mind that after the great devastations
everyone will prove his innocence.

Bear in mind:

nowhere on a map will you find Korea and Bikini,
but in your heart, you will find them.
Bear in mind that you are guilty of all the atrocious acts
committed far away from you. . . .

The Second Dream

CHARACTERS

Man   Wife   Gentleman   Lady   Boy

On November 3, 1949, the fifty-year-old daughter of the rice merchant Li When Chou in Tientsin had a dream that could, undoubtedly, cast the old girl in a bad light. Her parents and siblings, however, insist that she is a good-natured and harmless person. In this world, it is probably the villians who have the pleasant dreams.

    In the street.
WIFE: Fifty-seven B. This is the house.
MAN: You should have combed Chang Dou's hair better. He doesn't look very appetizing. And why don't you blow his nose!
    Sound of blowing nose.
BOY: Mother—do we have to go into this house?
WIFE: Yes, Chang Dou.
BOY: What for?
WIFE: Oh, nothing special.
MAN: Are you done with the kid now?
WIFE: Yes.
MAN: Then I'll ring the bell.
    Sound of doorbell.
BOY: That's a loud bell.
MAN: Didn't you bring a comb? His hair is all messed up.
WIFE: Well, it doesn't make much difference now.
MAN: It does make a difference.
BOY: Father—I can stay out here.
MAN: That's all we need.
WIFE: No one's coming to the door.

BOY: No—don't ring the bell again!

MAN: Why not?

CHILD: It's so loud. I'm scared.

MAN: Nonsense.

WIFE: Shush! Somebody's coming!

> *The door opens.*

MAN: We saw your advertisement in the paper.

LADY: The advertisement. Yes. Is this the child?

WIFE: It's so windy, his hair is all messed up.

LADY: Uh huh.

MAN: I hope you're still in need of. . . . Or did someone beat us to it?

LADY: He looks pale. Is he anemic?

BOY: Mother—let's go!

WIFE: He's only pale because he is scared.

LADY: Scared? But why? Does he know something?

WIFE: No.

LADY: Well, come on in.

> *They enter. The door closes.*

LADY: This is my husband. He is not well. Pi Gou!

GENTLEMAN *(feebly)*: Yes?

LADY: These people have brought a boy.

GENTLEMAN: Yes.

LADY: Six years old, I should think.

WIFE: Exactly.

LADY: Take a look at him, Pi Gou.

GENTLEMAN: Let him come closer.

MAN: His name is Chang Dou.

LADY: It really doesn't matter a whole lot what his name is.

BOY *(bursts into loud tears)*

WIFE: Chang Dou, what's the matter?

BOY: The gentleman has such cold fingers.

WIFE: Come, now. That's because he is ill.

BOY: I don't want to stay here.

MAN: Quiet now!

BOY *(sobs, more quietly)*

GENTLEMAN: He is pale.

LADY: Yes, he is.

MAN: He's not anemic.

GENTLEMAN: If he's anemic, I can't use him.

MAN: I guarantee that he is not anemic.

LADY: The blood's the most important thing, you know.

WIFE: Yes, yes, we know that. It said so in the advertisement.

LADY: It's the new therapy, you know.

WIFE: A great achievement of medicine, a blessing for mankind.

LADY: But I just don't know if little Chang Dou is suitable.

MAN: My wife has a child every year, sometimes twins. And all of them have been used for the new therapy.

WIFE: Six is the best age.

MAN: We provide nothing but healthy children, first-class. Here—I have references.

LADY: Let's see! Well.

WIFE: Chang Dou, let the gentleman see your neck.

BOY *(sobbing)*: Yes.

GENTLEMAN: See, An Ling—here's the artery.

LADY: Yes. But this time we'll let the maid do it.

GENTLEMAN: She knows how?

LADY: Of course she does.

GENTLEMAN: I don't really trust maids to know much of anything. . . . But, if you say so.

LADY: These references are excellent.

GENTLEMAN: All right, then.

LADY: Well, let's discuss the price.

MAN: Three thousand.

LADY: I beg your pardon. You must be out of your mind.

MAN: But that is how much we get for four- or five-year-olds! We've had to pay for his upkeep a whole year longer.

LADY: Two five. We can't afford luxury prices.

MAN: Three thousand, and that's final. You mustn't forget the spiritual values involved.

LADY: Don't be ridiculous.

WIFE: Come, Chang Dou, we're leaving.

BOY: Yes, mother.

GENTLEMAN: Wait!

LADY: What is it, Pi Gou?

GENTLEMAN: Write the check.

LADY: All right, if you say so.

BOY: Let's go, mother!

WIFE: Wait.

LADY: Here's your check.

MAN: Thank you. You won't be disappointed.

BOY: Can we go now?

WIFE: Your father and I have to go now. You'll stay here for a little while.

BOY: But I don't want to stay here.

WIFE: Don't make a fuss now. It's much nicer here than at home.

LADY: Would you like to take his clothes now?

MAN: We'll pick them up tomorrow. And, at that time, we would like to have a reference from you.

LADY: All right, then. Good-bye.

WIFE: Good-bye.

MAN: And many thanks.

WIFE: Chang Dou—we'll be right back. We just have to do a little shopping.

BOY *(sobbing)*: Yes, mother.

MAN: Well, come on then!

Man and wife leave.

LADY: I'll tell the girl to get things ready.

GENTLEMAN: Yes; do, An Ling. I'm starving.

LADY *(receding)*: Li By!

GENTLEMAN: Why are you looking at me like that, Chang Dou?

BOY: Your face is so white.

GENTLEMAN: Well, not for long, I hope. Listen: back there in the kitchen there's a train set, an electric one.

BOY: Really?

GENTLEMAN: You like playing with train sets?

BOY: Oh yes, I love them.

GENTLEMAN: Well, in a minute or two you can go to the kitchen, to Li By, and play with the train set there.

BOY: Great!

The lady's footsteps, approaching.

LADY: Everything's ready.

GENTLEMAN: Thank God. I'm getting really weak now. Young Chang Dou here would like to play with the train set.

LADY: With the train set?

GENTLEMAN: Yes, in the kitchen.

Lady and gentleman burst out laughing.

LADY: Well, why don't you go back there, to the kitchen?
BOY: Yes, ma'am.
>*He goes. From a distance:*
BOY: There's no train set here. . . .
LADY: Just go in there now. Li By, close the door.
>*Sound of closing door.*
GENTLEMAN: Are you sure Li By knows how to do it?
LADY: She's done it for her previous employers.
GENTLEMAN: I would have preferred for you to do it.
LADY: What do we have a maid for, if I have to do the dirty work myself?
GENTLEMAN: But, it's a matter of my health.
LADY: Darling, you have to forgive me, but I've been getting so sensitive lately. When I had to kill that dove the other day, I fainted.
GENTLEMAN: You could at least go there and make sure that it's being done right.
LADY: After you've had the blood, she'll fry up the heart and the liver.
GENTLEMAN: It's taking forever.
>*From the kitchen, Chang Dou's screams, fading away during the following exchange.*
GENTLEMAN *(angrily)*: See! You hear that? She didn't stun him right. And I have to sit here and listen to that.
LADY: Calm down. It's over now.
>*The door opens. Steps, approaching.*
Well, here it is, your bowl of blood. It's still steaming. That'll do you good.

Even when Zero Hour has arrived, I'll think that the earth was beautiful.
I'll think about my friends, about kindness
that makes a plain face beautiful,
and love that enchants the eyes.
I'll think about the dog, my playmate when I was a child,
about the blue lupins on the Samland coast on a vacation visit,
once more I'll see the long shadows of the spruce trees on the Alpine pasture
and hike up the Gederer with Emmy Gruber,

I'll remember the bird migrations above the airfield at Märkisch-
Friedland,

the smell of the beer cellar at the Sign of the Stag, my grandfather's
inn,

I'll remember the elder bushes, poppies, rapeseed fields seen rushing
by from the window of a train,

the blush on the cheeks of fourteen-year-old Gabriele Dembitza,

the red and green lights of an airplane under Cassiopeia,

the dancing under Chinese lanterns, on Le Quatorze Juillet,

the fragrance of fruit in the morning, by the stands in front of Celle
Castle,

I'll think about the heartbeat of the lizard that caught me watching
it,

and about a poem in Goethe's *West–East Divan* that consoled me.

The Third Dream

CHARACTERS

Father   Mother   Neighbor Woman   Bob   Elsie
    Mayor   Voice

*As we know, there can be many different kinds of Zero Hour: on
April 27, 1950, one of those was the subject of a dream seen by
Lewis Stone, an auto mechanic in Freetown, Queensland, Australia. For reassurance, it should be noted that Stone presently
enjoys the best of health and has long since forgotten this dream.*

> *Male, female, and children's voices, singing and laughing.
> When the hubbub subsides for a moment, one can hear the
> approaching Neighbor.*

NEIGHBOR: Hello! Hey! You there! (*end of noise*)
FATHER: What's up, neighbor?
NEIGHBOR (*close*): You're laughing!
MOTHER: And why shouldn't we be?
FATHER: We're happy.
NEIGHBOR: How can you. . . ?

FATHER: We have five kids, and our daily bread. What's your problem?

NEIGHBOR: Don't you know that the enemy's approaching?

FATHER: The enemy?

NEIGHBOR: They've seen him on the road from Sydney.

MOTHER: He can't be coming here.

NEIGHBOR: Where else does this road go?

MOTHER: He can't be coming to our house.

NEIGHBOR: No, but maybe he'll come to my house. *(angrily)* You shouldn't be fooling around! *(moving away)* See you later. Lock your doors. Good night.

FATHER: The gate to the yard is locked.

MOTHER: Look out there. All the lights have gone out!

FATHER: We'd better switch ours off, too.

MOTHER: Yes.

FATHER: That's better.

MOTHER: Bob, where are you? Elsie?

BOB: Here.

ELSIE: Here.

FATHER: Maybe it isn't true. We should have asked her who has seen him. The enemy—who can recognize him?

BOB: Mom—is it war now?

MOTHER: It is always war.

FATHER: Let's open the windows but keep the curtains closed.

>   *They do so.*

FATHER: Now, if we move the curtain just a little bit to the side, we can peek out.

MOTHER: It is dark. Nothing to see.

FATHER: It's the new moon.

MOTHER: And everything's really quiet.

ELSIE: It's not all quiet, Mom. I can hear something.

FATHER: What do you hear?

ELSIE: I don't know what it is, but I can hear something.

>   *In the distance, a lumbering noise, as if some shapeless creature were approaching.*

MOTHER: What is that?

FATHER: Footsteps. . . .

MOTHER: It doesn't sound human!

FATHER: Quiet!

>   *The lumbering steps come closer.*

ELSIE: Those are footsteps, Mom.

BOB: It's coming here.

> *The steps come thunderously close, then stop. The following lines are spoken in whispers.*

MOTHER: It stopped.

FATHER: Quite close to our house.

MOTHER: It could be somewhere else. You can't always tell. Take a look!

FATHER: I can't see anything. *(pause)*
No, I still can't see anything, but there's this light, like the green light on decayed wood—like the one on the clock, at night. . . .

MOTHER: Hush!

BOB: It's moving.

> *Three booming knocks on the gate to the yard.*

FATHER: It's knocking on our gate.

MOTHER: No, that's not our gate.

FATHER: Yes, it is.

MOTHER *(sobs)*: No—o.

FATHER: Quiet! Don't cry! He mustn't hear us.

MOTHER: Let's pretend we're asleep.

> *Three knocks, as before.*

BOB: Mom—does he want to come in?

MOTHER: Yes, he wants to come in here.

BOB: Well, maybe he'll think there's nobody here, and move on.

MOTHER: He's not going anywhere else. He's picked our house.

ELSIE: Why us?

MOTHER: Oh, child—maybe it's because we're so happy.

ELSIE: He doesn't like that?

FATHER: Keep your voices down!

MOTHER: What are we going to do?

> *Sound of something beating on the gate, as before.*

FATHER: We'll leave through the back. Hurry up!

MOTHER: But we need to take some things—clothes, food. . . .

FATHER: No! You know we can't take anything. He'll notice.

> *Muffled sounds of the gate being demolished.*

FATHER: He's breaking down the gate. Come on, let's go!

MOTHER: Come, children!

FATHER: Through here!

MOTHER: Are you there? Bob, Elsie?

CHILDREN: Here, here!

Their voices grow fainter during that exchange. After the gate collapses, the ponderous footsteps approach and come to a halt. Silence.
Outdoors.

BOB: Where are we going, Mom?

MOTHER: I don't know.

FATHER: To the neighbor's. She'll take us in. *(in an urgent whisper)* Hey, neighbor!

NEIGHBOR: Come in, come in. I've been expecting you.
   At this point, the sound environment changes to an indoor one, as the refugees enter the house.

NEIGHBOR: But I don't have that many beds. You'll have to sleep on the floor.

FATHER: No problem.

MOTHER: Can you see, from here, what he is doing back there?

NEIGHBOR: He's switched on all the lights. Seems like he's looking for something.

FATHER: We didn't take anything.

NEIGHBOR: Of course not.

ELSIE *(quietly)*: Hey, Bob!

BOB *(likewise)*: Yes?

ELSIE: I did take something. My doll.

BOB: Hush, don't say anything.

MOTHER: Why did he have to choose us?

NEIGHBOR: Yes, those are the honors one could do without.

FATHER: Do you think anybody's sleeping tonight?

NEIGHBOR: Nobody is.

FATHER: Maybe the ones whose doors he didn't bang on. . . .

MOTHER: It's beginning to get light.

NEIGHBOR: Tomorrow everything will be back to normal.

FATHER: Except for our home.

NEIGHBOR: You really didn't bring anything?

MOTHER: Nothing. It was dark. We wouldn't have been able to find anything.

NEIGHBOR: He's still searching.

MOTHER: What does he look like?

NEIGHBOR: He's a little fellow, sort of nondescript.

MOTHER: His face?

NEIGHBOR: I haven't seen it yet.

FATHER: Let me take a look.

NEIGHBOR: He's coming to the window. He's looking out.

FATHER: I can see his face. His eyes look like those of a blind man.

NEIGHBOR: Now he's looking over here. Get away from the window!

FATHER: I can tell that he's blind. And yet, his eyes are frightening.

NEIGHBOR: He's still looking over here. He's seen me. Maybe I should say hello to him? *(calls out)* Good morning, neighbor! *(silence)* He's not answering. Gosh, he gives me the shivers. He's just staring over here.

FATHER: He is blind.

MOTHER: You called him "neighbor"?

FATHER: You changed your tune pretty fast.

NEIGHBOR: He just keeps staring over here.

FATHER: You've written us off already—right?

NEIGHBOR *(shouts)*: Greetings, neighbor! *(Silence)*

FATHER: He's not answering. He may be deaf and mute as well.

NEIGHBOR: He just keeps staring over here. Listen, you have to leave!

MOTHER: Leave? Why?

FATHER: Where can we go?

NEIGHBOR: You have to leave. He doesn't want you here.

MOTHER: Have a little compassion! Look, the little one just fell asleep.

NEIGHBOR: Go! Hurry up! Go!

FATHER: Come on, we'll go to another house.

MOTHER: Come on, children.

Their voices grow distant.

FATHER: Bob, Elsie!

CHILDREN: Here. I'm tired. Here.

NEIGHBOR *(alone)*: Now he's not staring over here anymore. He's not blind, oh no, I know he isn't. He sees better than any of us. *(pause)*

Outdoors.

FATHER: All right, we'll ring this doorbell. The mayor is an old friend of ours. He'll find us a place to stay.

Bell. A window opens.

MAYOR: What do you want?

FATHER: You know what we want, Mayor. We had to leave our home.

MAYOR: Keep going. You don't belong here anymore.

FATHER: But—

MAYOR: No buts. You don't have a home here in Freetown anymore. And you're thieves.

MOTHER: Thieves?

MAYOR: Yes. Look at Elsie. Isn't she carrying her doll?

MOTHER: Her doll? Good God, Elsie, did you bring that doll. . . ?

FATHER: We have to take it back.

MAYOR: Too late now. You've broken the law, but we're really glad you did it. We all are. As a friend, I'm advising you to leave before they arrest you. That's all, 'bye!

Window slams shut.

FATHER: Come on, we have to keep moving.

ELSIE: May I bring the doll?

MOTHER: Yes, you may.

FATHER: But we're not allowed to—

MOTHER: But she loves it.

FATHER: All right, then. Because she loves it.

MOTHER: Where can we go?

FATHER: Maybe somebody else will take us in.

MOTHER: Nobody will take us in.

FATHER: Hello, neighbor!

VOICE: Damn it, I'm not your neighbor. Get out of town, you drifters!

FATHER: But we were all born here!

VOICE: Get out. Get out! You think we'll stick out our necks for you?

FATHER: Come on, let's go.

MOTHER: It's no use asking any of them. They're all standing behind their curtains, watching us go. No one will take us in. They're all glad to see us leave.

FATHER: They're afraid. All of them. We can't blame them for that.

MOTHER: No, I suppose not. They're miserable creatures, just like us.

FATHER: We still have our children.

MOTHER: And Elsie has her doll.

ELSIE: My doll.

FATHER: That was the last house. Thank God, we're out on the open road. It's really light now.

MOTHER: And where are we going?

* * *

There are signposts by the roads,
there are courses of rivers, easily followed,
lookout towers in high elevations,
maps on which lakes have been painted blue
and forests, green—
it is easy to find one's way around on earth.

But you who walk beside me, how hidden
from me is the landscape of your heart!
As I grope along in the fog, I am often overcome
by a fear of brambles, fear of a hidden abyss.
I know you don't want anyone to wander through your thoughts,
the echo of your words is designed to deceive—
the roads lead nowhere, there is no way out of this terrain,
and all the signposts have fallen into disrepair.

Every century gives us new things to hide, a landscape overgrown
to love's curious eye,
covered by the ever more luxuriant
foliage of loneliness.

The Fourth Dream

CHARACTERS

Anton   Vassily   Cook

On December 29, 1947, Ivan Ivanovich Boleslavski, a cartographic draftsman, lay sick in bed in his Moscow apartment. He was suffering from a feverish flu and slept for two days with minor interruptions. He dreamed a lot, mostly about countries he had never visited. It is of course possible that he may still get to visit these places during the remaining years of his life.

    Outdoors.
ANTON: We picked a good bunch of porters, don't you think?
VASSILY: Fifty pounds each, and no complaints.
ANTON: Through the jungle, eight to ten hours a day.
VASSILY: Loyal and inexpensive.

ANTON: But that cook! Vassily, how can we get rid of the cook?

VASSILY: Nothing wrong with his cooking. If one could only wipe that smirk off his face. . . .

COOK: Food is ready.

ANTON: Canned meat.

VASSILY: And this? Fresh vegetables?

COOK: Grows all around. Very good.

ANTON: Looks like leeks.

VASSILY: And tastes like wild mushrooms.

ANTON: Tastes good.

COOK: Very good.

VASSILY: Tell us, Congo, where did you learn to cook?

COOK: Never learned. It all look like leek, taste like mushroom.

VASSILY: Great prospects. . . .

> A *drum starts up, not too far away, followed by others at more distant spots.*

ANTON: The drums, again.

COOK: Because you now eating, white lords.

ANTON: Because we're eating. . . . You hear that, Vassily? They're transmitting every little twitch of our eyelids.

VASSILY: Well, we're interesting, for the first couple of days. They'll get bored eventually.

ANTON: I hope so. And why are they all squatting around us like that? *(changes tone of voice)* And you? Have you eaten?

COOK: Yes, have eaten. Everybody.

VASSILY: Leeks? Wild mushrooms? (Cook *giggles*)

ANTON: I don't want to be interesting. Twenty-three porters, one overseer, one cook—that's fifty eyes, staring at us *(angry)* Hey, you!

COOK: More vegetables?

VASSILY: That's enough. Good and filling.

ANTON: And every bite gets broadcast. As an added spice.

VASSILY: I'd prefer a dash of vinegar. Let's go into the tent.

ANTON: Yeah, let's smoke a pipe, one that won't be reported to the next village.

> *In the tent. The drumming continues, a little more distant.*

ANTON: Pitch tents, fold tents—is it really worth doing, just for a moment's peace and a pipeful?

VASSILY: Yes, we should have time—time as long as camp cot. . . .

And why don't we ever have any time? Why don't we just stay
here and let them drum us to sleep, under this canvas, that could
so easily be sewn shut . . . where we, where we, where we. . . .

ANTON: What?

VASSILY: I forgot what I wanted to say.

ANTON *(laughs)*

VASSILY: Anton—what are we doing here? Where are we going?

ANTON: (amused) You've forgotten that, too?

VASSILY: Totally.

ANTON: That's a joke, right?

VASSILY: I'm asking you, Anton, because I don't know anymore. I
don't know why we're here.

ANTON *(appalled)*: You don't know why we're here?

VASSILY: No reason to get upset. It must be the heat. A memory
lapse. *(he laughs)* It's funny, really.

ANTON: Or not funny at all.

VASSILY: Just a tiny little gap, a moment's oxygen deprivation in the
brain—these things pass. But, could you help me out?

ANTON: Of course.

VASSILY: Just tell me where it is we're going.

ANTON *(confused)*: Where we're going?

VASSILY: Whence, where to, and why.

ANTON *(after a brief pause)*: I knew it just a moment ago.

VASSILY: You knew it just a moment ago?

ANTON: I did.

VASSILY: But now you don't know it anymore? You don't know it,
either?

ANTON: Your forgetfulness is contagious.

VASSILY: Or it's the heat that's affecting both of us in the same way.

ANTON: Yes, it's the same heat, the same tent, and the same tobacco.

VASSILY: And the same memory. *(with forced cheer)* Well, never
mind, it'll come back. Don't you think?

ANTON: That's something to start out with. Now we just use logic
and deduction.

ANTON: It is obviously an expedition.

VASSILY: Right, an expedition. Whence, where to, why?

ANTON: We have those questions.

VASSILY: That's a good thing, too. It is Africa, in any case.

ANTON: And, as all expeditions have the same goal. . . .

VASSILY: All of them? Are you sure?

ANTON: The goal of all expeditions is happiness.

VASSILY: I doubt that. It's not a logical conclusion, anyway.

ANTON: But there is no other goal. Just think of it.

VASSILY: I just thought of—meteorology. . . .

ANTON: A thing of the past.

VASSILY: Really? Well. . . .

ANTON: The result of tent, drum, and jungle—

VASSILY: Happiness. But in what form?

ANTON: That's just the question we're asking with our expedition.

VASSILY: Right here?

ANTON: Why not here?

VASSILY *(forcefully)*: No, I don't believe any of that.

ANTON: There's no need to argue about it. We have our journals, our notes. We don't need memory.

VASSILY: Right, it's all written down there. You'll see that I was right.

ANTON: A waterproof briefcase, in baggage load number three.

VASSILY: Good thing you remembered that!

ANTON: We better go and check it out right away.
    Outside.

VASSILY: Congo alone? Where are the others?

COOK: All gone.

ANTON: Gone? What do you mean, gone?

COOK: Gone, up and away, left, *parti.*

VASSILY: And our baggage?

COOK: Gone, too.

ANTON: The waterproof briefcase in load number three?

COOK: Left, *parti.*

ANTON: Stolen! We're holding you responsible, Congo.

VASSILY: And just how do you propose to hold him responsible?

ANTON: Our instruments, our provisions! We have to go after them!

VASSILY: Unarmed? Listen, we don't stand a chance. *(yawns)* Let's just stay here. We still have the tent and the two cots.

ANTON: And the jungle, and the drums.

VASSILY: What does that add up to? *(laughs)* Logic and deduction, that's the stuff.

ANTON: And you? Why did you stay?

COOK: Do dishes, my white lords.

ANTON: No jokes, you rascal.

COOK: Duty, devoir, obligation. Drums tell me that.

VASSILY: The drums? Listen, Congo, you're not a rascal, you're an honest fellow, a loyal person: you are our friend.

COOK *(undecided)*: Can't stay.

VASSILY: You'll tell us everything, my friend Congo, won't you? What are they drumming now?

COOK: Then I should go.

VASSILY: But they're not saying that you can't tell us everything.

COOK: No. Remember food?

ANTON: Canned meat and vegetables.

COOK: It was the vegetables.

ANTON: It tasted good.

COOK: A root. Grow all around. You eat, memory gone.

ANTON: But I can remember the taste, exactly.

COOK: Like wild mushroom. But you forget soon.

VASSILY: Come on now. What's the antidote?

COOK: Don't know.

VASSILY: What are you going to do to us?

COOK: Nothing. We see.

VASSILY: We see? Would you mind elaborating on that?

COOK: If you stay alive, good, if not stay alive, also good.

VASSILY: Thanks a lot.

> *The drumming stops.*

COOK: Farewell, white lords.

VASSILY: Loyal and inexpensive. *(laughs)*

ANTON: Didn't I ask you how we could get rid of that cook? What conclusion can you draw from that?

VASSILY: Quite a logical one: that it wasn't hard at all to get rid of him.

ANTON: No: that we can still remember things, quite well. So it's not memory loss.

VASSILY: See, things aren't so bad after all. What's your name?

ANTON: Name?

VASSILY: Yes, your name.

ANTON: I don't know.

VASSILY: I'll call you One, and I'll call myself Two.

ANTON: Yes, that makes sense.

VASSILY: I feel so good. Quite empty. No effort at all.

ANTON: Ready for any life. One only has to decide, and the birth pangs begin. A feeling of happiness . . . everything still without any form . . . cocoon or seedpod. There are so many possibilities!

VASSILY: It is wonderful. An expedition that meets with success.

ANTON: Where are we?

VASSILY: Where do you think? Where we've always been.

ANTON: Weren't we somewhere else, before this?

VASSILY: Nonsense. We've always been here. That's our house.

ANTON: House? House? Don't you call that a tent?

VASSILY: Belongs to Africa, waterproof—all those words that are losing their meaning. At last.

ANTON: But that is not our house. We have to leave.

VASSILY: We'll stay, today, tomorrow, the day after, after, after. Where else would we go?

ANTON: Our goal is happiness.

VASSILY (*contemptuously*): Goal, happiness, Africa, waterproof. . . . Happiness is here.

ANTON: No, it is somewhere else. I'll go look for it.

VASSILY: You're a fool!

ANTON: Farewell!

VASSILY: I can't stop you.

ANTON (*from a distance*): Onward through the brambles.

VASSILY (*in a loud voice at first, then in a conversational tone*): Right, onward and on through, between leeks and freedom of the will, you think you'll find it there somewhere, the cuckoo's egg. . . . Fool, wretched fool! (*yawns*) Sleep is happiness, happiness, happiness. *(pause)* But something is still missing. There used to be something else. . . .

The drums start up quietly, grow louder.

VASSILY: Yes, that's it. Now I have everything.

Drums at full volume.

The Greeks believed that the sun, on its journey across the sky, kept grinding its own groove and thus produced a sound that was incessant, eternal, and immutable, and hence, imperceptible to our ears.

How many such inaudible sounds live around us? One day, they will become audible, and fill our ears with horror. . . .

The Fifth Dream

CHARACTERS

Mother Daughter Bill Radio Announcer
  Professor

. . . Mrs. Lucy Harrison of Richmond Avenue, New York, heard them on August 31, 1950, having fallen asleep one afternoon while mending the frayed hem of a skirt.

DAUGHTER: This is the living room. It's the nicest one of all.

MOTHER: What a gorgeous view! The river, and the boats, and the park over there, the tall buildings—God, it's beautiful.

DAUGHTER: Mom, I'm so glad you're visiting!

MOTHER: Well, I just had to come and see your apartment, at long last. I want to enjoy your happiness a little bit. It makes me feel young again, as young as when I was newly married. . . .

DAUGHTER: My darling Mom!

MOTHER: You really hit the jackpot. Bill doing so well in his job and all.

DAUGHTER: Yes, Bill is doing real well.

MOTHER: And he's spoiling you! I can tell. This cozy corner couch, the hi-fi. . . . Do you still play the piano sometimes?

DAUGHTER: I have to confess that I've gotten real lazy, ever since we got the TV, and the radio and the hi-fi. . . .

MOTHER: Well, you weren't concert material. But, yes, "Where Is My Rose of Waikiki"—you used to play that real nice. When does Bill get home from the office?

DAUGHTER: Around five.

MOTHER: Well, then, we've got some time together. *(with a sigh of relief)* I think I'll sit down right here, for a little while. This is such a charming apartment, I can't get over it! I like that tablecloth. It's different.

DAUGHTER: Bill got it for me the other day.

MOTHER: The other day? Was it a special occasion?

DAUGHTER: No—he just wanted to surprise me.

MOTHER: You have a good husband there. *(suddenly)* Hush!

DAUGHTER: What is it?

MOTHER: What's that sound?

A pause, during which we hear a quiet but steady and insistent scraping noise.

DAUGHTER: Oh, that's just the elevator.

MOTHER: Oh.

DAUGHTER: Can I offer you something—a snack, or a drink?

MOTHER: No thanks, just stay here. I had a meal on the train. Come on, sit down here next to me.

DAUGHTER: Would you like me to turn on the radio?

MOTHER: I don't want you to do anything, just sit here and let me look at you. You're looking good—I can tell that you're happy.

DAUGHTER: Oh, Mom—

MOTHER: My goodness. Tears?

DAUGHTER: Just because I'm so happy.

MOTHER: Oh Lucy, my dear little girl.

DAUGHTER: There, I needed that.

MOTHER: That elevator of yours seems to be running all the time.

DAUGHTER: Well, it's a large building, with many apartments.

MOTHER: But it's a strange elevator.

DAUGHTER: What do you mean by "strange"?

MOTHER: It makes a really strange sound.

Pause. We hear the same sound as before.

DAUGHTER *(with a forced laugh)*: Well, then, I'll turn on the radio— the elevator seems to be getting on your nerves. *(she turns on the radio)* And now I'll go and make you a cup of tea. No, you can't turn it down! I have to go to the kitchen anyway, to fix Bill's dinner.

MOTHER: If you insist.

Radio music.

MOTHER *(calls)*: Lucy—can you hear it?

DAUGHTER *(distant)*: What, Mom?

MOTHER: "Where Is My Rose of Waikiki". . . .

DAUGHTER *(distant)*: There you go! Your favorite song.

The mother hums along for a couple of bars, stops suddenly.

MOTHER: You can hear the elevator even with the radio on. I want to have a look.

She leaves the room.

DAUGHTER *(distant)*: What is it, Mom?

MOTHER *(distant)*: I want to see what's the matter with that elevator.

DAUGHTER: Oh, Mom, don't bother.

MOTHER (*distant*): The elevator isn't running at all. It's just sitting there. But you can still hear that sound.

DAUGHTER (*sounding pained*): Then it must be something else. Don't let it bother you.

MOTHER: But it's strange, all right.

DAUGHTER: Come on, go back and listen to the music.

MOTHER: You're right. It's silly to have such sensitive ears.

    Radio music ends. Announcer comes on.

ANNOUNCER: You heard "Where Is My Rose of Waikiki." And that was the end of our afternoon record hour. Now it is time for our afternoon lecture. . . .

MOTHER (*under her breath*): Lecture! Who needs it?

ANNOUNCER: At the gong, the time will be exactly five o'clock. (*gong*) Today we'll hear Professor Wilkinson address himself to the subject of termites.

PROFESSOR: It isn't pleasant to live where there are termites. With their insatiable appetite, these insects are capable of devouring practically anything, and we human beings are powerless against them. Their method of feeding is particularly unpleasant because we probably notice signs of their destructive activity only when it is too late. Termites have a way of hollowing out any object from the inside, leaving a thin outer wall, a skin, as it were, intact—at least until it crumbles to dust, which it does, sooner or later. You may go to sleep in your house one evening only to wake up in the great outdoors, the house having crumbled to dust overnight.

MOTHER: Did you hear that, Lucy? (*laughs*) Termites eat your house, and you wake up in the great outdoors.

DAUGHTER (*approaching*): Oh, Mom, turn that thing off.

    Radio is turned off.

MOTHER: I thought that was sort of interesting.

DAUGHTER (*despair in her voice*): No, it wasn't, no!

MOTHER: Lucy, what is the matter? You're pale as a sheet.

DAUGHTER: Nothing, nothing.

    Pause.

MOTHER (*determined*): Listen, Lucy—you weren't crying because you were happy.

DAUGHTER: But of course I was.

    Pause, in which the noise is heard, louder now.

MOTHER: It's termites! That sound is termites.

DAUGHTER: Termites don't eat reinforced concrete.

MOTHER: You don't want to admit it. But Lucy, dear child, I'm right, aren't I?

DAUGHTER: Yes, Mom.

   Pause, as before.

MOTHER: I don't understand you people. Why don't you move out?

DAUGHTER: It wouldn't be any use.

MOTHER: But, Lucy!

DAUGHTER: They're everywhere.

MOTHER: Oh, come on.

DAUGHTER: Haven't you noticed that you can hear that same sound everywhere? In New York, in California—in Mexico, in Canada. . . .

MOTHER: You can bet your life there aren't any termites in Albanville. My home is safe.

DAUGHTER: Believe you me: they're chewing away on your house just like they're doing here.

MOTHER: Someone would've noticed. No, it's just not true.

DAUGHTER: Once you've heard it, you hear it everywhere. In people's apartments and in the subway, in the trees and in the cornfields. I think they're even burrowing away underground. The ground we stand on is just a thin layer of skin. Everything, now, consists of just a thin layer of skin—it's all hollowed out inside.

MOTHER: No, that's not the way it is. That is a delusion, Lucy.

DAUGHTER: One strong tremor, and everything collapses. We haven't had a thunderstorm for a while. . . .

MOTHER: And you think that a thunderstorm—?

DAUGHTER: Yes. Yes.

MOTHER (*with a strained, choking laugh*): Well, seems to me it's been sort of hot and muggy all day. Why don't you open the window, Lucy?

DAUGHTER: All right, Mom. (*she opens the window*)

MOTHER: What do you know—it isn't like that at all, outside. Fresh air. Thank God. Clears the brain. So, listen, Lucy dear: you can't stay here any longer, it's out of the question. You come with me to Albanville, both of you, and we'll figure something out. I want to talk to Bill as soon as he gets home. Why isn't he here yet? It's way past five.

DAUGHTER: Maybe it isn't five yet.

MOTHER: Well, the radio should tell us the exact time. (*she turns the radio on*) Where people know what time it is, things are in good

order. And where things are in good order, there are no secrets.
Radio warms up slowly.

DAUGHTER: He's still talking about termites.

PROFESSOR: As the proverb of the Central African Ewe tribe has it: "The termite chews up things, it chews up God's things, but it cannot chew up God."

MOTHER: That's the end of it?

DAUGHTER: Probably so.

ANNOUNCER: You heard a lecture by Professor Wilkinson. At the gong, the time will be five-thirty.
Gong.

MOTHER: Half past five. Where is Bill?

DAUGHTER: Maybe we can find a bit of music on another station.
She fiddles with the dial. We hear various voices and kinds of music, until she stops at a station broadcasting quiet dance music.

MOTHER (*yawns*): If I could be sure he won't come in any minute now, I'd take a little nap. I feel terribly sleepy, all of a sudden.

DAUGHTER: But of course, Mom, just stretch out there on the couch.

MOTHER: It was a long trip, and now all this excitement. . . . I feel a little dizzy.

DAUGHTER: Just have a little nap. I'll get dinner ready.

MOTHER: That's nice music, puts you right to sleep. And it shuts out that terrible sound, most of it, anyway.
Pause, in which the music continues. Doorbell. The radio sounds very distant, as a door is opened close by.

DAUGHTER: Bill!

BILL: Hi, Lucy.

DAUGHTER: What's the matter? Why are you standing there on the landing?

BILL: Oh, Lucy, just go into the kitchen.

DAUGHTER: Bill—no kiss?

BILL: No, no kiss today. Don't touch me. I'm drunk. Let me in, but don't touch me.

DAUGHTER: You're not drunk, Bill. What on earth is the matter with you? Oh, everything is so horrible.

BILL: Come in here.
Door closes.

DAUGHTER: My Mom is here. She's come to visit.

BILL: Where is she?

DAUGHTER: In here—*(door opens, radio music sounds closer)* She's taking a nap, the trip made her tired. Are you hungry?

BILL: No.

DAUGHTER: Dinner's almost ready. Calf's liver.

BILL: I don't want to eat.

DAUGHTER: But that's your favorite dish!

BILL: I'm not hungry. Well, Mom is really fast asleep.

DAUGHTER: I'll finish fixing dinner, and then we'll wake her up.

BILL: Oh, don't worry about dinner! Stay here a moment.

DAUGHTER: All right.

BILL: Lucy, you're so beautiful. God, I love you!

DAUGHTER *(happy)*: Oh, Bill—

BILL: No, stay there, don't touch me. Oh Lucy, you're so beautiful I could cry. Or maybe you aren't so beautiful at all, but I love everything about you. But I'll never kiss you again, Lucy.

DAUGHTER: Bill!

BILL: Stay in your chair! Tell me: did Mom get tired all of a sudden? What I mean is—she didn't seem tired at all, before it happened?

DAUGHTER: She just said, all of a sudden, that she would like to lie down. She wanted me to wake her up when you got here. I'll do it now.

BILL: You can't wake her up anymore. She is dead.

DAUGHTER *(cries out)*: Bill! What are you saying!

BILL: Stay where you are! Don't touch her! Listen, be sensible, I don't have much time left to talk to you. You see, I'm feeling damn tired, too.

> *Crackling noise in the radio.*

BILL: We're going to have a thunderstorm. You can hear it in the static.

DAUGHTER: Bill, I want to go away.

BILL: Where? Turn off the radio—that static is terrible.

> *Radio is turned off. The termite noise is heard again.*

BILL: You hear that?

DAUGHTER *(whispers)*: I hear it. I want to go, Bill.

BILL: Oh, Lucy, please stay—don't let me die here alone.

DAUGHTER: We don't want to die, we want to live.

BILL: I'll die, just like your Mom.

DAUGHTER: No!

BILL: Now she's nothing but a thin layer of skin. She'll crumble to dust if you touch her.

DAUGHTER: But not you—not you!

BILL: Me, too. I noticed it on the way home. I had just looked at my watch, it was half past five, and that's when I noticed it. Now they've reached my heart. It doesn't hurt, but I'm all hollowed out inside. If you touch me, I'll disintegrate.

DAUGHTER: Bill!

BILL: No, don't touch me. I'm incredibly tired. It was so nice with you, it was so nice, living with you.

DAUGHTER: Bill!

> *Distant thunder.*

BILL: It's coming closer. When it gets here, the building disintegrates.

DAUGHTER: But you—you won't!

BILL: Yes I will, and so will Mom. Oh, Lucy—good night, my darling—good night.

> *The daughter cries out while we hear a loud, long, rolling thunderclap.*

Wake up, for your dreams are not good!
Stay awake, for the horror approaches.

Even to you it comes, who live far away from the sites where blood is spilled,
even to you and your afternoon nap,
the one you don't like disrupted.
If it does not come today, it will come tomorrow,
but rest assured.

"Oh, pleasant sleep
on these pillows with their red flowers,
a Christmas present from Anita, she spent three weeks embroidering them,
oh, pleasant sleep
after the juicy roast and the tender vegetables.
Nodding off, one muses upon last night's newsreel:
Easter lambs, awakening nature, opening of the Casino at Baden-Baden,
Cambridge beat Oxford by two and a half—

that's enough to keep the brain busy.
Oh, this soft pillow, filled with the best grade of down!
Resting on it, one forgets the troubles of this world,
that news item, for instance: The abortionist said in his defense
'The woman, mother of seven, came to me holding a baby.

She couldn't afford to buy diapers,
so she had wrapped it in newspapers.'
Well, that's a matter for the court, no concern of ours.
One can't help it if some people have a harder time of it than others,
and whatever the future holds, our grandchildren will have to deal
    with it."

"I see, you're asleep already? High time to wake up, my friend!
The current's already been switched on in the fences,
and the guards are at their posts."

No, do not sleep while the arrangers of the world are busy!
Mistrust the power they say they need to acquire for your sake!
Make sure your hearts are not empty
when they are counting on the emptiness of your hearts!
Do what is not necessary,
sing the songs they do not expect to hear from your lips!
Be troublesome, be sand, not oil in the gears of the world!

Translated by Anselm Hollo

DON'T GO TO AL-KUWAID!

CHARACTERS

MOHALLAB, *a merchant*
WELID, *his servant*
JEZID
A MAID
OMAR THE BANDIT
WILE, *his sister*
SAAD, *prince of the Parsees*
SHIRIN, *his wife*
OKBA, *the executioner*

Outdoors, outside Al-Kuwaid

MOHALLAB *(calls)*: Welid!

WELID *(farther away)*: Sir!

MOHALLAB: Come, ride ahead with me!

WELID *(closer)*: You're impatient, sir. The beasts are carrying heavy loads.

MOHALLAB: I'm not trying to make them go faster. But my yearning can't pad along on camel's feet.

WELID: It is only five days to Damascus.

MOHALLAB: From Al-Kuwaid, that is! Welid, your arithmetic is poor. That's why you haven't come up in the world—past the point of becoming my servant.

WELID: I do not wish for anything more. May the arithmetic be your responsibility. You are the merchant.

MOHALLAB: Welid, am I a stingy man?

WELID: Not with piasters. But with *time,* you are.

MOHALLAB: Not with piasters, but with time: that's true. Another five nights to be spent in dirty caravanserais, another five notches in the bamboo staff, another five times five calls of the muezzin, five times five my face toward Mecca—but why would that bother me, if it didn't have to do with—what, Welid?

WELID: Fatimeh.

MOHALLAB: Fatimeh. Yes. Speak to me of Fatimeh!

WELID: Sir, she'll be your wife, not mine.

MOHALLAB: Speak as if she were your beloved. Her hair—

WELID: —is as black as a moonless night. . . .

MOHALLAB: Why doesn't everybody speak of her? I long to hear about her.

WELID: Whomever she looks at, her eye sets on fire.

MOHALLAB: More!

WELID: Her eyebrows are curved like the horn of the moon. Her cheeks are as velvety as a peach.

MOHALLAB: Welid—you're in love with her!

WELID: Sir—

MOHALLAB: Say that you love her!

WELID: I love her.

MOHALLAB: Good. But who will possess her?

WELID: Mohallab, the merchant.

MOHALLAB: Fatimeh is loved by all: but she will be mine. Go on!

WELID: Her stature is that of a gazelle. Her words are sweet and gentle, her mouth—

MOHALLAB: Hush—only *I* know her mouth. But tell me this, Welid: what are we bringing home from India?

WELID: The camels are laden with silk, with carpets, with skins, with spices.

MOHALLAB: And all of it is—

WELID: For Fatimeh.

MOHALLAB: It's all for Fatimeh.

WELID: If I may say so, sir, you're getting carried away. When would Fatimeh ever set foot in your warehouses?

MOHALLAB: Oh, you're so sober!

WELID: Besides, aren't the goods the joint property of Hassan, your soon-to-be brother-in-law, and yourself?

MOHALLAB: And *you* accuse me of having a merchant's mind. Listen, Welid: would I have undertaken this journey, if Fatimeh didn't exist? Would I have piled up profit, had she not been my goal?

WELID: It is a good thing that we'll be in Damascus soon. If I had to go on telling you, every day, that I love Fatimeh—I just might end up really loving her.

MOHALLAB: Welid, I *order* you to love her. The envy of others sweetens possession. . . .

WELID *(his face turned away)*: Sir, that is Al-Kuwaid over there.

MOHALLAB: Those hovels in the valley?

WELID: It is bigger than it looks from here.

MOHALLAB: Whoa, Welid!

WELID: Sir, what is the matter?

MOHALLAB: I have seen these houses before!

WELID: You said you had never been in Al-Kuwaid before.

MOHALLAB: I never have.

WELID: Many places look the same. Nothing special: houses, gardens, date groves—

MOHALLAB: But I have seen *these* houses, *these* gardens, *these* palm trees.

WELID: We all know that feeling of having seen something before—or of having lived some moment once before.

MOHALLAB: I'm not saying it is anything special. Let us ride on.

JEZID *(approaching)*: Mercy, milord, mercy!

WELID: A beggar.

JEZID: May Allah protect you! See my crutches, my rags, my suppurating sores! May Allah protect your comeliness, and that of your spouse! May He protect your wealth and your journey!

MOHALLAB: Whoa, Welid. Here!

　　The clinking of coins on the ground.

JEZID: Milord, you gave me three piasters! I kiss your stirrup, I kiss the knees of your camel.

MOHALLAB: Onward!

JEZID: Wait, milord!

MOHALLAB: How dare you grab the reins of my horse?

JEZID: It's for your own sake, milord.

WELID: Give him a taste of the whip. Those piasters didn't agree with him.

JEZID: Don't listen to him, milord, listen to me!

MOHALLAB: Why are you staring at me like that, you bundle of rags? Where have I seen your eyes before?

JEZID: Nowhere, milord. And everywhere.

MOHALLAB: Go now. Your gaze makes me sad.

JEZID: I'm going, milord, but I want you to hear this: if your name is Mohallab, don't go to Al-Kuwaid!

MOHALLAB: Where do you know me from? Why shouldn't I go to Al-Kuwaid?

JEZID *(moving away)*: Farewell, milord! May Allah protect you!

WELID: Well, sir? Are you hesitating?

MOHALLAB: No.

WELID: So, on to Al-Kuwaid?

MOHALLAB: Should I turn around because of some beggar?

Al-Kuwaid, in the Street

The approaching sound of a blacksmith's shop.

WELID: Why are we stopping here, sir? The caravanserai is at the other end of Al-Kuwaid.

MOHALLAB: The forge.

WELID: I thought we had enough of those in Damascus.

MOHALLAB *(pensively)*: This moment happened once before. The two of us, stopping our caravan here on this dirty street of Al-Kuwaid. In front of us, a mangy dog, cowed and fawning in the dust; a bazaar and its chatter; the crimson weave of a carpet hanging from a window; and this forge. . . .

WELID: Why the forge?

MOHALLAB: Yes, this moment already happened once, and it fills me with sadness.

WELID: Damn that beggar we ran into! His words stick like barbs. How to pull them out of your heart?

MOHALLAB: No, it wasn't the beggar. He only said what was on the tip of my tongue. The forge, Welid! And the hammering: it is my own heartbeat. Welid—something is about to happen, and I am afraid of it!

WELID *(chuckling)*: But I'm telling you, sir, it's just that beggar.

MOHALLAB: I must think of Fatimeh. It has always helped me before! *(as if struggling to remember)* Her hair—her neck—her mouth—oh— *(he sighs)*

WELID: Sir?

MOHALLAB: Even her image has a shadow cast over it—I can't remember her clearly—Welid, help me!

WELID: That's easy enough, sir. You see that veiled woman over there? She has the stature of Fatimeh.

MOHALLAB: Yes—

WELID: She seems to be looking at us.

MOHALLAB: She's turning, walking away.

WELID: But first, she waved. That young woman would like to please you, sir.

MOHALLAB: Strange. She walks like Fatimeh. Come, let us see where she is going.

WELID: But sir, surely you don't care for a prostitute?

MOHALLAB *(farther away)*: Come on!

The hammering at the forge recedes; voices and noises of the bazaar come closer.

MOHALLAB: She's vanished.

WELID: Leave her be, sir. Let's ride on to the inn.

MOHALLAB: Why did that beggar say I shouldn't go to Al-Kuwaid?

WELID: Chase away your megrims, sir! Fatimeh's memory has always been helpful to you. Try it today.

MOHALLAB: I can't remember.

WELID: Her hair is as black as a moonless night. Whomever she looks at, she sets on fire; her eyebrows are curved like the horn of the moon, her cheeks velvety as a peach. Her stature is that of a gazelle—

MOHALLAB: Stop, Welid! *(after a pause)* Was that veiled woman not Fatimeh?

The street noises grow louder, then fade away.

A Room at Omar's

JEZID: A hundred and twenty camels. Carrying silk, carpets, skins, and spices.

OMAR: Armed men?

JEZID: About fifty.

WILE: I waved at Mohallab, and he followed me.

OMAR: Be quiet!

JEZID: The camels have been relieved of their loads. Mohallab and Welid are at the inn.

OMAR: And the armed men?

JEZID: With the camels.

WILE: I like that Mohallab. He has sad eyes. I love that.

OMAR: Be quiet. His eyes will get sadder still.

WILE: But not because of me, Omar.

OMAR: Because of you, too, Wile. Decoys are disappointing.

WILE: Really?

OMAR: I'll make sure that you disappoint him.

WILE *(laughs)*

OMAR: When the candle goes out, that's our signal.

JEZID: I warned him, I told him not to go to Al-Kuwaid.

OMAR: You warned him?

JEZID: He gave me three piasters.

OMAR: Jezid—for three piasters you throw away ten thousand?

JEZID: We'll take those more easily, because my warning confused him. Omar, you lack imagination.

OMAR: And what do you lack?

JEZID: Brawn. I'm too old. But I'd rather have my brain.

OMAR: Enough of your babble.

WILE: Jezid, we have to be quiet, both of us.

OMAR: We have more important things to do. *(claps his hands)*

WILE: You're calling the maid? Why?

OMAR: Do you want Mohallab to be woken up at midnight?

WILE: That'd suit me just fine.

    A door opens

MAID: You called, sir?

OMAR: Go to Mohallab, now!

Caravanserai

MOHALLAB: Welid, I can hear the hammering at the forge—even though it's a long way from here.

WELID: Sir, it is evening. No one is hammering anything now.

MOHALLAB: That is bad. The night has become loud in my ears. Can you hear the piping of the rats?

WELID: You can hear that in any inn. You never noticed it.

MOHALLAB: I'm telling you, things are not good. *(pause)*

WELID: Would you like to retire, sir?

MOHALLAB: No. The spiders are still spinning. In the cracks, the scorpions are still awake. Welid, I'll never get to Damascus!

WELID: May Allah protect you, sir! What are these thoughts that haunt you?

MOHALLAB: Welid, do you know me as a dreamer?

WELID: Well, yes, when you're thinking of Fatimeh.

MOHALLAB: Quiet, don't speak of Fatimeh. She is nearby, she may hear us. *(in a whisper)* She is nearby, but her hair is no longer as black as the night, the moon of her eyebrows has set, Welid, and the peach has rotted away. . . . Her head is a bony skull, Welid, with empty sockets, stripped of all flesh—but you will see her otherwise, and love her.

WELID: Sir, you must have a fever.

MOHALLAB: Probably so. But tell me, am I a dreamer, in your opinion?

WELID: Sir, you have a cool head, and you know your arithmetic.

MOHALLAB: Do I see ghosts? Am I a coward?

WELID: No, sir.

MOHALLAB: Have you ever seen me indecisive, or in a dither like a woman?

WELID: Never.

MOHALLAB: But now I am all those things, ever since this morning, when I saw Al-Kuwaid from those hills.

WELID: That beggar!

MOHALLAB: Not the beggar. Me.

WELID: Sir, you have been here once before, without really knowing it. Maybe as a child. Such things can be brought back—by a lark's wing, a note, an odor.

MOHALLAB *(laughs)*

WELID: Why are you laughing?

MOHALLAB: You breathe on the mountains and expect them to fall.

WELID: No, sir, I'd rather throw a rock at the shadow.

MOHALLAB: Is that better?

WELID: No. Where should I throw it?

MOHALLAB: I had Fatimeh for my dreams, and thus dreams did not require any room in the rest of my life. But there is no room for Fatimeh in Al-Kuwaid.

WELID: Well, sir, then let us depart now, tonight. The camels have been given water. We'll ride for a couple of hours and make camp along the road, as we've done many times.

MOHALLAB: No.

WELID: Let us leave, sir. I can see this is the wrong place for you.

MOHALLAB: It is too late, Welid.

WELID: Too late? Are you not free to do as you please?

MOHALLAB: You can't hear it, Welid, but the chain is being forged. It's becoming stronger and stronger.

WELID: Sir, you are ill.

MOHALLAB: The world is opaque to those who are well.

WELID: We can be ready to leave in an hour.

MOHALLAB: It is too late. Listen!

Approaching footsteps, outside.

WELID: Someone coming.

A knock on the door.

MOHALLAB: Come in!

The door opens.

WELID: What do you want, woman? Who are you?

MAID: I have a message for Mohallab, the merchant. Is that you?

MOHALLAB: I am he. Who sent you?

MAID: My mistress.

MOHALLAB: Her name is Fatimeh.

MAID: She waved to you, sir.

WELID: We do not know her.

MOHALLAB: I know her.

MAID: You know her, Mohallab.

WELID: What does your mistress want?

MAID: Nothing from Mohallab's servant.

MOHALLAB: What does your mistress want?

MAID: That Mohallab, the merchant, follow me so that I can lead him to her.

WELID: Mohallab is indisposed. He cannot come. *(pause)* Well, you've had your answer. What are you waiting for? Go!

MOHALLAB: I'll go with you.

MAID: My mistress knows the cure for your illness, Mohallab.

WELID: Don't go, sir, don't go!

MOHALLAB: Wait for word from me, Welid!

WELID: I'll wait for you.

MOHALLAB: Good-bye, Welid!

WELID: May Allah protect you, sir!

MOHALLAB: Allah protects whom it pleases him to protect.

MAID *(triumphantly)*: I'll walk ahead, I'll show you the way!
Mohallab *and* Maid *leave.*

Street at Night, and Wile's Place

MOHALLAB: Where's the moon?

MAID: It's the new moon, sir.

MOHALLAB: Not a good time to leave the house.

MAID: A good time for love! *(giggles)*

MOHALLAB: Love? You expect me to think about love, in these alleys?

MAID: Well, sir, they don't smell too wonderful—but I am taking you to a lovely house. A couch, redolent of ambergris. . . . *(giggles)*

MOHALLAB: Your laughter disgusts me, you servant of a whore.

MAID: Incense, if you like. Soft carpets.

MOHALLAB: Shut up!

MAID: But you came with me.

MOHALLAB: I'm driven by the same thing that makes dogs howl.

MAID: That's what I thought.

MOHALLAB: What did you think?

MAID: If it's not lust, it's fear.

MOHALLAB *(mumbles)*: It has to be something else, too! Remembrance. Or nonremembrance—what hovers above the tip of your tongue, but does not want to pass your lips.

MAID: A magic word, eh? Wile will unlock your lips, all right. *(giggles)*

MOHALLAB: Wile?

MAID: That is the name of my mistress.

MOHALLAB: She is no mistress of mine.

MAID: So you thought of that? Then she is. *(giggles)*

MOHALLAB: No, she is not.

MAID: Are you afraid?

MOHALLAB: I didn't forget my dagger.

MAID: Your dagger?

MOHALLAB: Why are you stopping here? Is this where we're going?

MAID: No. But it surprises me that you thought it necessary to bring a weapon.

MOHALLAB: It surprises you? Then I did the right thing.

MAID: We turn here.

MOHALLAB: And what if I turned back?

MAID: Don't listen to my toothless babble! You're not going to see me. You are going to see Wile.

MOHALLAB: I know I have another goal.

MAID: Which one, sir?

MOHALLAB: Which one? All I know is that I have it.

MAID: Come, then, up these steps. Here is our goal! *(giggles)* Through this door! Wile has a perfect body, sir. I am taking you to perfection.

> *We hear their footsteps on stairs and in hallways. They stop.*
> *A curtain is pulled aside, with a metallic tinkle.*

MAID: Mistress Wile, your visitor is here.

WILE: Good. Leave us alone.

> *Pause, during which we hear footsteps receding outside.*

Greetings, Mohallab.

MOHALLAB: Greetings, Wile.

WILE: Come closer.

MOHALLAB: Take off your veil. Let me see your face, Wile.

WILE *(with a quiet laugh)*: You'll be disappointed. *(pause)* Well? Why are you looking at me so hard?

MOHALLAB: I don't know you.

WILE: Where would you know me from?

MOHALLAB: But I expected to know you.

WILE *(laughs)*: Because I had her bring you to me?

MOHALLAB: No—not to know you, but to remember you.

WILE: Mohallab, I am not a ghost. Look here. I have hands, skin, a neck—why are you pulling your hand back?

MOHALLAB: Your skin is scorching me.

WILE: So let yourself burn!

MOHALLAB: It is burning me the way ice can burn.

WILE: Ice is a rare thing in our country. I don't know it. But you have traveled wide and far.

MOHALLAB: You are like ice—because there is a memory lurking somewhere inside you, I fear. And I suspect it to be a terrible memory.

WILE *(smiling)*: Mohallab!

MOHALLAB: But, perhaps that is why I have come to Al-Kuwaid.

WILE: Yes. That is why.

MOHALLAB: I'm feverish. I don't know if this is my body. I'd despise it, if it were.

WILE: Would you like something to eat or to drink?

MOHALLAB: No, nothing.

WILE: Come closer, Mohallab. Sit down beside me.

MOHALLAB: It doesn't surprise you that I came?

WILE: It doesn't surprise you that I sent for you?

MOHALLAB: I heard the hammer in the forge, I heard the howling of the dogs, I heard Welid, my servant. All of them warned me, but also impelled me—

WILE: To come to me.

MOHALLAB: Away from certainty.

WILE: But why?

MOHALLAB: Why?

WILE: Because you had a notion that I was beautiful? Because I waved to you? Say yes!

MOHALLAB: No.

WILE: Well, you *could* lie to me.

MOHALLAB: Once, in Persia, I was in an earthquake. Have you ever felt that the ground was no longer safe to stand on?

WILE: My ground is safe.

MOHALLAB: I would like to know who told you to wave to me.

WILE (*too quickly*): No one.

MOHALLAB: No one. But who is that?

WILE: It was a whim. I liked your looks. Allah's breath, if you wish.

MOHALLAB: Allah's breath. . . . And you can say that, just like that?

WILE: I waved to you for the same reason that you came here.

MOHALLAB: Then you should try to remember where you have met me before.

WILE: Maybe I do know you.

MOHALLAB: From where?

WILE: From a dream I had.

MOHALLAB: I have to know more about you—then I'll find the key.

WILE: Oh, Mohallab, you don't have to know anything! I don't want you to know. My mouth, my skin, my hair—it's all for you. That's enough.

MOHALLAB: But Wile, I need to know in whose life I belong. Here in Al-Kuwaid I understood that I was too sure of things. I have never been here before. Or have I, after all?

WILE: Now you belong to my life.

MOHALLAB: When did you come to Al-Kuwaid?

WILE: Mohallab, don't ask. (*quietly*) I don't want to tell a lie.

MOHALLAB: Why would you have to tell a lie?

WILE: I just would have to. Let's leave it at that.

MOHALLAB: Whatever is inside you, without your knowing it—*that* is what I have to rip out of you.

WILE: Mohallab, you frighten me.

MOHALLAB: We are afraid of one another.

WILE: I wish you could be with me in a different way.

MOHALLAB: Wile, I did not come here to make love to you.

WILE: But how else can you find out things?

MOHALLAB: If we made love, you wouldn't tell so many lies?

WILE: As if that was all—that I tell lies. . . .

MOHALLAB: Go on!

WILE: I have said too much already.

MOHALLAB: So—that's it, then: you are lying!

WILE: Forget what I said.

MOHALLAB: I brought this dagger along because the night was dark. Here, there is a light, but it is even darker.

WILE *(frightened)*: No, not the dagger!

> Mohallab *throws the dagger on the floor. The blade makes a metallic sound.*

MOHALLAB: There, my hands are empty. I am unarmed. Now you can tell me everything.

WILE: Mohallab, how can I tell you what I don't know?

MOHALLAB: Do not twine your arms around me. Be merciful.

WILE: Hush! I know how I can tell you. Embrace me, and you'll know everything. No, don't leave! Mohallab, we're running out of time.

MOHALLAB: Running out of time? Isn't the night still young?

WILE: It passes quickly.

MOHALLAB: Now listen to me: if you don't tell me your secret, you have to die!

WILE: Well then, let me die. Blow out the candle, Mohallab!

> Mohallab *blows out the candle.*

WILE: Here, my hand—my lips—

OMAR *(loud)*: Mohallab!

WILE *(sighing)*: It is too late.

OMAR: Bring the torches in here!

> *The sound of footsteps and the crackle of flaming torches.*

MOHALLAB: Wile, what does this mean?

OMAR: It means that I've picked up your dagger and stuck it in my belt.

MOHALLAB: Who are you?

OMAR: Tie him up.

MOHALLAB: Dogs!

> Mohallab *puts up a struggle, groans, is overpowered.*

OMAR: Why are you struggling, you fool—you think you're a match for twenty of us?

MOHALLAB: Wile, did you know this would happen?

WILE: I knew. It is why I sent for you.

MOHALLAB *(laughing)*: But of course! You told me you were lying.

WILE: I was lying, Mohallab. But I was honest with you, too.

MOHALLAB: What do you want from me?

WILE: Money.

MOHALLAB: I don't have any money on me.

OMAR: Don't take that so literally. You came here with a caravan.

MOHALLAB: I have a partner. I can't dispose of the goods without him.

OMAR *(with ironic compassion)*: Oh, well, Mohallab—that's not really one of *our* worries.

MOHALLAB: Why didn't you just attack our caravan?

OMAR: We're hoping this way will prove easier. We don't like to attract too much attention. Have you calmed down now? *(pause)* Because if you have, I'd like to suggest that we undo your fetters. I'd like to talk and come to an understanding with you, on friendly terms.

MOHALLAB: I'm touched by your offer of friendship.

OMAR: Well, thank you! Take those ropes off.

MOHALLAB: Just a simple ambush. . . . Yes: this knavery calms me down.

OMAR: Now isn't that the truth? An honest robber is more reassuring than an uncertain future. We'll understand each other, quite gloriously.

WILE: You are easily reassured, Mohallab.

MOHALLAB: Does that disappoint you, Wile?

WILE: It does.

OMAR: May I suggest that you take a seat on this carpet, Mohallab. Wile is going to sit a little farther away from you than before. But, that doesn't really matter, does it? She's no longer keeping any secrets from you.

MOHALLAB: You're not sitting all that close, either. Are you afraid? With two daggers in your belt?

OMAR: And two guards behind you. One to the right, one to the left.

MOHALLAB: Four armed men for one merchant? You're overdoing it.

OMAR: We know how to treat an honored guest. Are you comfortable?

MOHALLAB: You're very kind.

OMAR: I would regret it if those fetters had hurt you. Would you like a little ointment?

MOHALLAB: You are overwhelming me with your benevolence. But I am fine, I don't need anything.

OMAR: A little cake, perhaps? A goblet of camel's milk?

MOHALLAB: Let's get down to it.

OMAR: All right, then. *(sighs)*

MOHALLAB: Well?

OMAR: You have to understand my inclination to put this off as long as possible. I am a very sensitive man. Not as comfortable in the world of business as yourself. I love poetry.

MOHALLAB: Oh.

OMAR: Listen!

Let your hands get used to giving:
then, in the end,
you won't find it hard
to let go of your life.

MOHALLAB: Good advice.

OMAR: Isn't it? Harīrī wrote that, in the thirtieth year of his life.

MOHALLAB: It is always a pleasure to meet cultured people.

OMAR: The pleasure is mine, entirely. But, Mohallab, what I mean to say by quoting those lines is this: in his thirtieth year, Harīrī was thinking about his demise. And the message is, quite obviously, that one should start thinking about the end early on. How old are you, Mohallab?

MOHALLAB: In those terms, old enough to think about the end.

OMAR: I can see that you know how to apply the lessons of poetry to your life.

Here's another one by Harīrī:
Be content with little, grateful be.
Frugality brings true abundance.
Avoid greed: despicable is the vulture,
ignoble, the voracious hyena.
Though your garb may be tattered, let your soul
be as immaculate as the vestments of the swan.

MOHALLAB: Harīrī must have had *you* in mind, in that one.

OMAR: Come, come. We don't lay any claim to such golden lines— we make presents of them, to our guests.

MOHALLAB: So you are my host?

OMAR: Are you not sitting on a soft carpet? Did we not offer you cakes and camel's milk?

MOHALLAB: And fetters, as well.

OMAR: Oh, Mohallab, why not let prudence inform your words? Why remind me of the shadow that fell upon our friendship?

MOHALLAB (*impatiently*): All right, then. I am your guest.

OMAR: And will remain so for a long time, I hope.

MOHALLAB: How long?

OMAR: You sound so impatient. Do you have urgent business to attend to?

MOHALLAB: Regrettably, yes. An urgent journey to Damascus.

OMAR: Mohallab, you can't possibly leave us so quickly. Wile would be inconsolable. Wile!

WILE: I would be inconsolable.

MOHALLAB: I feel that way, too.

OMAR: Really? Oh, I'm glad!

MOHALLAB: But I don't know how I could postpone my journey.

OMAR: Oh, don't worry about that. We know how.

MOHALLAB: How?

OMAR: You simply tell your servant—his name is Welid?—a capable man, is he not?—

MOHALLAB: Yes, he is.

OMAR: Well, then you can trust him to obey your orders.

MOHALLAB: *Your* orders, I should think!

OMAR: Speak wisely, Mohallab. Remember our friendship.

MOHALLAB: Well, then, what orders?

OMAR: I was thinking that we might take care of your camels. We'll treat them well, and the goods will be undamaged.

MOHALLAB: All the things I bought for Fatimeh. . . . Half a fortune!

OMAR: Only *half* a fortune? How many have lost it all! Think about Harīrī:

> Be content with little, grateful be.

MOHALLAB: No.

OMAR: Why don't you give voluntarily what you are bound to lose anyway?

MOHALLAB: I am bound to lose it?

OMAR: You're bound to lose something in any case. Either your camels and goods, or—

MOHALLAB: Or?

OMAR: But Mohallab, have you already forgotten Harīrī's teaching:

> then, in the end, you won't find it hard
> to let go of your life.

MOHALLAB: Give me a day to think it over.

OMAR: Unfortunately, we have to leave Al-Kuwaid this very night. I don't think you'll want to come with us.

MOHALLAB: Didn't you just say that you hoped to have me as your guest for a long while?

OMAR: It is not wise to remind one's friend of his contradictions. *(suddenly tough)* Shall I have them tie you up again? You can have that, too.

WILE: Calm down, Omar. Mohallab won't refuse us.

MOHALLAB: I am in your hands. So be it.

OMAR: Mohallab, my dear friend, my blood brother!

MOHALLAB: So, what is going to happen?

OMAR: Pen and ink, please! You will write a letter to Welid. You'll tell him to bring the loaded camels here, and to pay and dismiss the armed escort. Tell him to stand by for further instructions.

MOHALLAB: Without a word of explanation?

OMAR: We do not want to upset Welid unnecessarily. Servants are under no obligation to share the emotional states of their masters.

WILE: Call the messenger!

OMAR: Did you get all that down?

MOHALLAB: ". . . bring them here without delay."

OMAR: Without delay, that's good. You surpass me in your attention to my interests.

MOHALLAB: They are mine, too. I want to be a free man again.

OMAR: Allow me to read it.

MOHALLAB: Friends have no secrets.

OMAR: You are a treasure trove of wisdom. A lesson to me.

MOHALLAB: I'm afraid I'm not always so wise.

OMAR: On your way now, with this letter!

A man's footsteps, receding.

OMAR: Well, Mohallab, perhaps you'd like to take this chance to get a little rest? It'll take a few hours for the camels to arrive here. I'll provide you with a room to sleep in, all by yourself. And, as you know, much good can be derived from solitude.

MOHALLAB: Let them take me there.

Outside the Caravanserai

WELID: Don't I know you?

JEZID: From where?

WELID: Before we came into town we met a beggar. He was lame and mangy, but he looked a lot like you.

JEZID: So you want to see me as a mangy beggar?

WELID: I see you as what you are.

JEZID: Then you must be equal to Allah.

WELID: Are the camels ready?

JEZID: As you can see, everything's ready.

WELID: Where are we headed?

JEZID: Where I take you.

WELID: I don't believe any of you—but the letter is in Mohallab's handwriting. . . .

Room at Omar's

A door opens.

OMAR: Forgive me, Mohallab, for disturbing your sleep.

MOHALLAB: I wasn't sleeping.

OMAR: You must have heard the camels arrive, the shouting of their drivers.

MOHALLAB: Is everything ready?

OMAR: Almost. Welid is waiting for your orders.

MOHALLAB: Take me to him.

OMAR: A while ago, you complained because we didn't invite you to be our guest for a longer time. I have thought it over. You can stay with us.

MOHALLAB: What does that mean? You promised to let me go. Is this how you keep your word?

OMAR: Mohallab, we have a deep desire to partake of your wisdom a little longer, both Wile and I. Wile, by the way, is my sister—did you know that? She is nobody's wife.

MOHALLAB: I don't care.

OMAR: That is a pity. She loves you so much. Both of us would be glad to have you stay with us.

MOHALLAB: No!

OMAR: As I asked you once before—why do you not, of your own free will, give what you will have to give anyway? How can you leave us if I don't want you to?

MOHALLAB: Your word!

OMAR: The word of a bandit isn't worth much.

MOHALLAB: For how long, then?

OMAR: Until Welid returns.

MOHALLAB: Returns? From where?

OMAR: From Damascus, of course.

MOHALLAB: How about some details, Omar?

OMAR: Losing this caravan, you lost half a fortune?

MOHALLAB: I said that. And it is true.

OMAR: Now all we need is the second half. I had the idea that Welid could bring it to us. After he has done that, we—with a heavy heart—will have to let you go with him.

MOHALLAB: As a beggar.

OMAR:

> *O put your trust in the veiled hand*
> *that leads no one where he wants to go,*
> *and always be prepared for change,*
> *for change is the fate of the world.*

MOHALLAB: More Harīrī.

OMAR:

> *Endure your suffering until the One*
> *who brought it to you tells it to be gone.*

MOHALLAB: A poet for all occasions.

OMAR: So, let us say: ten thousand piasters.

MOHALLAB: A nice round figure.

OMAR: Isn't it?

MOHALLAB: And who is supposed to come up with it?

OMAR: I have heard that you own, in partnership with your friend Hassan, a mercantile enterprise in Damascus. His sister was to be your wife. Surely, anyone would come up with a measly ten thousand piasters to save his brother-in-law's life? I'm assuming that your share in the business is the larger one by far—

MOHALLAB: No, it is smaller.

OMAR: Well, familial piety will have to account for the difference. In any case, Mohallab, friend and blood brother, I thought you could write a letter for Welid to take to Damascus. *(he claps his hands, calls out)* Pen and ink, please!

MOHALLAB: I want to speak to Welid.

OMAR: Oh, that won't be necessary. He'll do everything right, and to your satisfaction. I will tell him exactly where to bring the ransom money. And, dear Mohallab, I'd also like you to mention to Hassan that you have fallen into the hands of *bandits*. That might speed matters up. Even though it isn't true—

MOHALLAB: —Allah will forgive this lie.

OMAR: You know my words before they leave my lips. Yes, it is as you say, and we won't be offended if you describe us with such an ugly word—even though, in reality, we are your solicitous hosts. Ah, you're writing already. Truly, Mohallab, you are a wise man.

Outside a Tent

JEZID: What are you complaining about, Mohallab? I told you: don't go to Al-Kuwaid!

MOHALLAB: Welid's been gone a month. Maybe he is unable to find us?

JEZID: He'll find us.

MOHALLAB: Where are we now?

JEZID: I don't know. We move around so much. I have a poor memory for names.

MOHALLAB: I suspect that we're not too far from the Euphrates River.

JEZID: That's possible.

MOHALLAB: Even though you don't remember names, you know more than the others. Tell me: what exactly happened to me in Al-Kuwaid?

JEZID: Didn't you notice?

MOHALLAB: A kidnapping, extortion—that was all there was to it?

JEZID: That's not enough for you?

MOHALLAB: It was no more than that?

JEZID: You looked down into the valley, and down you went. Maybe poverty was waiting for you.

MOHALLAB: Poverty, for sure.

JEZID: Don't let it bother you. I'll give you the three piasters that you threw on the ground for me, back there.

MOHALLAB: Thank you, Jezid.

JEZID: There is always more than one word for the same thing. Why not substitute another word for "poverty"?

MOHALLAB: One that would be more palatable to me?

JEZID: Most people merely borrow their existence. Then they are surprised when they have to give it back, one day.

MOHALLAB: Then I'll become what I really am?

JEZID: If you achieve that, you have great wealth.

MOHALLAB: I will go back to Damascus. Hassan and Fatimeh will help me, and if Allah favors me, I'll recoup my loss in a few years.

JEZID *(laughs)*

MOHALLAB: Why are you laughing, Jezid?

JEZID: Then you would have gone to Al-Kuwaid for nothing!

MOHALLAB: Nothing? Twenty-thousand piasters is nothing?

JEZID: If you put a piaster value on it, it was cheap. But I'm afraid, Mohallab, you'll have to pay more than that.

MOHALLAB: How do you mean?

JEZID: You have to pay some more, but it won't be in piasters.

MOHALLAB: So tell me, what will it be?

JEZID: I don't know. I just have this premonition that that's how it will have to be.

MOHALLAB: Where does that premonition come from?

JEZID: I read it in your face. You drug yourself with hopes.

MOHALLAB: Be quiet! I don't believe you.

JEZID: You didn't believe me once before. *(turns away)* Look, over there—three riders!

MOHALLAB: Two. Omar and Wile.

JEZID: And a horse without a rider. Welid isn't with them.

MOHALLAB: Did you expect Welid? I only expect my freedom.

JEZID: So you think it'll come with these two?

> *Horses approach, halt.*

JEZID: A riderless horse?

OMAR *(grouchily)*: We didn't see Welid.

MOHALLAB: He didn't come?

OMAR: He most probably did come. They gave us a letter, at the inn.

WILE: We looked for Welid, but we didn't find him.

JEZID: And the ransom?

OMAR: Give Mohallab the letter. Let him read it.

MOHALLAB: It's very short.

OMAR: You can say that again. Very bad news for you, Mohallab.

MOHALLAB *(excitedly)*: I must go to Damascus.

JEZID: Let me see that letter.

MOHALLAB: Here.

WILE: We're sorry, Mohallab.

OMAR: But not for Mohallab. We're leaving. Jezid, prepare for departure.

JEZID: Aye aye, sir.

MOHALLAB: I have to go to Damascus. Omar, give me a horse or a camel!

OMAR *(laughing)*: A horse or a camel! Did you hear that, Wile?

WILE: Give it to him.

OMAR: And maybe ten thousand piasters as well? You have strange in-laws, Mohallab. What does the letter say? "To us, Mohallab is not worth ten thousand piasters." And now you think that you're worth a horse or a camel, to *me*?

MOHALLAB: I beg you, Omar! I have to know if I'm worth so little to Fatimeh.

OMAR: You think she doesn't know about this letter?

MOHALLAB: I can't believe it.

OMAR: I feel sorry for you, Mohallab, but I feel even sorrier for myself. You've made me lose ten thousand piasters.

MOHALLAB: "Made you lose"—Omar, you're joking!

OMAR: I was counting on that amount. Now I'll have problems.

MOHALLAB: By your kind of reckoning, I have lost the entire world.

OMAR: And that's why you're having problems now.

WILE: He can't *walk* across the desert.

OMAR: He won't have to walk. He can ride.

MOHALLAB: Thank you, Omar!

OMAR: You didn't expect such magnanimity, did you, Mohallab?

WILE: Take the horse we brought for Welid.

OMAR: Yes, he can have that one.

MOHALLAB: I'll leave immediately. Show me the way.

OMAR: We don't have to show it to you. We'll be riding with you.

MOHALLAB: You're going to Damascus?

OMAR: Damascus? Oh no. We're going to Basra.

MOHALLAB: I don't know where I am. Do I have to go to Basra to get to Damascus?

OMAR: No, it's in the opposite direction. But you have to go to Basra.

MOHALLAB: Does this mean that you're not setting me free?

OMAR: You are a poor substitute for ten thousand piasters, but we'll see what you're worth.

Market at Basra

WELID: How much is the white man?

JEZID: Ten thousand piasters, sir.

WELID: Who would pay ten thousand piasters for a slave?

JEZID: He's white.

WELID: The black ones are not so proud, and they work harder.

JEZID: He's very good. Show your muscles, Mohallab! Bend your arm!

WELID: I want to see his teeth.

JEZID: Open your mouth, Mohallab! Look at those gleaming teeth, sir. Go up close, he won't bite.

WELID *(quietly)*: Do you recognize me? I'm Welid.

JEZID: What did you say?

WELID: I say, he has good teeth, but he is about thirty years old. *(quietly)* Eight thousand is all I have.

JEZID: Thirty isn't old. Turn around, Mohallab. See that strong back?

WELID: Let's see him walk.

JEZID: Walk, Mohallab.

WELID: He is limping.

JEZID: So would anyone with a fifty-pound iron ball chained to his leg.

WELID: He is graying at the temples.

JEZID: So? We haven't dyed his hair. This is an honest transaction. But if you prefer, go ahead and buy one with dyed hair.

WELID: Five thousand.

JEZID: He knows how to ride and to use a dagger.

WELID: Not too good—who needs a slave who can stab his master and then ride away?

JEZID: He is strong and likes to work. And he's intelligent.

WELID: For ten thousand piasters, he ought to be a sage. Five thousand.

JEZID: You can use him as an overseer. He can write and do

arithmetic, he knows about buying and selling, and he knows how to deal with people.

WELID: It amazes me that he is a slave, if he knows all those things.

JEZID: Cruel blows of fate. Mohallab, write "Al-Kuwaid" in the air!

WELID: Did you teach him that trick?

JEZID: If seventeen camels are carrying burdens of silk valued at two hundred and thirty piasters a bolt, what is the monetary value of their total load?

MOHALLAB: Three thousand nine hundred and ten piasters.

WELID: Ah, he can speak, too. I thought he was mute.

JEZID: Intelligent men do not speak much.

WELID: Five thousand piasters.

JEZID: Ten thousand.

WELID: Six thousand.

JEZID: Ten thousand.

WELID: Seven.

JEZID: Ten.

WELID: Eight.

JEZID: Ten.

WELID: Consider: eight thousand piasters for a single slave. I could buy four blacks for that.

JEZID: He is white.

WELID: Oh, go to the devil!

JEZID: I'll give him your regards, sir.

WELID *(quietly)*: I'll sell the camels. I'll be back.

JEZID: What did he say?

MOHALLAB: He said he's going to buy a black one.

JEZID: A good decision.

MOHALLAB: But why didn't you sell me for eight thousand? Nobody is going to pay ten thousand for me.

JEZID: He was wearing a fake beard. I didn't trust him.

MOHALLAB: Why worry about a fake beard if he has eight thousand piasters?

JEZID: With someone else, I might've settled for three thousand. But I could tell that he was not well-disposed toward you.

MOHALLAB: Oh, Jezid, you are supposed to bargain to the advantage of Omar. Never mind me.

JEZID: I want to see you in good hands, Mohallab.

MOHALLAB: And that makes you cheat Omar?

JEZID: Yes.

MOHALLAB: Jezid, I am not grateful to you for this.

JEZID: I feel affection for you, Mohallab. I don't need your gratitude.

MOHALLAB: I hate you for it.

JEZID: That doesn't affect my feelings.

MOHALLAB: Oh, Jezid!

SAAD *(stepping close)*: How much is this slave?

MOHALLAB: Don't sell me to him, Jezid!

JEZID: He's white, sir. Show your muscles, Mohallab! He can write and do arithmetic and has a great deal of business experience. He is intelligent and strong. Show your teeth, Mohallab!

SAAD: How old is he?

JEZID: Twenty-five, sir.

MOHALLAB: Thirty.

JEZID: Shut up, son of a dog!

SAAD: How much is he?

MOHALLAB: Don't sell me, Jezid!

JEZID: Three thousand, sir.

MOHALLAB: Sir, I am worthless, I am lame, I don't know how to write, I can't do sums, I'm stupid.

JEZID: He is lying because he wants to stay with me. *(under his breath)* Idiot! I can tell that this is the right one for you.

SAAD: It's a deal.

MOHALLAB: Don't sell me, Jezid!

JEZID: Three thousand piasters, please.

SAAD: His name is Mohallab?

JEZID: Right, Mohallab. Four hundred, five hundred, six hundred. . . .

SAAD: Mohallab, don't be afraid. I am Saad, prince of the Parsees. We'll take good care of you.

MOHALLAB: I am not afraid of you, sir, but of the future.

SAAD: You would rather return to the past?

MOHALLAB: Yes, because I know it.

JEZID: Milord, he no longer has a past. Two thousand one hundred, two hundred. . . .

SAAD: Take off his chain.

JEZID: Eight hundred, nine hundred, three thousand. Thank you, milord. May Allah protect you.

SAAD: And you, too.

JEZID: Farewell, Mohallab, my son.

MOHALLAB: Jezid!

SAAD: Come with me, Mohallab.

MOHALLAB *(from a distance)*: I don't thank you for this, Jezid!

JEZID: May Allah protect you anyway! *(more quietly)* But Allah protects whom it pleases him to protect. *(louder again)* I have a heavy burden here. Three thousand piasters weigh as much as a slave chain. *(groaning)* Oh—

WELID *(approaching)*: Stranger, where is that slave? I want to buy him.

JEZID: For ten thousand piasters?

WELID: Nine thousand. That's all I was able to raise.

JEZID: I told you, that's not enough for such a fine specimen.

WELID: Oh, let him go for nine! Where is he?

JEZID: Look for him, you may get him for free. Farewell, Welid!

Hall in Saad's Palace

Loud voices can be heard approaching outside.

SAAD: Who is coming, Shirin?

SHIRIN: I heard the name Mohallab. . . .

>   *A door opens. The noise continues for a moment, then stops abruptly.*

OKBA: We found him by the river, three days' journey from here. He was hiding in the rushes.

SHIRIN *(quietly)*: He is pale and emaciated.

OKBA: You want me to execute him, milord?

SAAD: I don't want you to do anything. You can go.

>   *Steps recede. Door closes.*

Raise your head, Mohallab, and look at me. *(pause)* Mohallab, have you been treated badly in my house?

MOHALLAB: No, milord.

SAAD: Have you gone hungry, thirsty?

MOHALLAB: Milord, I have not been happy.

SAAD: Have I not made you the overseer of my house slaves? What more do you want, being a slave yourself?

MOHALLAB: I was born free, milord.

SAAD: Nobody is born free. One day, I may be a slave.

MOHALLAB: But I'll never be free?

SAAD: Mohallab, it pains me that you are not contented in my house. For, lo and behold, I like you. I will set you free, one day.

MOHALLAB: When, milord?

SAAD: When you are no longer impatient.

MOHALLAB: That will be too late, milord.

SAAD: How long have you been here?

MOHALLAB: Three months, milord.

SAAD: Is that a long time?

MOHALLAB: Not for one who wishes for nothing.

SAAD: Listen to what I tell you, and don't contradict me!

MOHALLAB: Milord, I am listening. I won't contradict you.

SAAD: Your life belongs to me, and you have forfeited it by your escape. I am being merciful to you: you may keep your life.

MOHALLAB: I thank you, milord.

SAAD: Serve me faithfully for twenty years, and at the end of those twenty years, I will set you free.

MOHALLAB *(hesitantly)*: I thank you, milord.

SAAD: Once again, I appoint you the overseer of my slaves. Furthermore, you will be the guardian of the sacred flame in the temple.

MOHALLAB: I thank you, milord.

SAAD: Thus, your escape has netted you a promotion. *(raising his voice)* But, Mohallab, don't think that my forbearance is endless. Okba, my executioner, has little to do in my domain. He has been pestering me for a death sentence for a long time. He would perform the execution with great pleasure. So, Mohallab, watch out.

MOHALLAB: Yes, milord.

SAAD: You may kiss my hand, as a sign of my mercy. Go now.

Garden

Sound of a distant flute.

SHIRIN: Mohallab?

MOHALLAB: Milady?

SHIRIN: What are you dreaming about?

MOHALLAB: I'm listening to that flute.

SHIRIN: Do you understand what it says?

MOHALLAB: I would like to understand it. I feel that it is telling me something.

SHIRIN: I understand it. Whoever is playing it is happy.

MOHALLAB: Then it isn't a song meant for me.

SHIRIN: It is meant for you. Happiness takes on many forms. But you, you know only one. You are blind.

MOHALLAB: Blind?

SHIRIN: Why did you run away, Mohallab? How could you do that to me?

MOHALLAB: To you, milady? I did not hurt you.

SHIRIN: You hurt me most of all, Mohallab.

MOHALLAB: Forgive me, milady, but I can't stay any longer. I must go to the temple.

SHIRIN: One moment more, Mohallab, for your princess.

MOHALLAB: I am listening.

SHIRIN: Mohallab, you are a slave in this household. I hold sway over you, just like Saad does. *(quietly)* And yet, you are my lord and master, and I am your slave.

MOHALLAB: Milady!

SHIRIN: Hush. Don't contradict me. I want you to be my lord and master, I order you to be that! *(Pause)* Mohallab, I belong to a royal family. You do not know my pride. It makes it possible for me to humiliate myself more deeply than anyone else.

MOHALLAB: Milady, there is not a single person in this household whom I respect as much as I respect you.

SHIRIN *(gently)*: I don't want you to respect me. I want you to love me.

MOHALLAB: You are the wife of my lord and master!

SHIRIN: I don't want to hear about it! Tell me, am I ugly?

MOHALLAB: Milady, one would have to be a liar to call you that.

SHIRIN: Mohallab, I loved you the first moment I saw you. Do you find my mouth pleasing? My hair?

MOHALLAB: I do, milady.

SHIRIN: Thank you, my lord.

MOHALLAB: Milady, I must go.

SHIRIN: Kiss me!

MOHALLAB: Kiss you, milady?

SHIRIN: Kiss me!

MOHALLAB: We're in the garden, in broad daylight.

SHIRIN: I'm telling you, I want you to kiss me!

> *The flute, closer.*

SHIRIN: Well, then did anyone see us?

MOHALLAB: I hope not, milady.

SHIRIN: But tonight, right here, Mohallab—are you listening?

MOHALLAB: I am listening, milady.

SHIRIN: —you have to kiss me even harder!

MOHALLAB: Someone's coming, milady.

SHIRIN: I'm gone.

> *In the meantime, the flute has come even closer.*

MOHALLAB: Hey, flute player, beggar! What song is that you're playing? Get out! This is Prince Saad's garden!

> *Flute playing stops abruptly.*

WELID: You don't recognize this song, sir?

MOHALLAB: I am no sir, I am a slave.

WELID: It's a song from Damascus—Mohallab!

MOHALLAB: Welid!

WELID: Yes, sir!

MOHALLAB: Where do you come from, Welid? Do you bring good tidings?

WELID: I got back too late to the market at Basra. I looked for you everywhere, but in vain.

MOHALLAB: Didn't Jezid tell you who bought me?

WELID: He wouldn't tell me, the devil.

MOHALLAB: I hope it was his intention to be vicious.

WELID: So I rode back and forth across the desert, from Mosul to Hadramaut. Finally, I picked up your track, and followed you here, via Damascus. I had a horse and money. But a day's journey away from here I ran into an ambush. A disaster, sir, because I now stand before you as a beggar. How can we get to Damascus without money, without provisions, without horses or camels, without weapons?

MOHALLAB: But why do you think I want to go to Damascus?

WELID: You don't, sir?

MOHALLAB: What about that letter?

WELID: Oh, we wrote that because we thought Omar would just let you go if no ransom was forthcoming.

MOHALLAB: That was a miscalculation. But you are giving me my life back, Welid. Do you have a message from Fatimeh?

WELID: Fatimeh—sir, I'll tell you later about Fatimeh. First of all let us figure out how we can get to Damascus.

MOHALLAB: Damascus—oh, to hear that word! Fatimeh—

WELID: To Damascus, with no money!

MOHALLAB: Let's just beg, like wandering dervishes. It doesn't matter—as long as we get to Damascus!

WELID: But sir, we can't cross deserts and mountains on foot.

MOHALLAB: Let me think.

WELID: The only thing I still have is a dagger.

MOHALLAB: I have an idea, Welid. It is shameful, but it is an idea.

WELID: It will have to work hard. Damascus is far away.

MOHALLAB: Can you find food and lodging for tonight?

WELID: I can always find those.

MOHALLAB: Come back early tomorrow morning. Maybe I'll have a chance to lay my hands on some money.

Shirin's Room

Shirin *is humming a melody. There is a rapid series of very quiet knocks on the door, executed, as it were, with fingernails. Shirin stops humming and opens the door. The conversation is conducted in whispers.*

SHIRIN: Mohallab!

MOHALLAB: Shirin!

SHIRIN: You come to my room? That's reckless!
     She closes the door.

MOHALLAB: Forgive me, but the day grew too long without you.

SHIRIN: It was longer for me. Look, I just stuck a rose into my hair, preparing to come to you—yet it's a long while until dusk.

MOHALLAB: Shirin, I'm on fire!

SHIRIN: Hush! If someone should hear us—!

MOHALLAB: Bolt the door!
     Sound of door being bolted.

In Front of the Executioner's House

Welid's *flute, coming closer.*

OKBA: Stop that noodling! I'll have no music in front of this house. Walk on by, cover your face!
  End of flute playing.
WELID: Why all that?
OKBA: This is the executioner's house.
WELID: Are you the executioner?
OKBA: I am.
WELID: Then your swords must be the sharpest in the land.
OKBA: I sharpen them myself. *He turns the grindstone, as if testing it, holds a blade against it, then stops it again.*
WELID: Mister Executioner, a poor wanderer asks you for a favor.
OKBA: These are hard times for the likes of me. Our prince does not enjoy seeing people in fear of death, the way a good ruler should. The ropes are rotting, the blades rusting. Go to hell! I don't have any money.
WELID: Mister Executioner, sir, I'm not asking for money. Could you sharpen this dagger for me? For free?
OKBA *(delighted)*: All right, let's see it! *(he starts sharpening it)* A Damascene blade. It'll shine like a diamond. But it needs blood on it, red as rubies. What a jewel!
  Noise of grindstone fades.

Room with Open Windows

Outside a nightingale is singing.

SHIRIN: The nightingale. . . .
MOHALLAB: My heart beats louder! Shirin, let us go away from here!
SHIRIN: But where?
MOHALLAB: Where I am not a slave, where I may love you, where you are nobody's wife! Let us elope, Shirin!
SHIRIN: Mohallab—if they catch you again, that is the end of you!

MOHALLAB: I'm not afraid of dying, as long as you are with me. Two days on the road, and we're in another country.

SHIRIN: I have to leave Saad?

MOHALLAB: Do you love him more than you love me?

SHIRIN: You are my greatest love.

MOHALLAB: Then come with me, Shirin.

SHIRIN: Oh, Mohallab—

MOHALLAB: Are you afraid?

SHIRIN: No.

MOHALLAB: To live with you, Shirin, where no one knows us—

SHIRIN: You, tempter, enchanter—

MOHALLAB: —where we can be happy together—

SHIRIN: What if I said yes?

MOHALLAB: Please do!

SHIRIN: But what will we do for a living?

MOHALLAB *(with a smile)*: I'll tell tales, in the marketplace.

SHIRIN: Hush, you teller of tales! You know, I have my jewelry.

MOHALLAB *(rapidly)*: I'll get some horses. For tomorrow night.

SHIRIN: So soon? No time to think it over?

MOHALLAB: Time engenders doubt, Shirin.

SHIRIN: I'll go with you. Here, this is my jewelry box. Use it sparingly!

MOHALLAB: You trust me with this?

SHIRIN: It surprises you that I trust you?

MOHALLAB: I am a slave.

SHIRIN: My king!

The song of the nightingale stops.

At Night by the Garden Wall

Hoofbeats, at a walking pace. They stop.

MOHALLAB *(calling out, quietly)*: Welid!

SHIRIN: Whom are you calling, Mohallab?

MOHALLAB: There you are, Shirin.

SHIRIN: Ready to elope, my lord and master. But you weren't calling my name.

MOHALLAB: I had a stable boy riding with me, but he has disappeared. He was a coward, afraid of the night.

SHIRIN: I'm not afraid of it. Which horse is mine?

MOHALLAB: Don't mount it yet!

SHIRIN: Why not?

MOHALLAB: You didn't forget anything?

SHIRIN: If you mean my cape, my gown, and my shoes—I have them all. I even brought a capsule of poison.

MOHALLAB: Poison?

SHIRIN: Just a drop, extracted from a thousand herbs. In case that which I forgot should catch up with me—

MOHALLAB: Don't say that!

SHIRIN *(laughs quietly)*

MOHALLAB: I am thirsty. Why don't you go and pick a couple of apples in the garden, while I adjust these saddles?

SHIRIN: We'll pass by a hundred orchards, Mohallab.

MOHALLAB: But Shirin, I'd like a couple from here—can't you see why?

SHIRIN: From the tree under which you kissed me? *(moving away)* I'm going, Mohallab.

MOHALLAB: Pick the two prettiest ones! *(to himself)* Now, up and away!

WELID *(calling quietly)*: Mohallab!

MOHALLAB: Welid! There you are, at last. Is everything ready?

WELID: Everything.

MOHALLAB: You are late. I almost had to ride with Shirin instead of you. To horse! And away!

    Hoofbeats, growing distant.

SHIRIN *(from a distance, calls quietly)*: Mohallab! *(closer)* Mohallab! *(close)* Did I hear horses? *(pause, then, quietly)* Mohallab? Oh . . . is that why you sent me away?

On the Road

Hoofbeats.

WELID: Spare the horses, Mohallab!

MOHALLAB: We need a head start.

WELID: No one is pursuing us.

MOHALLAB: Onward, on through the night! Away—from Shirin.

WELID: You fear her revenge?

MOHALLAB: No, but my face is red with shame. Praised be the darkness of the night that hides it. Onward, away, away from my shame!

Hoofbeats grow more distant and fade away.

By Open Windows

A rooster crows in the distance.

SHIRIN: Can you hear that rooster crow, Mohallab? See, I can talk to you as if you were here—and yet the night lies between us like a black mountain range, and every moment in which the hooves of your steed strike the ground is yet another cliff face of separation, impossible to scale, more final by the hour—Mohallab, Mohallab! And yet you are here, ever closer to me, and I was never able to speak to you the way I am speaking now. Out of one loneliness you came, now you ride into another—each kiss makes you more of a stranger, each embrace impoverishes you—I greet you the way a crag greets its eagle—that flies away, its wings becoming invisible in the icy distance; where its talons rested, a rock comes loose and falls into the abyss, that is all, the forests do not notice it. That is what you long for, the dwellings of people, the warm fur of animals, the consoling speech of the wind in the branches, just as I long for it, too. Do not listen to your heart, seal your ears with wax—for you will never reach what you yearn for, not here nor in Damascus. But ride on, Mohallab, don't ever come back! Your loneliness makes mine twice as great. I would not be able to endure it anymore.

Booming drum beats, in the distance.

Now! Now they have noticed that you are gone.

Other drums, far and near, join in. Silence.

Room in the Palace

OKBA: I'll bring him back, milord, dead or alive.

SAAD: Alive, Okba, alive! Guard him like the apple of your eye!

OKBA: Very well, milord. It is, indeed, better to execute a live one than a corpse.

SAAD: Any clues?

OKBA: It is said that two unknown horsemen left the palace quarter in a hurry, yesterday evening.

SAAD: Two?

OKBA: Maybe the devil came and got him.

Open Terrain

Hoofbeats at a walking pace approach and are heard throughout.

MOHALLAB: How many days to Damascus, Welid?

WELID: Twenty or so.

MOHALLAB: It is a long way.

WELID: A year can be short, a moment long. So, we don't really know how long twenty days are. We have to be watchful.

MOHALLAB: Who knows what may happen to us, Welid—we might be separated, before we know it—

WELID: Sir, what do you mean by that?

MOHALLAB: Take this pouch. I divided up the jewels.

WELID: All right, I'll take it, to get to Damascus.

MOHALLAB: Why else?

WELID: Mohallab, sir, I don't like being in your debt.

MOHALLAB: You mustn't feel indebted to me. But why don't you like it?

WELID: I'd rather not answer that.

MOHALLAB: It is *I* who have to be grateful to you, Welid. You came to me across deserts and mountains. You were loyal.

WELID: I wasn't loyal to you, Mohallab.

MOHALLAB: How, then, do you define loyalty?

WELID: It would be better not to discuss that until we get to Damascus.

MOHALLAB: First you make me anxious, and now you don't want to talk about it?

WELID: Well then, Mohallab, sir: after we get to Damascus, I will be your enemy.

MOHALLAB: But—if you'll be my enemy in Damascus, you must be my enemy now?

WELID: Yes, I am your enemy. Even here.

MOHALLAB *(pain in his voice)*: Welid!

WELID: I am no longer your servant, Mohallab.

MOHALLAB: No, but does that make you my enemy? Oh, Welid—

WELID: Hear, then, what you were to be told in Damascus. Do you remember the letter?

MOHALLAB: "To us, Mohallab is not worth ten thousand piasters."

WELID: I advised Hassan to write that.

MOHALLAB: Nothing so terrible in that. You thought Omar would let me go.

WELID: That was what I said, Mohallab, but I had something else in mind.

MOHALLAB: What was it?

WELID: I thought that he would kill you.

MOHALLAB *(startled)*: Welid!

WELID: You want that pouch back?

MOHALLAB: Keep it. But—go on.

WELID: Omar didn't kill you. He sold you into slavery. I was overcome with remorse, and decided to rescue you.

MOHALLAB: You are a better man than you claim to be, Welid. Every human being has evil thoughts.

WELID *(furious)*: Don't think that I am a good person! Don't expect anything from me! I wanted to help you, but that was to be the *last* thing I ever did for you. I wanted to escort you to Damascus, and from then on, I wanted to be your enemy. Well, I've started a little sooner.

MOHALLAB *(chuckles, then laughs out loud)*: But Welid, why do you insist on being my foe?

WELID: I am not insisting. You are.

MOHALLAB: I am? Welid, you're dreaming.

WELID: Listen to me, Mohallab! I told you that I am no longer your servant.

MOHALLAB: You are not a slave. I can't stop you from leaving my service.

WELID: I have become a merchant.

MOHALLAB: I see. You must have brushed up your arithmetic?

WELID: I hope so, Mohallab. I am now a partner of Hassan, your brother-in-law.

MOHALLAB *(surprised)*: Oh—

WELID: Well, it's really a joke to call him your brother-in-law.

MOHALLAB (*taken aback*): Welid!

WELID: Old habit of mine, now an empty phrase.

MOHALLAB: Welid—what about Fatimeh?

> *The horses stop.*

WELID: Don't grab my reins, Mohallab, I can't stand it when you do that. Yesterday, I had my dagger sharpened. Look at it! And watch out, so I won't have to use it!

MOHALLAB: What about Fatimeh?

WELID: Do you want your jewels back? Mohallab, Fatimeh will be my wife.

MOHALLAB: You are worse than Omar—you sold me worse than he did!

WELID: Watch out, Mohallab! Hands off!

MOHALLAB: I'll strangle you!

WELID: Take that!

MOHALLAB (*cries out*)

WELID: You reckoned wrong, merchant Mohallab.

MOHALLAB (*slides groaning from the saddle*)

WELID: You want your jewels back?

MOHALLAB (*groans*)

WELID: I guess you won't need them anymore. (*he spurs his horse and calls out, from a distance*) I'll give Fatimeh your regards!

MOHALLAB (*quietly*): Welid—help me!

> *Hoofbeats fade away.*

Back at the Palace

OKBA: Milord, you told me to bring him back alive. It is not my fault that he is more dead than alive. Could I have known that when I sharpened that dagger?

SAAD: Stop babbling, Okba! How many times do you want to tell me that story. Take him to the dungeon.

SHIRIN: A sick man, to the dungeon?

SAAD: And call my personal physician to attend to him.

SHIRIN: He must get well.

OKBA: Milady, we'll do everything we can, but—"well"?

SAAD: Go, don't waste time!

> *Footsteps of the men carrying the stretcher. A door is opened and closed.*

SHIRIN: Saad—should I take care of him?

SAAD: You? He is in good hands. A princess does not have to nurse a slave in a dungeon, even if he is worth three thousand piasters.

SHIRIN: Don't be hard on him.

SAAD: They found this little box of jewels next to him. Look!

SHIRIN: It's mine.

SAAD: Had you noticed that it had been stolen?

SHIRIN: No, I hadn't. You think he stole it?

SAAD: Who else?

SHIRIN: The other one, the one who stabbed him.

SAAD: Then why didn't *he* take the jewels?

SHIRIN: Well, what if Mohallab noticed the thief and followed him, and took the jewel box away from him—and then got stabbed in the melee—

SAAD: And then the thief leaves the box lying there, next to his unconscious victim? Take a look, see if anything's missing.

SHIRIN: Yes, a bracelet is missing, and a piece to be worn round the neck . . . a pair of ruby earrings, a belt buckle. . . .

SAAD: So the thief only took half of your things?

SHIRIN: Oh, I don't know.

SAAD: If Mohallab ever wakes up to life again, we'll know. Oh, Shirin: I wish he wouldn't wake up.

Dungeon

OKBA: This ointment on the wound, in the morning and at night. Oh, Mohallab, what pains I have to take to bring you back to life, just so I can take it from you again! "Moisten lips with chamomile tea." For three days I have moistened his lips with chamomile tea. What becomes of a man when all he takes in is a little moisture flavored with chamomile? Starving to death is a horrible way to go. Come on, Mohallab, wake up, have a bite to eat, be glad that it is *I* who'll dispatch you! Mohallab, I am a master of my trade. Believe me, starvation is a bloody poor executioner. Hey—did you say something? He's moving his lips. No. Or? Mohallab, you know how to torture a man. You'd make a good apprentice.

MOHALLAB *(quietly)*: Welid!

OKBA: What? You're talking. Mohallab, my friend, my dear friend, you are talking! *(even more beside himself)* And you've opened your eyes! God knows, maybe you've been peering at your friend Okba for three days, just pretending to be dead! And here I boil water for chamomile tea and cover you with white and yellow ointments. . . .

MOHALLAB: Where am I?

OKBA: That, indeed, is the appropriate question in cases like these. But all right, let's not talk about where you are. It's really a very simple place, austere, one might say. But straw keeps you warm. Just you wait, I'll see to it that you soon find yourself in a much nicer place.

MOHALLAB: You are Okba, the executioner.

OKBA: You recognize me? Boy, am I delighted! Let me embrace you, my friend! Truly, Mohallab, you are the one I love the most.

MOHALLAB: I seem to have heard that before.

OKBA: But no one means it as sincerely as I do. *(in a sly tone)* Just tell me one thing, Mohallab, just between you and me—

MOHALLAB: What?

OKBA: Did you steal the jewels of the princess?

MOHALLAB: Yes.

OKBA: Let me embrace you, Mohallab!

Hall in Saad's Palace

MOHALLAB *(in a firmer and louder voice than in the preceding scene)*: Yes, milord, I stole them.

SAAD: Mohallab, consider that your life hangs in the balance. Try to remember exactly! Think back! Perhaps the other man stole them?

MOHALLAB: Welid? No, milord.

SAAD: Or maybe you just found them?

MOHALLAB: Of course I found them. I couldn't have taken them, otherwise.

SAAD: No jests, Mohallab! Perhaps you found them accidentally, without knowing whose property they were.

MOHALLAB: I knew they belonged to the princess.

SHIRIN: Perhaps someone gave them to you.

MOHALLAB: No, milady, no one gave them to me. I stole them.
SAAD: That is a pity, Mohallab. Okba!
OKBA: My lord.
SAAD: Take him.
OKBA: Is it time, milord?
SAAD: It is time.
SHIRIN: Wait! Saad; I gave that jewel box to Mohallab.
SAAD: You did?
SHIRIN: Yes.
SAAD: You gave him the jewels?
SHIRIN: To help him escape.
MOHALLAB: Oh—milord, the princess is being kind, and full of compassion. She feels sorry for me because I must die. But—I stole the jewels.
SHIRIN: Who do you believe—the princess or the slave?
SAAD: I believe . . . him.
MOHALLAB: I thank you, milord. Okba, let us go.
SHIRIN: Wait! Saad—do you recognize this capsule?
SAAD: You must have taken it from my cabinet! It is poison. Give it to me!
SHIRIN: Now look—I'm swallowing it.
SAAD: Shirin!
SHIRIN: There's still time to tell you what I have to tell you. Will you believe me now?
MOHALLAB: Shirin!
SAAD: He is calling your name, Shirin.
SHIRIN: I gave him the jewels because I love him, and because I wanted to flee with him. But he left me behind. Do you hear: he spurned me!
SAAD: Shirin!
SHIRIN: No, don't hold me, Saad! I love him, him, him, do you hear? Now you have no reason to kill him. Oh, Mohallab. . . .
OKBA (whispers): She's dying.
SAAD: Stop standing around and gawking! Get out of here, I'm telling you, get out!
MOHALLAB: Yes, milord—?
OKBA: Shall I execute him, milord?
SAAD: What are you waiting for?
      Mohallab *and* Okba *leave.*

Outside and in the Caravanserai

MOHALLAB: Where are you taking me?

OKBA: To the Cliff of Silence.

MOHALLAB: A reassuring name. Listen, the fetters are hurting my hand.

OKBA: It'll soon be over.

MOHALLAB: You're right.

OKBA: It goes quite quickly, you see—I give you a little push, and you fall two hundred fathoms, down into the gorge.

MOHALLAB: As long as you do it right.

OKBA: Most of them don't even scream. Probably black out, right away.

MOHALLAB: I am glad for your sake. At long last, you have a job to do.

OKBA: I thank you, Mohallab. You are the first one to understand me. But I hope I'll have more work now. Shirin is dead, and the prince will remember a ruler's ways. . . .

MOHALLAB: So it was the princess who made things hard for you?

OKBA: She was too gentle.

MOHALLAB: Yes. She was very gentle.

OKBA: And here we are.

MOHALLAB: You can see a long way.

OKBA: Right. It is my favorite spot. Other people don't like to come here.

MOHALLAB: I can believe that.

OKBA: Now, do you have a wish?

MOHALLAB: No, not really.

OKBA: Well, then—

MOHALLAB: Okba—something just occurred to me.

OKBA: Let's hear it, Mohallab. I have often thought of compiling a collection of last thoughts. What do you think of that idea?

MOHALLAB: I think it's a good one.

OKBA: It is, isn't it? There's only one snag: I can't write.

MOHALLAB: Some think death is just a moment. But sometimes death takes a whole lifetime.

OKBA: Oh, Mohallab, I wish I knew how to write!

MOHALLAB: My death began in Al-Kuwaid. Jezid, the beggar, told me "Don't go to Al-Kuwaid!" But, come to think of it, he was wrong. It was safe for me to go there. The only thing I did wrong was that I followed the maid who took me to her mistress. I shouldn't have done that. That was wrong. Oh, Okba, if I could have that moment back, I'd do it differently.

OKBA: Yes. Hindsight, as they say.

MOHALLAB: If that moment could repeat itself—

OKBA: Mohallab?

MOHALLAB: Yes?

OKBA (*cross*): Time for you to fly!

MOHALLAB (*cries out*): No!

His cry grows more distant . . .
. . . and returns at full volume in an enclosed space, then breaks off.

WELID: What's the matter, sir?

MOHALLAB: Welid!

WELID: Why did you cry out, all of a sudden?

MOHALLAB: I thought I was falling.

WELID: You were just sitting there, quite calm.

MOHALLAB: Welid, where am I?

WELID: Two hours ago, we rode into Al-Kuwaid. Now we are at the inn. The camels have been relieved of their burdens. They're in the stable.

MOHALLAB: Oh, I must have been dreaming.

WELID: Sir, it seems you lost consciousness for a moment.

MOHALLAB: A moment? Oh, Welid, wasn't it months, years?

WELID: You must have a fever.

MOHALLAB: What was it I dreamt? I can't remember any of it. Where are we?

WELID: In Al-Kuwaid, sir.

MOHALLAB: Go on, Welid, refresh my memory.

WELID: We're bringing a caravan from India. The camels are carrying silk, carpets, skins, and spices.

MOHALLAB: And a while ago I met a beggar who told me, "Don't go to Al-Kuwaid!"

WELID (*laughing*): Yes, that's what the fool said. See, now you're remembering things. Think about Damascus!

MOHALLAB: Ah—Fatimeh. . . .

WELID: Her hair, as black as a moonless night—

MOHALLAB: Wasn't there a blacksmith, hammering in his forge? And a woman, waving?

WELID: Sir, that wasn't Fatimeh. Fatimeh's eyebrows are curved like the horn of the moon.

MOHALLAB: Enough about Fatimeh. There is no room for her in Al-Kuwaid.

WELID: That beggar put the fear in you, sir. If this place disturbs you so, we should leave.

MOHALLAB: Leave? To go where?

WELID: To Damascus.

MOHALLAB: I'll never get to Damascus.

WELID: Let us go now!

MOHALLAB: Welid, it is too late. Do you hear those footsteps?

　　Outside, footsteps approach and stop. A knock on the door.
Come in!

　　Door opens.

Who are you, woman?

MAID: My mistress invites the merchant Mohallab to visit her.

MOHALLAB: Who is your mistress?

MAID: She waved to you.

WELID: A prostitute, sir.

MOHALLAB: I'll go with you.

WELID: Don't go, sir, don't go!

MOHALLAB: Good-bye, Welid.

WELID: May Allah protect you, sir! But do not go!

MOHALLAB: Allah protects whom it pleases him to protect. I'm going.

Translated by Anselm Hollo

Ingeborg Bachmann

Ingeborg Bachmann was born in Klagenfurt, Austria, in 1926. She studied German literature, philosophy, and psychology, and concluded her studies with a PhD in 1950 on the reception of the philosopher, Martin Heidegger. Restlessly moving from place to place, she worked for a period as an editor for a radio station and visited Paris, London, and the United States. She was invited to Lecture at Harvard University in 1955 and held the newly created chair for poetics at the University of Frankfurt in 1959. From 1953 to 1957 she settled in Italy as a free-lance writer. Back in Germany, she worked briefly as a dramaturgist for a television station, then began to move again. Rome, Zurich, and Berlin were stopovers; she traveled to Prague, Egypt, and the Sudan. In 1973 she visited Poland and saw Auschwitz. She died in 1973 after having suffered severe burns in an accident at home.

Bachmann was discovered in 1953 as an outstanding poet at a meeting of the Group 47, the literary guild of the postwar years. In her short life, she received many literary prizes, including the Georg Büchner Prize, and for *The Good God of Manhattan,* the prestigious prize for radio plays of the War Blind. Critics and writers alike praised her intellectual competence and her aesthetic finesse. Bachmann was the author of poems, radio plays, libretti, essays, short stories, and novels. Bachmann was the author of poems, radio plays, libretti, essays, short stories, and novels. She first became known as a poet and the author of radio plays such as *Zickaden (Crickets,* 1955) and *The Good God of Manhattan* in 1958. She eventually abandoned poetry. Her first novel, *Malina,* was finished in 1971. Her almost completed second novel, *Der Fall Franza,* appeared posthumously in 1978. As in her radio plays, she

145

inscribes in her novels and stories distinct female and male discourses to expose the unexamined ideologies that determine and govern our social identity.

A melancholy mood pervades all of her writings, sustaining a reflective, introspective imagination. Ingeborg Bachmann was acutely conscious of the price paid for Hitler's rise to power and the ensuing decline of human values. Long before the women's movement of the 1970s, she held strong opinions on the public neglect of female sensibilities and of her own commitment as a woman writer to explore the relationship of women and men. In her works, the motives of a divided self, of unrequited love, of pain and destruction mirror personal and public conditions. She believed that the postwar era showed unmistakable signs of continued inhumanity and the forceful as well as concealed subjugation of the *other*.

The God of Manhattan is her best known radio play. The principle of montage connects the frame with the main story and a chorus of unidentified voices. The character of the good god accused by a judge of the death of the girl Jennifer, maintains that love and chaos are too close together to uphold the precarious balance necessary in everyday circumstances to guarantee a normal, happy life. Orpheus and Euridyce, Tristan and Isolde, Romeo and Juliet, and all legendary passionate lovers prove the point. But at the end of the play there is another message. The love of Jennifer and Jan cannot survive because Jan's love is not strong and unconditional enough: his self asserts itself in the end and he survives. The woman is sacrificed, the man returns to a fixed order and a conventional life. The intervening chorus warns the audience of intoxication, self-abandonment, and the impossibility of real love in our world.

The radio play was first produced in 1958 and has become a classic example of the genre. Bachmann's sensitive disposition, her sense of doom, and her mourning over the inadequacy of a woman's position in private and public life have been considered major elements in the creation of her literary works.

M.H.S.

THE GOOD GOD OF
MANHATTAN

CHARACTERS

THE GOOD GOD
THE JUDGE
JAN, a young man from the old world
JENNIFER, a young woman from the new world
BILLY
FRANKIE   2 squirrels
A WARDEN
A COURT USHER
A GYPSY (FORTUNE TELLER)
A BEGGAR
A WOMAN
HOTEL REGISTRAR
AN ELEVATOR OPERATOR
A POLICEMAN
TWO CHILDREN
A BARTENDER
VOICES, genderless, monotonous

In the Courtroom

The fan is on because it is the height of summer.

USHER *(calling into room from doorway)*: Your Honor. . . .
JUDGE: Yes?
USHER: May I bring in the accused?
JUDGE: Yes. And please turn off the fan.
USHER: Excuse me. In this heat. . . ?
JUDGE: Turn it off!
   Door opens. A Warden *brings in* The Accused.
WARDEN: Your Honor, The Accused! *(aside)* Over here. You'll have
   to stand during the hearing . . . understand?
   Fan slows down and stops.
JUDGE *(different voice)*: Sit down!
WARDEN *(quietly, busily)*: Sit! Sit down. It's permitted. . . .
JUDGE: And you can go, Sweeney. You too, Rossi.
WARDEN: As Your Honor wishes.
USHER: Thank you, Your Honor.
   The two men leave the room. Moment of silence. The Judge
   riffles through his papers.
JUDGE *(murmurs indistinctly while making some notes)*: New York
   City . . . August, nineteen hundred and . . . fifty. . . . *(then more
   rapidly, in a clear, indifferent voice)* Your name? Place of birth?
   Time? Date? Color of skin? Height? Weight? Religious affiliation?
   Average alcohol consumption? Mental illnesses. . . .
ACCUSED: I wouldn't know.
JUDGE *(in the same tone of voice)*: Accused of the murder of. . . .
ACCUSED: Of?
JUDGE *(friendly, inconsequently)*: Murderous, this heat. There has
   never been a summer this hot! Can you remember? Except per-
   haps six years ago, when Joe Bamfield and Ellen . . . Ellen. . . .
ACCUSED: Ellen Hay.
JUDGE: Correct. When they were both killed by a bomb. That
   summer was as hot as this.
ACCUSED: I remember.
JUDGE *(apologetic)*: Of course we're not here to talk about high
   temperatures.
ACCUSED: I should hope not.

JUDGE: But it would be stupid to have you answer questions to which I already know the answers.

ACCUSED *(condescending)*: You?

JUDGE *(while making further notes, casually)*: For example, isn't it correct that you lived in three rooms of an old building on the corner of 63rd and Fifth Avenue near the zoo. . . ?

ACCUSED: Ah.

JUDGE: . . . and that you were arrested by officers Bondy and Cramer in the hallway of the Atlantic Hotel shortly after it happened . . . as you were hastening to the exit. . . .

ACCUSED *(ironic)*: Hastening!

JUDGE: Isn't it correct that you. . . .

ACCUSED: Of course it's correct. But if you'll forgive me, I'd like to go back to your first question. I suppose you also know who I am?

JUDGE *(after a short pause reluctantly, timidly)*: The Good God of Manhattan. Some also call you The Good God of the Squirrels.

ACCUSED *(weighing this)*: The Good God. Not bad.

JUDGED *(hastily)*: Three bags of squirrel food were found in your home.

ACCUSED: And confiscated? A pity. I was good business for Manhattan, no? Or have you ever actually seen a person use any of those peanut machines in the subways?

JUDGE: So you bought those nuts for the animals? Are you an animal lover? In some countries squirrels are shy and innocent. But our squirrels look mean and corrupt, and there's a rumor that they are in league with the devil. Are you an animal trainer, a breeder? I call your attention to the fact that the hearing has officially begun now.

ACCUSED: I don't know if I can satisfy anyone's curiosity. What do you expect of me? Self-justification? At best I could enlighten you. But if you'd permit an old man to give you some advice—

JUDGE: I must be well-preserved. I'm no spring chicken myself.

GOOD GOD: Begin at the beginning, or at the end, but be systematic about it, sir. I can see you've cleaned out my office. You've got my card file and all my correspondence right there. Your job couldn't be easier. My work was tedious, painstaking detective work. I couldn't have done it without the squirrels. They were my messengers, mail carriers, scouts, agents. I employed several hundred of them. Two of them, Billy and Frankie, were my captains. They were really dependable. I never planted a bomb unless those two had found the exact spot and calculated the precise moment to make dead sure. . . .

JUDGE: Dead sure . . . of what?

GOOD GOD: That it would kill those it was intended for.

JUDGE: Who were they?

GOOD GOD: Oh! You mean you don't know? *(curiously)* How do you see the case?

JUDGE: I don't see it . . . anymore. I saw a series of assassinations of people who had harmed no one, perpetrated by an unidentifiable lunatic.

GOOD GOD: I thought you would take the expert testimony of your psychiatrists seriously.

JUDGE: I only thought it was a lunatic until I became aware that you were the originator of these acts.

GOOD GOD: Originator. Very good. The originator.

JUDGE: The investigations are closed. Except, of course, for the last case.

GOOD GOD: The last "case"—to use your questionable jargon— isn't closed for me either. Since I didn't have the chance to finish my work properly. I'd like to know what happened to the young man who escaped?

JUDGE: Escaped?

GOOD GOD: Without a scratch, it seems.

JUDGE: Physically unhurt, yes. But. . . .

GOOD GOD: Didn't he leave immediately?

JUDGE: Certainly. He took the ship to Cherbourg that very evening.

GOOD GOD: Ah! You see! And this is the man who had sworn not to take the ship, but to live and die with her. To suffer uncertainty and trouble; to forget his origins and his mother tongue; and to speak with her in a new language to the end of his days. And yet he took the ship and didn't even stop to bury her. And went on shore over there and forgot that when he saw her mangled body he had felt less firm ground under his feet than at his first sight of the Atlantic.

JUDGE: It's true, he didn't bury this girl.

GOOD GOD: Didn't even bury her! Oh, he deserved to live!—But now I'll tell you how it all happened. How does it go?—the whole truth, and nothing but the truth. I am also state's witness for the prosecution and will soon stop being the accused.

JUDGE *(coldly)*: I am ready.

GOOD GOD: Barely two weeks ago I received a message about an incident at Grand Central Station. The messenger was a very inferior animal, whose services I hadn't attached any importance to before and who was still serving his apprenticeship.

JUDGE: What happened at the station?

GOOD GOD: Nothing special. Toward five o'clock, shortly after the express train from Boston arrived in the underworld of Grand Central Station, when the travelers had dispersed through the halls and exits following the glowing red and green arrows, when the organ music seeped from the walls—when all the clocks were ticking and the neon lights flickered in the eternal darkness—two newcomers arrived. You could say, that's nothing special, and you'd be quite right. And yet, it is always a particular place, the position of the clock hands, an unearthly music, a quivering train on the tracks, and a babble of human voices, which make a new beginning possible.

JUDGE: A beginning of what?

GOOD GOD (lost in memories): She walked beside him in pink and white. There were so many voices and hers was inconsequential. There were so many possibilities, and this was the least likely one—but she tried it anyway.

> VOICES (*without timbre, without expression, clear and measured):*

GO ON GREEN GO ON
THINK ABOUT IT WHILE THERE IS TIME
YOU CAN'T TAKE IT WITH YOU
SLEEP FASTER GO ON
FASTER DREAMING WITH US
CLOUDBURSTS SHOWERS FASTER
EASIER SAFE EARTHQUAKES
REMEMBER AT THE GREEN LIGHT
BEWARE OF THE RED AND THE BROWN
THE BLACK AND THE YELLOW PERIL
WHAT WILL OUR MURDERERS THINK
YOU CAN'T DO IT STOP!
STOP AT THE RED LIGHT!

At Grand Central Station

JENNIFER: Are you looking for the exit?

JAN (*disconnected, defensive*): Excuse me?

JENNIFER: I just thought—because I saw you in Boston—that you may be a stranger here.

JAN: Don't worry. I'll find my way around.

JENNIFER: How did you like Boston?

JAN: Well. . . .

JENNIFER: And New York? Do you like New York?

JAN: Thank you. I don't know it yet.

JENNIFER: I rode in the same compartment with you for the whole trip. Two rows back. You were at our last college dance.

JAN: Yes, coincidentally.

JENNIFER: I'm Jennifer. You looked my way once and I thought you were going to ask me to dance.

JAN: I can't dance.

JENNIFER: I could tell! *(as though answering a questionnaire)* I like Europeans. *(hesitant)* And . . . what brings you to New York?

JAN: The wish to leave. I've only got a few hours, or a few days, until my boat sails.

JENNIFER: That's terrible. Do you *have* to go back?

JAN: I don't *have* to, but I *want* to. Didn't I say that already?

JENNIFER *(dismayed)*: No!

JAN *(politely)*: Yes. Good-bye. It's been a pleasure.

JENNIFER: Now I'll take this lilac taxi and you can get the blue and white one behind it. The taxis will meet each other often on Broadway and going up to the Bronx. But neither of us will be in them anymore.

JAN *(after a moment's thought)*: Listen, Miss. . . .

JENNIFER: Jennifer.

JAN: Lilac doesn't suit you. How old are you?

JENNIFER: Twenty-three.

JAN: And what do you do?

JENNIFER: Right now I'm studying political science—but I'd really like to see the world. I know hotels in Boston and Philadelphia—and maybe soon in Paris—but I don't know one in New York. Crazy, huh?

JAN: Please.

JENNIFER: So I can't even give you any help.

JAN: Then you can come with me, because it's too crazy that you don't know your way around. I don't know any hotels either, but it doesn't bother me. Right now I'm hungry. I need something to eat before I can think further.

*People passing by, voices interrupt the two. Jennifer moves
on a few steps.*

JAN: Jennifer!—Hey, wait a minute! *(breathless, closer)* What are
you doing?

JENNIFER *(breathless)*: Nuts! I'm getting nuts from the vending
machine because you're hungry. This is how it works—

*When she pulls the handle it plays a few bars of music—
music which will often be heard again.*

JENNIFER: The music is free. For some change you get some nuts and
music for a lifetime.

JAN *(amused)*: Good God, that looks like squirrel food.

JENNIFER: They're quite fresh, I swear. *(slyly)* And I swear that the
squirrels spend all their money here to make sure that there will
always be a fresh supply of nuts.

JAN *(cheerfully)*: Guess what I just saw, Jennifer? A squirrel *(mysteriously)* And it handed me a letter.

JENNIFER: Really!

JAN: Which says: "Tell no one!"

JENNIFER: And what else?

JAN: "You will spend this evening with Jennifer on the heavenly
earth. . . ."

JENNIFER: Why "the heavenly earth"?

JAN: This is it, right here: Ma-na Hat-ta. At least that's the way the
Indians explained it to me. But they were all in costumes and
looked about as genuine as buffalo trained to run on a racetrack.

JENNIFER: Who is the letter from?

JAN: I can't read the signature. *(chewing)* These nuts are very good,
but we also have to eat something sensible. What is sensible food?

JENNIFER: Italian and Chinese, Spanish and Russian. Artichokes
swimming in oil; pale tea with birds-nest soup; leeks with tender
snakes; and the foods of all the seas followed by the fruits of all
the lands.

JAN: I'd love some ice-cold air because it's so hot, and a dim room;
some snowgeese and a cocktail from Greenland with ice floes in
it. And I'd like to look at you for a few hours, Jennifer—at your
cool shoulders, cool face, cool round eyes. Do you think that is
possible?

JENNIFER *(with great conviction)*: Absolutely possible!

An After-Hours Bar: then On the Street: later A Seedy Hotel

The music up and abruptly out.

JENNIFER *(slow drawling voice):* It isn't true that you can't dance.

JAN: Come, let's go.

JENNIFER: Ouch, my poor hands. My poor bruised shoulders. Please don't do that. Don't hurt me.

JAN: It's two o'clock in the morning.

JENNIFER: Where are we? Where are the singing waiters?

JAN: Stop drinking now! That was earlier on—the waiters here don't sing.

JENNIFER: Why not?

GYPSY *(joins them suddenly)*: A moment, please! Give me just one moment. Show me your palm, pretty lady. I want to read your future.

JAN: Come on!

JENNIFER: My future, yes, hey, wait a minute! She wants to predict my future. Show her your palm too. She's a real gypsy: brown and red and so sad. Are you real, dear lady?—Well?

GYPSY: I can't read anything from your palm. Did you hurt your-self?

JENNIFER: He did it. He dug his nails into me. It still hurts a lot.

JAN: Jennifer!

JENNIFER: Nothing? Nothing at all?

GYPSY: I could be wrong.

JAN *(coldly ironic)*: Impossible.

JENNIFER: And his palm?

GYPSY: You will have a long life, young gentleman—and you will never forget.

JAN *(ironically)*: I hardly dared to expect that.

JENN *(indignant)*: But you didn't even look at his palm.

JAN: Calm down. All a gypsy needs to see is the dregs of your drink. Mine still has a lemon peel floating in it. That's very significant.

GYPSY: Yes, it is. Good night.

JENNIFER *(low voice)*: She refused the money.—You know, I'd like to know all the places I've been to with you.

JAN: For the diary? For the notebook?

JENNIFER: I don't think it's right for the diary.

JAN: The fresh air will do you good. Careful now, it's three steps up.

JENNIFER: Two o'clock in the morning. And who is this still sitting on the steps? My poor man, aren't you going to go to sleep?

BEGGAR: Thanks for the inquiry. For what can a poor man like Mack do. . . .

JENNIFER: Are you an actor?

BEGGAR: Swallowed by the pain-filled city and the everlasting torture, lost among the lost. I beg you for a small gift for me and my kind.

JENNIFER *(whispering)*: I have a bag of nuts, two dollars, and a scarf. Take them.

BEGGAR: In the name of no one. And without anyone's blessing. There are too many of us here, miss, in this city of beggars. We're colorless. We envy both blacks and whites. Bowery—end of the line. But you belong on the elevated with your gentleman, before they tear it down. Here it stinks to high heaven. The station is just round the corner. Wish you a good night's sleep.

JENNIFER: Thank you. *(sighing as she goes)* My gentleman. I'm too tired to ride home. Let's go.

JAN: No later than ten A.M. tomorrow, I should . . . I'm sorry. We'll go to the first hotel we can find. Is that all right with you?

JENNIFER: Say something about my eyes, again!

JAN: It doesn't make sense to go on looking—it's so late.

JENNIFER: Or about my mouth. How did it go? You touched my lips with a straw and my knees with your knees . . . and then you said:

JAN: *Pas d'histoire.*

JENNIFER: No.

JAN: I'd appreciate it if you stopped making a fuss.

JENNIFER *(shivering)*: Let's walk on farther, much farther.

JAN: It will soon be morning, my child. What do you usually do at this time?

JENNIFER: I sleep. But on the weekends when there's a dance, I stay up this late. And Arthur kisses me goodnight, or Mark, or Truman. Don't you remember Truman? He was with me that night. He's really sweet. You have to kiss me good night now.

JAN: I'll leave that to Truman and Mark.

JENNIFER: Of course you don't *have* to. Tell no one. *(they come to a halt)* Why are you stopping in front of this dreadful dump?
JAN: Be sensible.
　　　They enter the hotel.
WOMAN *(with sleepy, unpleasant voice)*: What'dya you want?
JAN: Is there a room available?
WOMAN: On the ground floor. Number One. Pay in advance. Key. Check-out time noon.
　　　They go, without talking, down the hallway. He unlocks the door, and locks it again behind them when they enter.
JENNIFER: One shouldn't go to a hotel with a stranger, right?
JAN: I've heard that speech before.
JENNIFER: Phew, this stuffy air. There isn't even an air conditioner.
JAN: Is that so terrible?
JENNIFER: No. But I just can't right now, I can't. I don't know anything about you. Oh, please tell me something about yourself. Let's talk and think it over.
JAN: Get undressed!
JENNIFER *(tearfully)*: My poor hands. My poor, poor hands. Just look at them.
JAN: It's your fault, you asked for it. I never even dreamed of hurting someone so much before.
JENNIFER: If only the room wasn't so dark and filthy—a home for flies and roaches. And I'm dirty too—from this moist, sticky air. Doesn't the air taste syrupy to you?
JAN *(more warmly)*: You are very sweet, Jennifer. Don't think about it. Close your eyes. *(stops a moment, then with slight irony)* No, did I say "sweet"?
JENNIFER *(trembling)*: Yes.
JAN: I wanted to say something completely different—it just came out automatically. Actually I was thinking that I have to go to the ship's office early tomorrow.
JENNIFER: What did the gypsy really say?
JAN: Something different than the handwriting analyst who came to our table just before her. He said the long tails of your letters indicated sensuality, and my cramped capitals showed I had something to hide; and the dashing T-crosses meant a soaring imagination. Assuming goodwill and compatible signs, a harmonious

companionship is not out of the question. But—sweet Jennifer—
we'll end this short night without knowing about the long days
each of us has spent!

JENNIFER *(toneless)*: Shall I put out the light?

JAN: Put it out. Believe me, I'd love to cover you with snow to make
you even cooler than you were—and to make you feel more sorry.
Perhaps I'll feel sorry too—or I'll forget about it, if I'm lucky. One
knows so little beforehand. And even less afterwards. One night is
too much—and not enough.

JENNIFER *(irrelevantly)*: I could turn on the radio. There must be a
late-night program. When I come home I always listen to music
before I go to sleep. It's very pleasant.

JAN: Music. My dear Jennifer, you are not going to listen to any
now. *(and yet the music now begins to play softly)*. I won't stand
for it.

JENNIFER *(crying)*: No? You're so awful to me. Why? Why do you
do that? Why, why, why?

JAN: Why are you kissing me then? Why?

> The music, which has grown louder, ends, and it is quiet for
> a moment.

JAN: Jennifer! Wake up! Please, wake up.

JENNIFER *(sleepily)*: What time is it?

JAN: Twelve o'clock. I should have gone hours ago. . . .

JENNIFER *(comprehension dawns)*: Hours ago? Of course. . . .

JAN: It's only still dark inside here because the window is below
street level. A light shaft without light. By the way, you were right
about the dirt.

JENNIFER: Why don't you go? I didn't ask you to wait for me. You
won't get a ticket and you'll miss the boat.

JAN: Don't talk like that, Jennifer. You were delightful, and I'm very
grateful.

JENNIFER *(changed, frank)*: It's horrible, isn't it?

JAN: What?

JENNIFER: To wake up in the dark way down here. With this awful
taste in our mouths.

JAN: We'll go have breakfast, that'll make you feel better.

JENNIFER: I won't—I won't feel anything anymore.

JAN *(tortured, carefully)*: If you'd only get dressed, sweetheart. Then we can talk about it in peace. If we could just get away from this place.

JENNIFER: Hand me my clothes. You can touch them. You don't have to turn your back. *(coldly)* Why are you suddenly treating me with such politeness and distance?

JAN: I'm sorry.

JENNIFER: Even though I was so delightful?

JAN *(warmly)*: Please forgive me. I should have known better.
   Loud knocking on the door.

WOMAN *(from outside)*: Are you clearing out or staying?

JAN: We're just going.

WOMAN: Get going, then! *(farther away)* When're we goin' to clean up? Unbelievable. Past noon already. I shoulda thrown. . . .

VOICES:
   GO ON GREEN LIGHT GO ON
   TRUST US TELL US
   WHY NOT ENJOY WITHOUT GUILT
   TELL EVERYONE, TELL THE WORLD
   ORDER UP THE SUN AN ACCOUNT ON THE MOON
   DREAMSPUN THICKER BRIGHTER INFLAMMABLE
   YOUR LAST SHIRT THE WAY OF ALL FLESH
   WHY BLAME OTHERS
   PEP UP INCITE INTOXICATE
   GO AFIELD LOOK INTO THE FUTURE
   THINK ABOUT IT AT THE RED LIGHT:
   STOP! YOU CAN'T DO IT—

JAN: A letter from the squirrel?

JENNIFER *(with finality)*: No letter from the squirrel.

In the Courtroom

GOOD GOD: That's how it all began.

JUDGE: It seems like the end to me.

GOOD GOD: You don't understand. There was danger ahead—I could smell it—it was all beginning again. From this moment on I began to persecute them.

JUDGE: Why should you persecute them? I don't see anything

unusual about a young man *(clears his throat)* Ahem—looking for a little adventure on his travels. You know, travel acquaintances—that sort of thing. Not very noble, mind you, a bit thoughtless. But a common occurrence.

GOOD GOD: No mere occurrence. It was bright daylight. The shades of night were gone.

JUDGE *(feeling his way)*: Are you a moralist? Does this sort of thing scandalize you?

GOOD GOD: Oh no. I don't mind the thoughtless, the bored, or the lonely ones who fall into little adventures. They don't want to spend time alone. But can't you tell—*it* had begun? And notice how it started. He said: "A letter from the squirrel?"—he was a little hesitant, a little unsure. He should not have asked this question. She answered: "No letter from the squirrel." She should never have given this answer, for he then continued. . . .

Back at the Hotel

JAN: Hungry?
JENNIFER *(uncertain)*: Is that so important right now?
JAN: Yes.
JENNIFER: Hungry!
JAN: For fresh coffee and hot toast and orange juice?
JENNIFER: Hungry! Hungry—for everything.

Continued in the Courtroom

GOOD GOD: With these words she looked at him again, and day had come.

JUDGE *(turning pages)*: So they went for breakfast. From the cafeteria he called the shipping company who told him to call again tomorrow or the next day, to confirm a passage on the *Ile de France*.

GOOD GOD: Day had come. All the horizontals and verticals of the city had come alive with the great angry hymn to work, and salaries and high profits. The roaring smokestacks stood like the columns of a revitalized Nineveh or Babylon; and the blunt or pointed skulls of the skyscrapers rubbed against the gray tropical sky, which oozed and dripped moisture like a repulsive sponge on the roofs below. In the great printing houses, rhapsodical typesetters began to pound out the news and predict the future. Tons of cabbage heads rolled in the markets, and hundreds of corpses were manicured, painted, and displayed in the funeral parlors. Yesterday's garbage was incinerated at high temperatures, and in the store shoppers rummaged for novelty foods and tomorrow's throwaways. Packages rolled down conveyor belts, and escalators bore clusters of people up and down through swags of soot, polluted air, and exhaust fumes. The wild summer inspired new colors in the spray booths of the auto-body shops, in the hats of the ladies swaying down Park Avenue, and in the gleaming containers for rice and honey, turkeys and crabs. The people felt wherever they went, and as though they belonged to this city—the only city ever invented and designed to fill all their needs and desires. This city of cities, with its feverish pace and all its agony, ready to receive everybody, and to let everything flourish! Everything. Even this.

JUDGE: Crime. Murder.

GOOD GOD *(taken aback)*: I was thinking of something else.

JUDGE *(short)*: All right. So after making the phone call the two of them left the cafeteria and took the subway to 125th Street in Harlem. They stopped at a bar from which they got two plastic swizzle sticks as souvenirs; then at a church from which they took two paper fans with scenes of the life of St. Catherine of Siena. Next, they were seen in a record store listening to cuts of popular music in the company of some blacks; after which—on the advice of a travel agency—they went to the Atlantic Hotel on Lexington Avenue, and took a room.

GOOD GOD: There's just a small detail I don't want you to lose sight of. The point about the floor. If you really want the whole picture.

JUDGE: The point about the floor?

In the Lobby of the Atlantic Hotel

REGISTER: I still have a room on the seventh floor, sir—number 703. Overlooking the courtyard. Very quiet.

JENNIFER *(whispers to Jan)*: No view of the street? No higher floor?

JAN *(to* The Registrar*)*: That's the best you can do? Is nothing else available?

REGISTRAR: No, I'm sorry. If you stay longer I can put you down for a room on the street side, higher up. But one never knows.

JAN: Well, we don't know either—if we'll still be here then. But keep us in mind. *(while going, to Jennifer)* Are you unhappy?

JENNIFER: No, it's all right. Nothing will bother us.

ELEVATOR OPERATOR: Going up! Over here, please.

    Elevator starts up.

JENNIFER *(ecstatic, over sound of elevator)*: Going up! What a trip! I can feel it in my ears. And you'll see what else they have up there: an air conditioner with cold air, lots of water, and regular maid service.

ELEVATOR OPERATOR: Seventh floor!

    The elevator stops. They go through the hallway to their room.

JAN: I'm looking forward to your wet hair and wet mouth, to thick drops on your eyelashes. You'll be light-hearted and happy and sensible, and we won't accuse each other of anything.

JENNIFER: When your ship sails, it will sail. If I have to wave to you, I'll wave. If I can kiss you for the last time, I'll do it quickly, like this, on the cheek. Unlock the door.

In the Room on the Seventh Floor

JAN: Yes, my eager little Jennifer. But since I am not a trusting fellow I have to test you some more. Tell me: when is tomorrow?

JENNIFER *(precisely)*: At the earliest—tomorrow.

JAN: And today?

JENNIFER: At the latest—today.

JAN: And now?

JENNIFER *(slowly, embracing him)*: Right now.

In the Courtroom

JUDGE: So there were further intimacies.

GOOD GOD: No, no! That's not the point. Stop using those ridiculous phrases. It was an agreement to—distance.

JUDGE: Get to the poinit.

GOOD GOD: But this distance can't be maintained. It keeps breaking down. There's the laughter, for example. Yes, to be quite correct, it started with the laughter. *(darkly)* With those indescribable smiles. Without any apparent provocation, they keep laughing.

JUDGE: Who keeps laughing?

GOOD GOD: Those, to whom it's beginning to happen.

JUDGE: Lunacy.

GOOD GOD *(strong assent)*: Lunacy. Yes! They laugh in public but also in private. Or they smile at passersby, secretly, smugly, like conspirators, who are not going to let the others know that the rules of the game will soon be abolished. That smile sits there like a ruthless question mark.

JUDGE: What does it matter? It seems harmless.

GOOD GOD: To the contrary. They are like glowing cigarette butts in a carpet, beginning to burn a hole in the world's crust. With this constant smile.

JUDGE: Get to the point!

GOOD GOD: Towards midnight they got up. Naturally that's an hour at which no one gets up except bankrobbers, barmaids, and nightwatchmen. They went to the Brooklyn Bridge.

JUDGE: Right. To the bridge. —Why?

GOOD GOD: No reason. They went and stood there leaning against the girders, to be silent for awhile, and then they began to talk again.

Outdoors

JAN *(playfully, cheerfully)*: If you'll come with me to Chinatown, I'll buy you a dragon shirt.

JENNIFER: Then I'll be protected.

JAN: If you'll come with me to the Village, I'll steal a ladder, so you can escape if there's a fire. Because I want to keep on loving you for a long time.

JENNIFER: Then I'll be rescued.

JAN: If you'll come along to Harlem, I'll buy you a dark disguise so no one will recognize you—because I alone want to love you, and for long.

JENNIFER *(not playing along)*: How long?

JAN: Play along, Jennifer! Don't ask how long? Say: "Then I'll be sheltered."

JENNIFER *(sighing, relieved)*: Then I'll be sheltered.

JAN: And when you walk along the Bowery with me, I'll give you the long lifelines of the beggars' hands—because I want to keep loving you even when you're old and decrepit.

JENNIFER *(breaking out):* A letter from the squirrel! At last—another letter from the squirrel!

JAN: What does it say!?

JENNIFER: "Tell no one. Tonight Jennifer will be waiting for you on Broadway under the Pepsi-Cola waterfall, next to the Lucky Strike smoke ring."

JAN: I won't tell anyone.

JENNIFER: Will you come?

JAN: Come on! I'm coming now.

In the Courtroom

GOOD GOD: Now they were playing. They played at love. They played it everywhere, on dark streetcorners and dim Broadway bars; under the flickering neon signs of 42nd Street movie houses, in the lightshowers of artificial suns and comets. But their play was like their laughter—it violated every rule of normal behavior.

JUDGE *(pedantically)*: Towards five o'clock in the morning they came back to the hotel.

GOOD GOD: Weary and wrung out with their intoxication and self-abandon. They walked side by side, not looking up, further removed from each other than in their play, their laughter, or their sleep. Then, up in their room, came the silent embraces, silent duties, performed without objection, still according to the rules. But not for much longer. Not much longer.

JUDGE *(grudgingly)*: This wallowing in what happened is completely pointless. It reveals no motive. The facts don't prove anything. Now, finally—I want to know your motive. Why did you do it? Outrage? No. Envy?

GOOD GOD: Give me time. I am of goodwill.

JUDGE *(cold)*: The words of a benevolent God.

GOOD GOD: I was of goodwill all along, even then. You won't believe me, but I gave them every chance.

By the third day, the hotel clerk still didn't have another room for them. In the afternoons they drove around Central Park in a horse carriage and got into a parade. The drum majorettes danced along in front kicking up their legs, indestructably young and firm ballerinas of the street, turning cartwheels for the veterans and victors. Streamers festooned the treetops, car tops, and people's heads; children jubilated, and the squirrels took possession of the scraps of lawn. They marked their territory with discarded nutshells. By the water-lily pond, near the vendor's booths, a few boards had been set up and a curtain hung across them. For five cents, anybody could enter here and take in a unique theatrical performance. The performers who manipulated the puppets were the two squirrels, Frankie and Billy. Yes, my hoarse, bloodthirsty captains, who loved to spend their spare time treating people to the horrifying spectacles that our poets have clothed in such beautiful words.

Whenever a dozen spectators had gathered, the curtain was closed behind them. Two other squirrels gripped the cloth with their claws and hung onto the boards like living hooks. Inside it was dark, the floor of the little stage glowed phosphorescent, ready for corpses. The two actors announced the program and directions from backstage.

In the Theater

FRANKIE: Ladies and gentlemen . . . for only five cents: five of the world's most beautiful love stories!

BILLY: Orpheus and Euridyce.

FRANKIE: Tristram and Isolde.

BILLY: Romeo and Juliet.

FRANKIE: Abelard and Héloise.

BILLY: Paolo and Francesca.

FRANKIE: To hell with them. To Hell!

BILLY: Shut up! *(louder)* And now, about the first scene: How

Euridyce is turned into stone, and comes to a sad end in the realm of the dead. How Orpheus, the singer, is torn to pieces by crazed women, and at the end, the lament of Nature.

FRANKIE: Dead. Torn to pieces. The End!

BILLY: Next, Tristram and Isolde—the story of a long-haired queen and her hero, a strong love potion, a black sail at the right time, and a long, painful death.

FRANKIE (*beside himself*): To hell with them!

BILLY: That comes later, you idiot. And immediately following—the sweet death of the beautiful Romeo and his Juliet in darkest Verona. With grottoes, old walls, a moon, and much enmity as set pieces.

FRANKIE: Bravo. Don't forget the daggers!

BILLY: And now. . . . An excursion into medieval France. Abelard and Héloise.

FRANKIE (*begins a soft ghastly laugh*): Oh Billy, I can't take those two seriously. Such a crazy love—how Héloise will languish! Oh, it's going to be so embarrassing. It's always made me itch when proud Titania embraces the ass. But this is the limit—please, I'll just die. To hell with them!

BILLY: Hell doesn't come till the end!

FRANKIE: I know: Paolo and Francesca. But it tickles me to death.

BILLY: Ladies and gentlemen! Two lovers, once again in distant Italy, a story book and its seductions as background, and the Inferno as future.

FRANKIE: What did I tell you: To hell with them!?

BILLY: Don't be afraid. You're going to see and taste and smell a lot of blood. Screams, curses—

FRANKIE: And hell!

BILLY: And you will gaze straight into hell. So, that's our modest program for today. The preview for tomorrow: The terrible loves and deaths of a few other couples, as handed down through chronicles, well-known melodramas, and the newspapers; from all countries including India's valleys of the dead, the bestial Rhineland, and stinking Venice, which have all provided excellent backdrops for the development of beautiful sentiments.

FRANKIE: And now, your attention, everybody, your attention!

The music comes up, as though it were the signal for the beginning of the play.

Outdoors

JENNIFER: They put a lot of effort into their performance, and they're so funny. Didn't you like it?

JAN: Sure. But didn't any of the squirrels sneak us a letter?

JENNIFER: I didn't notice anything. They do it so secretly. Let me look in my purse. *(opens purse)* Here's a note which says:

JAN: "To Hell."

JENNIFER *(laughing)*: Oh no! It says *(whispering)* "Go home, please."

In the Courtroom

GOOD GOD: And always they returned to that hotel room. Imagine—what those four walls must have seen.

JUDGE: Walls are built for that reason too—so that natural healthy feelings—

GOOD GOD: —can find an outlet? But it is neither natural nor healthy. When they embraced, they were already thinking about the next embrace. They gave themselves up to a desire unimagined at their creation, with a spirit of utter solemnity. With each glance, each heavy breath, they affirmed the present moment; seizing this fleeting flesh, tasting its bitter sadness—this flesh in which they lay captive, condemned for life.

In the Hotel Room on the Seventh Floor

JAN: Are you listening to me?

JENNIFER *(tired)*: Yes.

JAN: I know it will soon get to the point where I'll promise to write to you when I return to Europe. But you shouldn't trust me. Do you want to know what I'll write?

JENNIFER: Yes.

JAN: "My darling: I have thought about everything carefully. . . . You have become so important to me, so precious. . . . Write to me immediately, in care of general delivery, because—but I'll explain that later . . . and by return mail, if for you too these days were . . . dadam . . . across this great distance. Take you in my

arms, my little sweetheart, dadam . . . dadam . . . . we must see
each other again, we will. . . . find a way, we will, we should, we
must, in spite of the distance. Write to me!"

JENNIFER *(pulling herself together, innocently)*: Will you really write
to me?

JAN: No. That was a joke. And I don't think I'll be up to any jokes
after this.

JENNIFER: I'm not sure I understand you.

JAN: You'll understand soon enough. *(quoting, playfully)* "I am
drunk with you, my soul, and mad with desire for you. You are
like wine in my blood, and you take shape out of dreams and
drunkenness to cause my ruin."

JENNIFER: What is that?

JAN: Words.

JENNIFER: For your feelings?

JAN: I have stripped off my feelings and thrown them in a heap with
my clothes.

JENNIFER: Is that your inner self speaking to me?

JAN: My inner self! I've searched and dug for years but I have never
met my inner self.

> *The telephone rings*

JENNIFER: The phone! Shall I answer it?

JAN: Please.

JENNIFER: Hello. Yes. I understand.—Thank you. That's all right.

> *Pause*

JENNIFER: You have a reservation on the ship. You can sail.

VOICES:

> THINK ABOUT IT WHILE THERE IS TIME
> GIVE GOD A CHANCE
> BRIGHTEN UP YOUR LIFE
> CHEER UP AND STEEL YOURSELVES
> DO GOOD AND DO IT FAST
> FASTEST THING ON WHEELS
> REMEMBER TO REACT
> DAMAGED WIVES HUMAN LIVES
> TUNE IN TUNE OUT LET GO
> YOU CAN'T TAKE IT WITH YOU
> GO ON KEEP GOING
> AT THE GREEN LIGHT THINK ABOUT IT!

In the Hotel Room on the Seventh Floor

JENNIFER: I'm ready. My suitcase is packed. It's light as a feather. A flight bag. What should I say to you now? Good-by?

JAN: Don't say anything, Jennifer. If you can, say it was easy, it was lovely. It will be easy.

JENNIFER *(copying him)*: It was lovely.

JAN: I'd better not say anything.

JENNIFER: Are you going first? Or shall I? You can check to see if I've left a handkerchief behind. I always leave one. A handkerchief for waving good-bye, with a drop of perfume on it—no tears.

JAN: Let's go together!

JENNIFER: No.

JAN: At least down to the street.

JENNIFER *(indifferent)*: If you like. It makes no difference anymore. Don't you agree?

JAN: Yes, that's right.

> *They open the door, go through the hallway to the elevator. Take elevator down.*

ELEVATOR OPERATOR: First floor?

JAN: First floor.

JENNIFER *(to herself)*: It will be easy, it will be easy.

JAN: I still have to pay the bill.

JENNIFER: I'll go on ahead—I'm going, *(and as she starts to run)* I'm going.

> *Street sounds and over them the*

VOICES:

> DON'T BE AFRAID OF MONDAYS AND TUESDAYS
> LAST STOP FOR LEMMINGS
> YOU CAN'T TAKE IT WITH YOU
> HANDS OFF YOUR HEARTS AND FLOWERS
> FEEL FOR YOURSELVES SEE FOR YOURSELVES
> LISTEN AND GO ALONG GO ON
> CLOSER TO HIM CLOSER TO THE VOID
> THINK ABOUT IT BUILD ON US TRUST IN US
> THINK ABOUT IT WHILE THERE'S STILL TIME!

On the Street

JAN *(loud, then louder, finally in despair)*: Jennifer!—Jennifer!—Jennifer!

VENDOR: Convention of veterans! Meeting of idiots! Convention of old war heroes.

JAN *(turning to the shouting vendor)*: She must have passed by here with a suitcase. In pink and white, with curls falling over her ears. And such a look: How do you like me? Please, have you seen her?

VENDOR: Seen. I seen nothing. Pink and white? They're all like that, happened to me too once upon a time. You won't see her again. Why don't you ask the cop over there? Yeah! That guy with the helmet on his head and the billy club.

JAN *(approaching the policeman)*: She can't have gone far. Did you see—a girl like any other, but the only one to me.

POLICEMAN: Are you a relative?

JAN: I started to run the minute I realized things had changed. She had a hundred-yard start on me.

POLICEMAN: Oh, that's nothing. You're a very nice fellow, but first I have to help those kids cross the street, then we can talk. Right, kids?

CHILDREN: Take us across! Carry us! Come on, you dear old uncle policeman.

JAN *(walking on and shouting into distance)*: Jennifer! Jennifer!

    His shouting dies down and there is a sudden silence, then:

JENNIFER *(without surprise)*: You?

JAN *(out of breath)*: Give me your suitcase.

JENNIFER: Jan!

JAN: Are you crazy?—Standing here blowing into your cupped hands, and wiping the hair out of your eyes? We're going back.

JENNIFER: Yes?

JAN: How could you just leave? I'll never forgive you.

JENNIFER: Jan.

JAN: I should beat you in front of all these people—I *will* beat you. . . .

JENNIFER: Yes, yes.

JAN: Will you leave again, when I send you away!?

JENNIFER: No.

JAN: Do you remember now where you belong, even though you've lost your mind?

JENNIFER: I don't know of any place for us to go anymore. But if you knew one, I would know it too.

JAN: I know one. Tell me, if that wasn't a sign. . . .

JENNIFER: Yes? yes?

JAN: When I asked for the bill, I heard that a room had become vacant, overlooking the street, on the thirtieth floor. It stopped me cold. I knew I had to follow you and tell you. Was I right?

JENNIFER: Oh yes, yes.

JAN: Because that's what you wished for, and because I haven't granted any of your wishes and haven't yet given you a present.

JENNIFER *(slowly)*: Kiss me. Right here on the street . . . in front of this window full of oranges and brown pineapples. And in front of the ambulance, and all the peach stones and green date pits thrown away by the circus barkers.

JAN: And you're not afraid to be embarrassed on the street?

JENNIFER: No. And I know why.

JAN: Tell!

JENNIFER: Because it's obvious to everyone, that I'll soon be completely lost, and they can sense that I have no pride, and that I'm longing for humiliation; that I would allow you to kill me now, or throw me away like a plaything after every game you invent.

JAN: You must have been very proud once, and now I'm very proud of you. *(suddenly concerned)* Jennifer!

JENNIFER: It's nothing. I feel a bit dizzy. Because you once loved me or because you'll love me again. Hold me tight.

JAN: Don't talk any more! We're almost there. I'll tuck you between clean sheets, give you a drink, put some ice on your forehead, and a cigarette in your mouth. Not another word!

JENNIFER: I think I almost fainted. Forgive me. I didn't know one could pass out like that.

In the Courtroom

JUDGE: Some refreshment? A cigarette?

GOOD GOD: Just a sip of water.

JUDGE: The thirtieth floor is better than the seventh, of course—and either one is a lot better than the ground floor. Especially here.

GOOD GOD: Everywhere. The air is thinner up there. The walls repel the sound waves. Everything sinks away as though into a riverbed with driftwood. Seen from such a distance, the normal human mind seems to shrink until it resembles a speck of idiocy.

JUDGE *(thoughtlessly)*: So the two had lost their minds, had they?

GOOD GOD *(heavily)*: What are you saying?

JUDGE: Just a hunch.

GOOD GOD: Yes? There's something about those heights where no eagles nest. Freedom. A monster that seizes the ranks of lovers and blindly protects them, yet leaves no footprints. Love, I suppose, which we can never apprehend and bring here. Love, like that gypsy woman, casting a spell. . . .

JUDGE: Unbelievable. No, we can't summon that here. But what we can try to understand are the facts. . . . *(riffling through papers)* What is it like on the thirtieth floor?

GOOD GOD: The room is brighter than the day. When they return from shopping expeditions, they fry fish with pale fish-eyes in the kitchenette. Wash a pair of stockings or socks in the bathroom, and hang them up on the steel bar where they could also do a few gymnastics if they have nothing better to do. They already call it "home"; lean out of the window sometimes; pull straw out of an ad for brooms and stick it on the wall to make the room more like a nest. They double-lock the door and then get up a third time to check if it is really locked. They go out less and less. They run out of cigarettes and one of them offers to go buy some, but in the end they go together.

JUDGE: Any letters from the squirrel?

GOOD GOD: Heaps. The mail piles up. And Billy and Frankie danced up and down in the hallway and peeped through the keyhole.

In the Hotel Hallway

BILLY: Oh what fun that no one knows!

FRANKIE: What I don't know won't hurt me so.

BILLY: Poet, madman. What are you thinking of doing with the girl?

FRANKIE: To hell with her!

BILLY: And with him?

FRANKIE: He's clever, but it got him anyway. Smart aleck, bad-mouth, the world is rotten!

BILLY: What's it going to be?

FRANKIE: Spanish torture.

BILLY: Spanish?

FRANKIE: You'll die of laughter. Thumbscrews are nothing compared to it. Burning matches under the fingernails—a colonial officer's game. Whipping would be a pleasure compared to it. Come, I'll whisper it in your ear.

    Whispers incomprehensibly.

BILLY: Hoho?!

FRANKIE: Oho!

BILLY: Agreed?

FRANKIE: Agreed. If our stern master permits.

BILLY: Permits?

In the Courtroom

JUDGE: We're not in the Middle Ages anymore, you know.

GOOD GOD: No. At the beginning of the New Age. Or the Last Age. As you like.

JUDGE: It's unbearable. This heat. And it's getting dark already.

GOOD GOD: I assume that like most people today, you're in favor of mass destruction, not individual destruction. But I've had to come up with an old-fashioned method for those individuals who've separated from the pack—and I don't expect much mercy from them.

JUDGE: Mercy from whom? And for what?

GOOD GOD: I have to make a correction here. I only guided and used the vulgar imagination of my henchmen—they were repellent to my sober nature. Such excrescences can only be found in the lower creatures. I have no homicidal tendencies.

JUDGE: You're contesting the charge?

GOOD GOD: Only justice was done.

JUDGE: You're contesting? Why expect mercy then?!

GOOD GOD: No mercy, then.

VOICES:

> GOOD ADVICE AIN'T EXPENSIVE
> DIRT CHEAP DO OR DIE
> NO MERCY FOR STOOLPIGEONS
> THINK ABOUT IT WHATEVER HAPPENS
> GO ON VOLUNTEERS IN FRONT
> JACKALS AND WOLVES IN BACK
> PEACE RARELY COMES ALONE
> NO MERCY THIS TIME
> STRONG MEASURES STRONGER
> DOWN WITH ALL BARRIERS
> YOU CAN'T TAKE IT WITH YOU
> STOP! LOOK AT IT UNDER THE LIGHT: STOP!

In the Hotel Room on the Thirtieth Floor

JENNIFER: Rescue me!

JAN: Is that what's become of you? Is that what you've turned into? From a pink and white girl with diaries, good night kisses, necking in cars, with Truman, and scribbled notebooks under your arm, very cute, and how do you like me?—Why do all the buildings have fire escapes? so one can escape when there's a fire; why are there fire extinguishers in all the rooms? so one can extinguish the fire and save oneself.

JENNIFER: Save me! From yourself and from myself. Do it so we stop fighting each other, and I can be quieter around you.

JAN: Are you crying? Go on, cry!

JENNIFER: Do you think we're crazy?

JAN: Perhaps.

JENNIFER: Do you despise me?

JAN: Only a little. Only enough so you never cease to amaze me. But I also amaze myself.

JENNIFER: Will you sail today?

JAN: No.

JENNIFER: But I know it's just a postponement, just another postponement.

JAN: Don't ask! Perhaps because there's still something left undone.—But where's your curiosity? You wanted to ask me very

different questions, and give me answers to questions you think I
have.

JENNIFER: Yes, yes. Let's just lie here quietly and talk. You begin!

JAN: About my childhood? Stories about the country and the city,
parents, aunts, uncles? About my school days? About mean
teachers, chalk fights, and passing exams?—I was born, and then
it was too late already.

JENNIFER: Yes. Perhaps I'm being silly . . . but I keep thinking I need
to know all about you.

JAN: I could also tell you what ideas and views I experimented with;
how much money I now earn for mindless work, and what my
prospects are. Or describe the country, its mountains, apple trees,
and latest border conditions. But here you all just call it: Europe.
Europeans. How can I be so limited then and talk about our
apple trees, and leave out the pines and the beaches that may also
exist. Anyway, it's all very far away and doesn't seem to mean
much to me anymore.

JENNIFER: And . . . but. . . .

JAN: What now?

JENNIFER *(quietly)*: There were . . . others. And what do I mean to
you now?

JAN *(after short pause for thought)*: Have I intimidated you so much
that you only dare to ask about that now? The inevitable, favorite
question. Of course I'm ready for it. But why do you want to
bother with it? If I told you something now, about a few women
or lots of them, disappointments—is that what it's called?—or
unforgettable experiences? I know the script by heart, and I've
made up a few versions of my past. On the spur of the moment.
There's a tragic and a comic version, one with a story and one full
of statistics. But wouldn't it be better if you let me have them all?

JENNIFER: Yes. Only when you talked about the letter you're not
going to write me, you said: "write me in care of general delivery
because—but I'll explain that later."

JAN: Perhaps I wanted to give myself away. Because there really is
someone over there waiting for me. There's always somebody
waiting. Or it would never have been allowed to start in the first
place. We're simply handed on, one relationship replaces the
other. One hops from one bed into the next.

JENNIFER: What will you say when you get back?

JAN: Nothing.

JENNIFER *(tortured)*: As though nothing had happened?

JAN: I didn't say that. I don't even mean to say that I'll go back there. But one way or the other, there's nothing to say.

JENNIFER: Because it is easier. Oh, everything is so easy, easy!

JAN: Go on, cry! But don't forget that you also said: Tell no one!

JENNIFER: Yes. Because that's what it says in the letters that come from the squirrels.

JAN: They ought to know what they're writing.

JENNIFER: And even if they don't know!—So, I'll never get to know you then.

JAN: What would you gain by knowing about my weaknesses, and about the few good deeds I did along the way. I don't want to know anything about you—I want to extract you from your life story. When you walk, or move, or look at me, when you obey me and give in wordlessly, you identify yourself in a way that no document, no report could ever do. I'm not worried about your identity. *(changed, wounding)* But we could try to find a common basis, if it's so important to you.

JENNIFER: Don't! Don't!

JAN: What do you know about interferences and automation, about quantum moods and intersubjective verifications?

JENNIFER: Not that!

JAN: About nuclear changes, psychopathology, and the paleolithic?

JENNIFER *(frightened)*: Please don't!

JAN: So we won't be able to discuss that.

JENNIFER: No. . . .

JAN: Perhaps there are other things?

JENNIFER: Whatever you want. I'll make an effort.

JAN: Why make an effort?

JENNIFER: To get closer to you.

JAN: Would you express an opinion?

JENNIFER: Which one?

JAN: That's what I'm asking you.

JENNIFER: Is that so important to you?

JAN: No. But since we're into it now, I just want to find out what possibilities are left if you have no opinion, but want to try hard, and so on.

JENNIFER: Don't push me away.

JAN (*increasingly alert, ironical*): There are still other means of communication. We could go to the theater and exchange ideas in the intermissions about the cleverly fabricated incendiary effects.

JENNIFER: What play are you talking about?

JAN: About one I'll never see with you.—And what about music? When we have the leisure, we can listen to an important piano concerto with brilliant phrasing, and a seductively intelligent structure.

JENNIFER: You mean some serious music?

JAN: And if that doesn't work out, we'll visit some galleries and strain our eyes to get a sense of the color values. And if that doesn't work either, you'll learn to cook and entertain me with pancakes, sauces, and desserts. Evenings there's always the movies to escape to. Together one stares at the screen and relaxes. You can depend on it, something will be found to keep us together. Children, for example, worries, and bad weather. You can depend on it!

JENNIFER: It's all fine by me.

JAN (*angry*): Me too.

JENNIFER: You're beautiful when you get angry.

JAN: I'm not angry now. But I'd like to break away from all the years, and all the thoughts of all the years: and I'd like to tear down the structure that is my self, and be the other, that I never was.

JENNIFER: You're beautiful, and you already are as you never were.

JAN: And I'll tell you something else: it is impossible that that should happen to us:

YOU MINE, I THINE.

TRUST EACH OTHER. LET'S THINK OF THE FUTURE.

LET'S BE GOOD COMPANIONS. REMAIN FRIENDS.

PROTECT EACH OTHER, SUPPORT EACH OTHER.

BE A COMFORT. BE A COMFORT.

You are the first person who is no comfort to me. I could stand my friends and my enemies, even when they paralyzed me and wasted my time. I could bear it all. But you I can't bear.

JENNIFER: You are beautiful and I adore you. I kiss your shoulders and think nothing of it. Is that being no comfort?

JAN: Yes. But it's only the first attack, the first strike against a chain that doesn't want to break. But listen, you can hear it rattle and if it should break in the end without a sound, you won't think anything of it either. But then the law of this world can also no longer bind us.

In the Office of the Good God of Manhattan

BILLY: Those two aren't going to last much longer. They're rolling their eyes. Staring into the void. Blaspheming.

FRANKIE: O.U.T. spells Out! What does our Master say?

BILLY: Wait. Wait it out.

> *Scratching noise.*

Stop scratching up the munitions cupboard. He'll smack your paws.

FRANKIE: I'm itching to get on with it.

BILLY: Shall we send them another letter?

FRANKIE: Yeah, one that'll raise their blood pressure, put the screws on. To hell with them.

BILLY: What shall we write?

FRANKIE: "Tell no one."

BILLY: Goes without saying.

FRANKIE: I could tear my fur out. I can't think of anything.

BILLY: So tear out your fur!

FRANKIE: Ouch! Ouch! Ouch!

BILLY: Still nothing?

FRANKIE: I've got it!

BILLY: This could be good.

FRANKIE: They have to go higher.

BILLY: You're nuts. Want a crack on your nut?

FRANKIE: Keep your nuts! A room must become available on the top floor. Give me the card file! Who's roasting up there now?

BILLY: How high up? The fifty-seventh floor? That would be the top.

FRANKIE: Give me that! Ah, Mr. Missismister. Let's try it.

BILLY: How?

FRANKIE: He's got to get out. We'll come skipping along. I'll take a flying leap at his chest. And he packs his bags in terror.

BILLY: So he moves out, they move in. Then what?

FRANKIE: They'll float up there and have to keep house in the stuffy air. Lose the ground under their feet. Feel dizzy. *(he whistles)* And not give a damn for the heavenly earth.

BILLY: Heavenly. That'll speed things up.

FRANKIE: Oh, what fun!

BILLY: Oh, what fun, that no one knows, I'm called Billy—

FRANKIE: I'm called Frankie—

BILLY: The tame one, the shy one—

FRANKIE: The speedy squirrel boys.

In the Courtroom

JUDGE: A man actually did move out of the top floor—for these or other reasons.

GOOD GOD: The desk clerk remembered a tip the two had given him, and moved them up. The view from the room was a strange one. Below lay a world abandoned in flight. With one eye you could see the moon while the sun still shone in the other. The sea curved away, visibly pulling ships and smoke down with it to other continents.

JUDGE: That move was quite a maneuver! Did you think you could operate up there unobserved?

GOOD GOD: No, just faster. I only moved things along, which couldn't be stopped anymore. I also felt sorry for them because they had hardly any money left. I wanted to save them from distracting worries. You know how expensive rooms at the top are.

JUDGE *(dismissingly)*: Compassion, too. Yes, I know. *(leafing)* Now we're about to get to the last night—right?

GOOD GOD: A night that preceded the last day, like the last night of all. A night of burning heat. Feverish. The air conditioner was useless.

JUDGE: Like today.

GOOD GOD: Ice melted in the glass, before one could bring it to one's lips.

JUDGE: And the two had no premonitions?

GOOD GOD: They had received the letter and believed its message.

In the Hotel Room on the Fifty-Seventh Floor

JENNIFER: You see, it's another tip. Another sign. *(tenderly)* Good, dear little squirrels.

JAN: Moving in the evening. Moving into the night itself.

JENNIFER: I will put my hairbrush next to yours. Set up your books. Hang your jacket next to my skirts. I'd like to put everything in its place, as though it were forever. I want to engrave this moment in my memory forever: the breathless night and the moist heat, the shining island over which we float, and the lights we will burn here to add to the glow, in the honor of nobody.

JAN: Come! Drop that stuff in your hands. Let everything drop forever. I sense that I'll never know more clearly in which longitude and latitude I am, nor on what everything is grounded, than in this indifferent room. It can be felt here precisely because there is so little ground. Here we have space—and you give shelter to me, the stranger.

JENNIFER: Because he has come from far away, and must go on, I make up his bed and place the water pitcher next to him.

JAN: But he still fumbles in the dark and can't find his way. He still provokes distance because his accent is harsh, and he doesn't inspire trust yet. Now I'd like to have a map that explains me to you: with all my sand-colored deserts, and white tundras, and an unexplored territory. But there's also an expanding new green area, which proves that the polar sea in my heart has begun to melt.

JENNIFER: At last. At last.

JAN: And I'd like to have a book in which I could look up on you, Jennifer. Your climate, vegetation, and animal life. The causes of your illnesses and their silent, stubborn enemies in your blood; and the tiny life forms I pick up from you in my kisses. I'd like to see through you now, at night, when your body is all lit up, warm and excited, ready for a party. I see transparent fruits and jewels, carnelians and rubies, shining minerals. Magical traceries of blood. To see right inside you, Jennifer. Reveal all the layers: the blankets of delicate flesh and white, silky skin that cover your joints, the relaxed muscles and beautifully polished bones, and the luster of your bare hip sockets. The smoky light in your breast and the daring curve of these ribs. I want to see it all, look at everything.

JENNIFER: If only I could do more, tear myself open for you and give myself over to you completely—every fiber of my body, skin, hair, all yours.

JAN: And to listen. Put my ear up against you because it's never quiet inside you; there's always the rising and falling wind in your lungs, a sound like a piston in your heart chamber, an anxious sound when you swallow, and a ghostly crackling in your limbs.

JENNIFER: Sound me out. I can't have any secrets from you.

JAN: But can I ever know everything? I'll be consumed by jealousy until I know every hidden color, and the secret passages through your cells; the salt spilling through your tissues and your microscopic inhabitants, mosaics of vanished myths. Spongy tissue and bone marrow. The whole profligate structure that is you, which will fade away without being known.

JENNIFER: Am I fading away already? Am I fading away because of you?

JAN: There's too little time in this world. Even when all is known and formulated, I still won't grasp the laser of your mobile eyes and the blonde fur on your skin. When everything has been known, done, and destroyed again, I'll still be seduced by the labyrinth of your gaze. And the sobs that rise in your throat will still have the power to alarm me like nothing else.

JENNIFER: So little time. Much too little time.

JAN: Because of this, my skeleton will still want to embrace you when you are a skeleton, and to hear this chain rattle against your bones on the day of the last judgment. Your decayed heart and the handful of dust you will become will fill my mouth and choke me. Your nothing will be filled with my nothingness. I'd like to be with you to the end of all time, to reach the bottom of the abyss into which we are falling. I want to reach an end with you, an end. And to revolt against the end of love in each moment and to the end.

JENNIFER: My end. End it now.

JAN: There is a deception from the beginning, and no blasphemy will take its measure. Why must we reproach ourselves with love, this fiery script, only to see it extinguished as we draw closer? Who screamed that god is dead? Or toppled into the halls of thunder! Or that he doesn't exist? Hasn't there been too little complaining in this little time? Are we tearing out our hearts for nothing, just to fill the emptiness with our cries, are you dying for this? Oh no. Love me so I won't fall asleep and stop loving you. Love me, so we will understand. For why shouldn't I embrace you, torment you, and find the depths of despair in you? And why should I let anyone prescribe for me how often and how long I should still embrace you, though I desire it and you forever. I don't want to desert you now, to betray you in the land of dreams and to be betrayed in sleep. I want what has never been: no ending. What will remain is a bed—at one end icebergs knock against each other, and someone is setting the lower rim on fire. And on either side stand not angels, but great tropical plants, raucous parrots, and wilted vines from famine lands. Please don't go to sleep, I beg of you.

JENNIFER: I'll sleep no more, leave you no more.

JAN: Come then. I am with you and against everything. Counterclock time begins.

In the Courtroom

JUDGE: What are they talking about?

GOOD GOD: About a different level of being. About a crossing of boundaries. About something that you and I can't fathom.

JUDGE *(reserved)*: We've dealt with all sorts of cases here.

GOOD GOD: You're only dealing with me, you can't touch them.

JUDGE: So you claim. . . . Do you mean to say that the case of Ellen Hay and Bamfield, and all the others, whom you—

GOOD GOD: Whom I? I?

JUDGE: —who were murdered, were similar to this case?

GOOD GOD: I can't claim that. Each story happened in a different language. They all became speechless in a different way. And they were immersed in different time periods. But one who hasn't really studied the cases might see similarities in them. Just as there appear to be similarities between two-legged species. But all of them loosened their natural bonds and were inclined to free themselves of their attachment to the world. Isn't it said sometimes that the victims are guilty, not the murderers?

JUDGE: Don't try to confuse things! And stop twisting words around.

GOOD GOD: I'm not trying to do anything of the kind. I just want to make clear to you that the two had stopped believing in anything, while I acted in good faith.

JUDGE: You, sir?

GOOD GOD: Do you want my confession of faith?—I believe in a fixed order for everyone to live by every day. I believe in the great power of an all-encompassing convention in which all ideas and feelings have their place, and I believe in the death of its adversaries. I believe that love is the dark side of life, more corrupting than any crime, or all heresies. I believe that where love blossoms, chaos erupts like before the first day of creation. I believe love is innocent and leads to downfall; that it can only lead to further incrimination, and from trial to trial. I believe it's right that lovers should fly up into the air, and have always done so. There they may be set among the constellations. Didn't you say: He didn't even bury her? Didn't you say so?

JUDGE: Yes.

GOOD GOD: I'm just repeating it. Not buried. Understand. Set among constellations.

JUDGE *(matter of fact):* You have a sick imagination. One could point to any number of happy couples: the childhood friend who later married a doctor; the country neighbors who already have five children; the two students who show such an earnest devotion to life and to each other.

GOOD GOD: I'll grant you countless happy couples! But who wants to bother with people who make a short foray into freedom and then begin to show sense. People who have tamed that bit of initial heat, and made it a cure-all against loneliness, a companionship and an economic partnership. A respectable status in society has been achieved. Everything is balanced and in order.

JUDGE: Nothing else exists, or is possible.

GOOD GOD: Because I have eradicated it and frozen it out. I did it so there could be peace and security, and so you could sit here quietly examining your fingernails, and that everything would go along as we prefer it to.

JUDGE: There can't be two judges—just as there can't be two orders.

GOOD GOD: Then you must be on my side, only I don't know it yet. Then perhaps you didn't intend to take me out of action, but only to be able to talk about something that's better not talked about. Then two keepers of order may be one.

VOICES:

ONE CONSTELLATION DOESN'T MAKE A SKY

GIVE IN BE SMART
TRY KEEPING SOME POWER IN RESERVE
ROCKETS RED GLARE BURSTING BOMBS
HEAVY WATER EASIER TO ADVERTISE
BREAK UP BREAK IT UP BREAK UP THE WORLD
AT THE TONE THE TIME WILL BE ZERO HOUR
RISE AND FALL BLOW BY BLOW
IF YOU THINK ABOUT IT YOU CAN'T DO IT
MAKE IT SHORT AND SWEET
GRIN AND BEAT IT—STOP!

In the Room on the Fifty-Seventh Floor

JAN: Can you do it? Can you bear it? Even though it means "Good-by"—which isn't a word that applies to us.

JENNIFER: The only thing I can't bear is that you are still here and that I have to look at you, during these last moments. Soon I will become nothing. Oh, if it would just end—and end my pain. If I could be beside myself. Can I say it all?

JAN: Yes. Say it!

JENNIFER: Don't touch me anymore. Don't get too close. I would catch on fire.

JAN: How far away shall I go?

JENNIFER: Stand by the door. But don't turn the handle yet.

JAN *(from distance)*: I. . . .

JENNIFER: Don't speak to me anymore. And don't embrace me one last time.

JAN: And I!

JENNIFER: Now turn the handle and go, without turning around. Don't turn your back to me. Even though my eyes will be closed and I won't see your face again.

JAN: But I can't just. . . .

JENNIFER: Don't hurt me anymore. No more postponements.

JAN *(as he crosses the room towards her)*: Now I can never leave again.

JENNIFER: No. Don't touch me!

JAN: Never again. Look at me. Never again.

JENNIFER *(slowly, while sinking to her knees)*: Oh, it's true. Never again.

JAN *(shocked)*: What are you doing? Stop that!

JENNIFER: Stop kneeling at your feet and kissing them? I will do this forever. And walk three steps behind you wherever you go. Drink only after you have drunk. Eat when you have eaten. Watch when you sleep.

JAN *(quietly)*: Get up now, dear.—I'm going to open the window and let in some air. You'll wait here, without crying, while I just run out to give back the ticket, so the ship can sail away forever. I'll take the bright red taxi, the fastest one. Because the time has come.

The only thing I'm sure of now is that I want to live and die here with you, and to talk with you in a new language; I can't practice my profession or do any business anymore; can't do anything useful. I want to break with everything, divorce myself from everything. And if I never regain my taste for the world, it will be because I cleave to you and to your voice. And in our new language—for this is an ancient custom—I will declare my love for you and call you "my soul." This is a word I never heard before and that I just found, and it is no insult to you.

JENNIFER: Oh, tell no one!

JAN: My spirit, I love you deliriously, there is nothing else. That is the beginning and the end, the alpha and the omega.

JENNIFER: It is an ancient custom: if you declare your love for me, I must confess my love for you. My soul—

JAN: Immortal, or mortal: Yes, there is no other answer.

In the Courtroom

GOOD GOD: Yes, they must fly away, without a trace, for no one and nothing must get too close to them. They are like the rare elements that are found here and there, whose powerful radiation destroys everything and calls the world into question. Even the memories that remain of them contaminate the places they have touched. This trial will be unprecedented. If I am found guilty, it will endanger everyone. For those who love must be destroyed, or else they will never have existed. They must be hounded to death—or they won't live. One may counter my argument saying: this feeling will play itself out, it will pass. But it isn't a matter of feeling, it is doom! And it will not pass. And it is important to be evasive, to adapt oneself! Answer me—by everything you hold sacred. Answer!

JUDGE: Yes.

GOOD GOD: Yes—there is no other answer. If I had to do it all over again I would go and do the same thing.

In the Room on the Fifty-Seventh Floor

Knock on door.

JENNIFER: Come in.

GOOD GOD: You are alone?

JENNIFER: Yes. What is it?

GOOD GOD: I just want to deliver a package. It was sent to you.

JENNIFER *(without reaction)*: I know nothing about it.

GOOD GOD: It is supposed to be a surprise for you.

JENNIFER *(slightly happy)*: A present, yes?

GOOD GOD: Can I put it down here? And you won't be inquisitive, but wait until you're not alone anymore?

JENNIFER: Oh, sure. I'm not inquisitive. I can wait. Wait.

GOOD GOD *(changed tone)*: He'll be right back.

JENNIFER: Yes, right away. He just . . . *(breaks off)* . . . just went out for a moment, in a hurry, although there isn't anything to hurry for anymore. It is a day of surprises today. *(goes silent)* You see, it is a special day.—Thank you.

> *Silence.*

That's fine. Thanks. Aren't you going?

GOOD GOD *(unmoved)*: You're thanking me?

JENNIFER: Yes. *(whispering)* But now I want to be alone. You understand. Because tonight a ship will sail that will not take him away from me, and I want to rip off my clothes with joy. Please go now, because I may not speak to anyone. I love. And I am beside myself. My insides are burning with love, and love is burning up the time in which he will be here but hasn't arrived yet. I have gathered myself for that last moment and I love him. Go away

now. Don't look at me like that. Don't breathe this air. I need it
because I love. Go away. I love.

GOOD GOD: No letter from the squirrel?

JENNIFER: Oh, my God!

GOOD GOD: A letter from the squirrel which says: Tell no one.

JENNIFER *(in terror, quietly)*: Don't say it. Not you. No one.

GOOD GOD: No one knows.

JENNIFER: No one.

> *The door closes.*
> *The Music.*

In a Bar on Forty-Sixth Street

JAN *(entering)*: Good afternoon.

BARTENDER: What'll it be?

JAN *(taken by surprise)*: I don't know. What?

BARTENDER: A double whiskey. Lots of ice. Something like that?

JAN: Yes. And make it quick. What time is it anyway? My watch
seems very slow. I expect it'll stop soon because I haven't wound it
up in a few days.

BARTENDER *(making the drink)*: It's a damn hot one today. *(Puts the
glass on the counter)* Just coming up to the hour, I think. Want
me to turn the radio on? Then you'll get it exactly.

JAN: Thanks. That's nice of you.

BARTENDER *(going through the dial on the radio)*: The baseball
game is over. Now we're getting commercials, of course.

VOICES *(quietly, from the radio)*:

GO ON KEEP GOING GO ON

JAN: I have to get going.

BARTENDER: You can't keep going on Forty-sixth Street. They've
torn up the whole street. Lost all my clients. You have to go back
and around the whole block.

JAN: So—that's why this place is empty.

VOICE *(quietly)*:

THINK ABOUT IT WHILE THERE'S STILL TIME

JAN: Another double whiskey, please. You know something? . . .
Sometimes I would really like. . . . I'm not holding you up?

BARTENDER: Of course not. I know how it is. Nobody to talk to.

JAN: No, that's not it. But a few casual words feel good sometimes, you know.
BARTENDER: You are a very nice guy. *(puts the glass in front of him)*
JAN: Is that today's paper?
BARTENDER: Sure, take it!
JAN: Just a quick look. . . . I haven't seen a paper in days. *(opens paper)*
VOICES *(quietly)*:
    THERE IS NO MERCY THINK ABOUT IT
JAN: In our country—I mean, over there—the government has changed. I had no idea.
VOICES:
    NO MERCY NO TIME FOR MERCY
JAN *(jumps up)*: The time! Can't you look for another station?
BARTENDER: I can try.
    Flips through dial looking for another station.
VOICES *(break through, accompanied by other sounds)*:
    THINK ABOUT IT YOU CAN'T DO IT
    STOP! STOP AT THE STOP LIGHT!
BARTENDER: I'm trying.
    He keeps turning the dial and finds the music, which suddenly comes through loudly and is then interrupted by a muffled explosion.

In the Hallway of the Fifty-Seventh Floor

FRANKIE: Lovely flight, lovely sight.
BILLY: But he wasn't there, he didn't come back. *(tearfully)* What a mess.
FRANKIE: And I've singed my fur. Almost flew along with her. What are we going to report?
BILLY: Successful explosion, bad timing. One body missing. And the Master's waiting in the lobby. Wanted to hear the whole thing.
FRANKIE *(affectedly)*: I don't dare to face him. I singed my fur.
BILLY: Listen! They're coming already. Gapers, tourists. We'll have to climb down the outside walls. Quick, hop through the room and out of the window. Let's get out of here!

FRANKIE: Yuck, look at that mess. Black as hell. Charred. Still smoking. *(coughs)* Oh, what fun!

In the Courtroom

JUDGE: She died alone.

GOOD GOD: Yes.

JUDGE: And why? *(continues immediately, with assurance)* Because—after making the fateful decision—he suddenly felt the desire to be alone. To sit quietly for half an hour, just thinking, as he used to think, and talking, as he used to talk, to people who didn't matter, in places of no consequence. He had relapsed, and order held out her arms to him for a moment. He was normal, healthy, and upright like a man who peacefully takes a drink before dinner, to banish the enchanting whispers and scents of his beloved from his ears and nostrils; a man whose eyes have come alive again at the sight of newsprint, and whose hands get sticky at a bar.

GOOD GOD: He had been saved. The world had got him back. By now he's back in his country and, given bad moods and moderate views, he'll live a long time.

JUDGE: And perhaps he'll never forget. Yes.

GOOD GOD: Do you really think so?

JUDGE: Yes.

GOOD GOD: Are we finished?

JUDGE: Yes. You may go. Down this long hallway to the elevator. Take the side exit next to it. Nobody will stop you.

GOOD GOD: And the charges?

JUDGE: Remain in place.

GOOD GOD: And the verdict? Your sentence—will I never hear it? What lightning springs to your eyes, Your Honor? What reservations did you have when you questioned me, and which do you have now as you answer? Silence—to the end?

He goes and the door closes behind him.

JUDGE *(alone)*: Silence.

Translated by Faith Wilding

Peter Handke

Peter Handke was born in Griffin, Austria, in 1942. He studied law but gave up his academic pursuits after the publication of his first novel in 1966 (*The Hornets*, followed by *The Peddler*). He changed his residence frequently, living both in France and Germany. For about a year he traveled in the United States and his prose text *Short Letter, Long Farewell* became an instant success in German-speaking countries (1972) and in its English translation (1974). Eventually Peter Handke returned to live in Austria. Recently he completed a tour of the Far East. There seems no end to his wanderings. His literary production of novels, plays, stories, essays, and sketches is profuse. Next to the Austrian playwright and novelist Thomas Bernhard, he has become the most discussed and controversial contemporary Austrian writer. His plays, narrative fiction, and essays in English translation have also achieved considerable acclaim in America. (*A Sorrow beyond Dreams*, 1974; *A Moment of True Feeling*, 1977; *The Left-handed Woman*, 1978). Practically all of his plays, particularly the so-called Speak-ins, *Offending the Audience* (1966), *Prophecy* (1966), *Self-Accusation* (1966), *Calling for Help* (1967), the critically acclaimed *Kaspar* (1967), *The Ride across Lake Constance* (1970) and *They Are Dying Out* (1973) have frequently been performed on American stages.

Peter Handke has received several prizes, among them the Gerhard Hauptmann Prize (1967), the Schiller Prize (1972), the Georg Büchner Prize (1973), the Prix George Sadoul (1978), the Kafka Prize (1979), and the Literary Prize of the City of Salzburg (1986). It is noteworthy that he refused to accept the Anton Wildgans Prize of the Association of Austrian Industrialists in 1985.

Peter Handke's preoccupation with literary form and linguistic experiments stands in the Austrian tradition of philosophical investigations into the manifestations of linguistic alienation, as for instance in the writings of Hugo von Hofmannsthal and Karl Kraus. In many of Handke's plays there is an echo of the Austrian philosopher Ludwig Wittgenstein and his speculations about the possibilities and limits of language *(Tractatus logico-philosophicus)*. If philosophical problems can only be solved by analyzing the workings and meanings of language, then Handke in turn affirms the importance of the linguistic basis of the literary discourse in his works. The sine qua non for Handke is the living language, and that the meaning of the word is its usage. He also shares Eugène Ionesco's belief that the possibility to form, influence, and restrict an individual life through the dominant words of an adversary leads to the disintegration of the personality and reality itself. (Both Ionesco's *The Lesson* and Handke's *Kaspar* show a person under "speech torture.")

Peter Handke's Speak-ins, his plays *Kaspar, The Ride across Lake Constance,* and his radio plays of the 1960s are characterized by a constant flow of words corresponding to the barrage of repetitions, nonsequiturs, normative pronouncements, and clichés used in everyday life. Neither the Speak-ins nor the radio plays provide any action, plot, or development of characters in the traditional sense. Words alone supply a concept of the world, and the abstract world of his stage and radio plays cannot be measured with conventional expectations. At any given moment, however, the listener should be mistrustful of the spoken word. The inability to name and hear the truth is a familiar exposition in his works. A new sensibility toward language as a lived experience informs Handke's plays and the following texts by Jürgen Becker and Reinhard Lettau. Peter Handke once wrote that the invention of a story is entertaining but nothing more. Although Bertolt Brecht helped to educate him, the dialectics of Brecht's plays, the attempt to lay bare the contradictions in capitalist society and present the world on the stage as being capable of change, according to Handke, fall short of capturing reality and do not disturb anybody or change anything.

Handke trusts that to pay attention to speech and calling it into question in order to deconstruct the ideological position may perhaps enable us to reconstruct the world. The analysis and its presentation to the way in which language is being used show the power and torture emanating from the cross fire of words. As in his Speak-ins and in *Kaspar*, his radio plays are concerned with the possibilities inherent in human discourse. The radio plays published in the late 1960s under the title *Wind und Meer* (*Wind and Sea*, 1970), include in reverse order of their chronological existence, *Geräusch eines Geräusches* (*Sound of a Sound*, 1969), *Hörspiel 2* ("Radio Play" 2, 1968), *Hörspiel 1* ("Radio Play" 1, 1968). After his successful plays, radio broadcasts, and film scripts (with Wim Wenders), there was a noticeable change of mood in the plays *They Are Dying Out* (1973) and *Uber die Dörfer* (*Through Villages*, 1981). Peter Handke had developed a new relation to the real world. He had rediscovered the calming and inspiring effect of classic literary works (Goethe, Stifter, Fontane) and the soothing, humanizing qualities of nature. Pictures of the past and evocations of a friendlier future are reflected particularly in his last play and in his prose writings of the 1970s and 1980s (*A Sorrow Beyond Dreams*, 1979; *Slow Homecoming*, 1980). The reflective, descriptive, and evocative aspect of naming the objects of the world have replaced the haunting and destructive power of words.

The radio play included in our volume belongs to the earlier texts of the author. None of the characters has a name. Voices are heard of the questioner and the questioned about the past interrogation, alternating with the voice of the questioner addressing the interrogators, shifting to the reenactment of the interrogation of five interrogators and the interrogated. It is a play on questions and answers, about a process of discovering the truth. As it turns out, the questioner is as guilty as the interrogators themselves in obtaining answers by scheming, flattering, tricking, and threatening the victim.

The deliberately unintelligible and confusing discourse of the interrogators and their victim, who tries to withstand brute force by words and deeds, is heightened by the sound effects used in this radio play as an autonomous *gestus*, as banal and ominous as the discourse. The objective to make the victim confess and to relive the experience is to empty him of his arguments and break his resistance. The end is the drying up of sentences, words, sounds; and the rest is silence.

If Handke described his play *Kaspar* as a drama that "shows what is possible with someone" through the impact of the spoken word, that man can be constructed and deconstructed through the use of language, then the radio play in our volume is a play to show the trial of a person to subdue the human spirit and make her or him speechless.

With this play and the two following ones, the radio plays of the 1950s have undergone striking changes. In recent radio drama there is a strong emphasis on the spoken word. Neither plot nor the delineation of characters are of importance. Time, space, and meaning have to be distilled from the speech patterns, from sound and music.

Still relying on word and sound as the dominant features of the genre, the new radio play has come into its own. The play that ends in silence is but a step in the direction of radio drama which dispenses with language altogether to become a play of pure sound, as in Handke's *Wind and Sea*.

M. H. S.

"RADIO PLAY" (No. 1)

CHARACTERS

QUESTIONER
QUESTIONED
THE INTERROGATED
INTERROGATOR A
INTERROGATOR B
INTERROGATOR C
INTERROGATOR D
INTERROGATOR E

Sound Effects: *All sorts of radio-drama sound effects used briefly and abruptly—they are never complete.*

Questioner *and* Questioned *are always closer to the microphone than the* Interrogator, *and the* Questioned *closer than the* Interrogated.

The delivery is never realistic, but always painful, just as the sound effects are always used musically rather than realistically—to surprise, not to explain.

> *The sound effect of water being poured into a glass. A shrill whistle on two fingers.*

QUESTIONER: Can you recover from a scare like that?

QUESTIONED: They buttoned up my jacket and pulled it down over my shoulders, so I couldn't move my arms anymore.

QUESTIONER: How can you recover from a scare like that?

QUESTIONED: They threw my coat over my head and tied it around my neck with a cord.

QUESTIONER: Did you pick up your feet on the level ground as though climbing stairs; and then on the stairs, did you expect stairs?

QUESTIONED: A fat drop—or was it soft butter?—plopped on the floor next to me.

QUESTIONER: Were the walls soundproof?

QUESTIONED: It was dark in the room so at first I thought it was night.

> *The sound effect for distant wind.*

QUESTIONER: What kind of cigarettes do you like?

INTERROGATOR A: Sorry, we can't offer you any other chair.

INTERROGATOR B: What can we do for you?

INTERROGATOR C: Don't you think it's ridiculous that you've got your clothes on?

INTERROGATOR D: We'll have to jog your memory a little.

INTERROGATOR E: Can you sit down standing up?

INTERROGATOR A: Sit down.

The sound effect of a ringing glass.

QUESTIONER: Were you able to keep your mind off it?

QUESTIONED: The toe of the shoe caught me on the chin.

QUESTIONER: Maybe you were desperate because you had to keep comparing the situation you were in with some other situation you might have been in?

QUESTIONED: When they kicked me I tried to read the brand name on the sole of their shoes.

A very short, stately violin solo, falling away, on two notes.

QUESTIONER: Didn't it feel good that you could at least move a finger?

The very short violin solo again.

QUESTIONED: They flexed their fingers before they grabbed hold.

QUESTIONER: Are you a light sleeper?

QUESTIONED: At first they frightened me with plays on words.

QUESTIONER: How much water do you take in your whiskey?

INTERROGATOR C: Can you imagine anything these hands wouldn't do?

Scraping sound effects that very suddenly cease.

INTERROGATOR D: Why do you wear sunglasses at night?

INTERROGATOR C: Do you want me to spell it out?

INTERROGATOR D: Who said you could sit down?

INTERROGATOR C: Did it make you speechless?

INTERROGATOR A: Out with it.

Pause.

QUESTIONER: Would you like a little ice with that?

QUESTIONED: They sat me on a chair without a seat.

QUESTIONER: Do you feel all right?

QUESTIONED: They showed me a photo of many people. I couldn't find myself in it.

QUESTIONER: When cannonballs are fired over the water, don't the drowned all rise to the surface?

The doorbell buzzes.

QUESTIONED: They tore the buttons off my jacket.

QUESTIONER: Do you feel better?

QUESTIONED: They told me to lean back in the chair, but it didn't have any back.

QUESTIONER: Who was that shot meant for?
  The doorbell buzzes.
QUESTIONED: They flew into a rage because I didn't notice they were being contemptuous.
  The doorbell buzzes.
QUESTIONER: Who expects to get punched just as he is eating an apple?

INTERROGATOR B: People will say that you looked a lot younger while you were still alive.
INTERROGATOR E: We can get very disagreeable.
INTERROGATOR A: Why did you hesitate at this word?
INTERROGATOR E: Why did you walk on tiptoe?
INTERROGATOR B: We're really very easy to get along with.
INTERROGATOR A: Did you ever get it from both sides at once?
INTERROGATOR C: Why are you blinking?
INTERROGATOR A: You'd give anything in the world to rub your nose right now, wouldn't you?
INTERROGATOR B: Is that right, you'd like to rub your nose?
INTERROGATOR D: Doesn't your nose itch at all?
INTERROGATOR E: You'd like to rub your nose? I hope not.
INTERROGATOR C: And your armpits?
  A railroad train passes by.

QUESTIONED: I was glad when it suddenly started to rain.
  Children's cries are heard.
QUESTIONED: They were very satisfied to see me sweat.
  Children's cries are heard farther away.
QUESTIONED: A bird flew up screaming.
  Children's cries are heard farther away.
QUESTIONED: They deliberately walked around the room just to show me *they* could move freely.
  Children's cries are heard very far away.
QUESTIONED: Gradually the walls of the room took on screaming colors, so that I had to—no, wanted to—cover my ears with my hands.
  Children's cries are heard, very near.
QUESTIONER: How much sugar do you take in your tea?
  Pause.

QUESTIONER: Or do you prefer to smoke cigars?
   Pause.
QUESTIONER: How often do you usually take a bath?
   Pause.
QUESTIONER: Do you change your underwear every day?
   Pause.
QUESTIONER: Do you like to sleep on your back or on your stomach?
   Pause.
QUESTIONER: Aren't your shoelaces too frayed to use for garrotting?
   Pause.
QUESTIONER: Did anything heavy ever fall on you when you opened a closet?
   Pause.
QUESTIONER: Have you ever heard a child laugh behind someone who was dying?
   Pause.
QUESTIONER: Is the hand crawling over your body your own?
   Pause.
QUESTIONER: Why are all the dogs suddenly starting to bark?
   Pause.
QUESTIONER: Isn't it very still?
   The very quiet sound of a sigh.
QUESTIONER: Have you ever patted a dead man on the back?
   A heavy object smacks the water very loudly.
QUESTIONED: Fear made my body very heavy.
QUESTIONER: While someone was talking to you and smoking at the same time—and there was a pause in the conversation—have you ever heard the cigarette crackling between his fingers?
QUESTIONED: Once when I told the truth I got very embarrassed and corrected myself by lying.
QUESTIONER: Are you sitting comfortably?
QUESTIONED: They persecuted me so much with words that even in my sleep I was not in control but the words controlled me; they hounded me into my sleep with their words.
   The sound-effects of an unoiled door.
QUESTIONER: Weren't you able to get used to them?
QUESTIONED: A minute was a long time for me.
QUESTIONER: Couldn't you at least get a rest between questions?

QUESTIONED: They drummed on the table with their fingertips when I owed them an answer.
  The low sound of wind.

INTERROGATOR A: You know more than you're willing to admit.
INTERROGATOR C: Aren't you finally going to come out with it?
INTERROGATED: Could I scratch my ear?
INTERROGATOR B: We only want to talk to you a little.
INTERROGATED: Could I just scratch my ear a little?
INTERROGATOR D: Don't you have something to tell us?
INTERROGATED: I haven't heard a thing.
INTERROGATOR E: Did you say something?
INTERROGATED: I don't hear a thing.
  A teakettle whistles louder and louder.

QUESTIONER: Did they look at you while they questioned you?
QUESTIONED: It seemed to me that my heartbeat shook the chair I sat on—no, what I meant to say is that I didn't hear a thing meant for other ears—no, no, what I really meant to say is that it calmed me down, the way one of them secretly pointed at me with his finger—no, with a burning match.
QUESTIONER: Did *you* look at the questioners?
QUESTIONED: One of them held a hot iron up to my face—no, he showed me the iron from a distance, but I could feel how hot it was—or better: I saw cigarette burns on the door—or, wait a minute, I turned my face away in pain, no, that's not quite right either, I only shook my head because I wanted to see if I could still move.
QUESTIONER: Did your cigarette go out?
QUESTIONED: When one of them tried to spit at me, he choked or at least whistled under his breath, no, he growled, no, he really seemed to be looking down an empty street or, no, as if I was just not *possible* at all, or as if in spite of everything the room really had a nice view.
  The sound of a waterfall. The whistling of a locomotive entering a tunnel.
QUESTIONER: Do you like to hear yourself talk?
QUESTIONED: One of them wanted to reach into his jacket, under the arm, but the zipper was jammed, or I ought to say he struck a

match on his shoe sole, no, his boot sole, or the wall, no, he tore a
calendar page off the wall, no, he took a picture off the wall, no,
no, in fact he took the photo out of my hand or, to tell the truth,
he, no, another one, took me by the hand and tore the cloth off
my eyes or anyway tore the lining out of my coat, out of my
pants—to be more exact—turned my pants pockets inside out,
yanked me out of the chair and stood me up against the wall, yes,
that's how it was, that's how it is.

A door slams shut.

QUESTIONER: How often do you have to water your flowers?

INTERROGATOR E: This isn't a coffee break.
We didn't bring you here to exchange formalities.
We have something to talk over with you.
We want to take a little walk with you.
We want to chat a little with you about the weather.
This isn't a coffee break.
We didn't bring you here to exchange formalities.
We have something to talk over with you.
We want to take a little walk with you.
How are you feeling?

Loud honking.

INTERROGATOR E: How are you feeling?

Loud honking.

INTERROGATOR E: How are you?

A great church bell tolls.

INTERROGATOR E: We're not here to talk about the weather with
you.

Cicada chirp.

QUESTIONED: Every time they looked at me I appeared to be caught
in the act.

The great church bell tolls. Suddenly the cicadas chirp.

INTERROGATOR C: The fresh air will do you good.
We'd like to put a few questions to you.
What are you laughing about?
You'll get used to your new surroundings soon enough.
Please sit still.
Didn't you cough differently the last time?
Where do you get the nerve to say "Hello!"?

That you deny it, already proves you know too much.
Please take off your coat.
  Seagulls scream.
QUESTIONED: While they smiled at me sincerely they held their teacups in the *most natural way* in the world.
  Seagulls scream.
Whenever I avoided their eyes, I didn't know where to look.
  Seagulls scream.
They told each other jokes in front of me to show me that I wasn't one of them.
  The seagulls scream.
When my head got heavy and I leaned it a little to one side, they thought I would finally start talking.
  The seagulls scream.
They even searched the color and pattern of my shirt for something to give me away.
  A small bell tinkles.
INTERROGATOR D: We've softened up lots of others.
QUESTIONED: On the windowsill I saw a tin can with the date on it showing that the contents could still be eaten, and right away I believed nothing could happen to me as long as the canned goods were still edible, so I felt better.

QUESTIONER: I myself know the situation you're in. I too have been so frightened that I called strangers by their first names. I too have often found that I couldn't go to sleep in a strange room. Often I too have suddenly heard the shutters slam. Like you, I just stared dumbly once when I was threatened with death, and it has happened that I too have stuck my finger into a water faucet because I couldn't stand the dripping anymore.
  Pause.
Do you talk to yourself sometimes too?
QUESTIONED: Yes, it bothers me to hear others greedily sucking on their cigarettes when they get desperate.
QUESTIONER: And are you ashamed when you catch yourself talking to yourself?
QUESTIONED: No, it wasn't soft butter, but a thick newspaper that plopped onto the street from the top floor.
QUESTIONER: And do you look around to see if anyone or, better, if

most likely no one heard you?

QUESTIONED: Yes, my heart has started beating faster when I filed my fingernails.

QUESTIONER: And do you hum then or whistle from embarrassment?

QUESTIONED: No, I don't have a vaccination scar on my upper arm.
Pause.

QUESTIONER: Have you made yourself comfortable?
Can I get you anything?
Do you feel at home?
Have you stretched out your legs?
Is the light bright enough for you?
Do you need an ashtray?
Can I give you a refill?
Pause.

INTERROGATOR A: He has a really guilty way of chewing.

INTERROGATOR B: He feels so guilty he can't swallow.

INTERROGATOR E: He feels so guilty that his cheeks are full.
Pause.

INTERROGATOR C: He only has flesh wounds.

INTERROGATOR D: He won't live to an old age.

INTERROGATOR C: In the old days they would have cut off his eyelids and put him out in the sun.

INTERROGATOR D: At least the pain would help pass the time.

INTERROGATOR A: He'll yell himself out soon enough.

INTERROGATOR C: And we could be such good friends.

INTERROGATOR B: We have to get him to the point where his pain makes him look *disgusting*.

INTERROGATOR D: He's no good to us dead.

INTERROGATOR E: We'll make sure he doesn't forget us.

INTERROGATOR C: He'll sing beautifully.

INTERROGATED: I'd like to wash my hands.

INTERROGATOR A: He'll sing beautifully.

INTERROGATED: I'd like to swallow.

INTERROGATOR B: He'll sing.

INTERROGATED: I'd like to button up my pants.

INTERROGATOR D: You'll *sing*.

INTERROGATED: I'd like to scratch my head.

INTERROGATOR E: Sing.
INTERROGATED: It's nice here.
> *He bites into an apple. The apple is eaten, for a while. At the same time there is humming, and periodically a child's trumpet is blown.*

QUESTIONER: Could we finally get less formal?

INTERROGATOR A: What occurs to you when you hear the words "clam chowder"?
INTERROGATED: It's not enough to call for help only *once*.
INTERROGATOR A: What occurs to you when you hear the word "silkworm"?
INTERROGATED: At first I thought the clotted blood was a joke.
INTERROGATOR A: What occurs to you when you hear the word "abdominal"?
INTERROGATED: The shoes have steel toes.
> *The ringing that signals a hit in a penny arcade, but very short.*

INTERROGATOR A: What occurs to you when you hear the word "glove"?
INTERROGATED: The foam is popping in the sink.
> *The ringing.*

INTERROGATOR A: What occurs to you when you hear the sentence "He's sitting with his back to the wall"?
INTERROGATED: He's a passionate hiker.
> *The ringing.*

INTERROGATOR A: What occurs to you when you hear the sentence "The dead man's children are snuggling up in the neighbor's bed"?
INTERROGATED: No one has any spot remover handy.
> *Ringing.*

INTERROGATOR A: And when you hear "A nail bent while being hammered"?
> *Pause.*

INTERROGATED: Nothing can happen.
> *Ringing.*

INTERROGATOR A: And "The telephone book is open at a particular place"?

Pause.

INTERROGATED: It's a hole the size of a child's fist.

Ringing.

INTERROGATOR A: "He stepped on something soft"?

Pause.

INTERROGATED: The price tag is falling off the meat hook.

Ringing.

INTERROGATOR A: "In his desperation he's very precise about every word"?

Short pause.

INTERROGATED: They don't have to be ladies' shoes.

Ringing.

INTERROGATOR A: "She is dressed up in stockings"?

INTERROGATED: Glove.

INTERROGATOR A: "The toothbrush lands with the bristles up"?

INTERROGATED: Silkworm.

INTERROGATOR A: "The matches are damp"?

INTERROGATED: Silkworm.

INTERROGATOR A: "The drainpipe elbow is unscrewed"?

INTERROGATED: Silkworm.

INTERROGATOR A: "All the dogs wake up"?

INTERROGATED: Meerschaum pipe.

A fanfare, short, broken off, disordant.

QUESTIONED: Actually I can't really complain of mistreatment. I use every word to get off the subject. When I drop things, I can actually kill time picking them up. When they tell me stories that supposedly happened to *me,* actually it just gives me something to listen to. What I *see,* the pain makes me believe I actually *hear.* My hand lay in the water so long that I'm actually just happy for it to be out of the water. Actually I'm also happy that the torn-out hair was curled, that is actually *I'm* happy that the torn-out hair ... actually, to kill time I can also read the label on the matchbox. I admit to them that I'm right-handed and actually that's about all it takes to satisfy them. Luckily the room has four walls. Luckily I can distract myself by thinking that before a dying man dies, he eats one last apple, and actually that's about what it takes to satisfy me too. Actually they can't really do anything to

me because you always see the wedding pictures of murdered men
and there aren't any wedding pictures of me.

QUESTIONER: May I—can you describe what happened?

QUESTIONED: The door opened like. . . .

They yelled at me as if. . . .

One of them pounded the table like. . . .

One of them yanked left and right on my turned-out pants
pockets like a. . . .

One winked at me as if he had. . . .

The ash fell from the cigarette exactly like a. . . .

One of them sniffed at his fingers as if he. . . .

One had a black leather strap around his knuckles like a. . . .

The knife blade didn't flash any longer than. . . .

*Crockery shatters. Glass shatter. A clock strikes. The child's
trumpet. The wind.*

QUESTIONER: You needn't say anything if you don't want to. It
would be easy to understand if you didn't want to tell. It would be
entirely excusable if you didn't want to tell anything.

QUESTIONED: When I didn't feel like reassuring them anymore,
they started reassuring *me*.

QUESTIONER: You needn't tell anything about it.

QUESTIONED: They didn't even let me rub my eyes.

QUESTIONER: If it's hard for you, you needn't tell anything.

QUESTIONED: They sat me on a chair with such high legs that I
couldn't even reach the floor with my toes.

QUESTIONER: No one will demand that you remember.

QUESTIONED: I slept with my teeth clamped together.

QUESTIONER: Just stop talking when you feel you can't go on.

QUESTIONED: Even when I toyed with my shoelaces they thought I
might be revealing something.

QUESTIONER: Talk about it only if it feels good.

QUESTIONED: When I went to dip the spoon back into my soup, the
bowl wasn't there anymore.

QUESTIONER: Just talk it out.

QUESTIONED: I didn't close my lips very tightly, so they wouldn't
think there was anything I wanted to hide.

QUESTIONER: Even if it's hard for you—you have to tell about it.

QUESTIONED *stays silent.*

QUESTIONER: It'll help us get on with it.
QUESTIONED *remains silent.*
QUESTIONER: Tell how it was.
QUESTIONED *remains silent.*

> *Birds' voices. The door creaks. Pause. A radio dial goes quickly through all the stations. Pause. Birds' voices. The door creaks. Birds voices.*

INTERROGATOR C: Tell how it is.
INTERROGATED: It's like when someone dives into the water and after he's been under for a long time and still hasn't come up, the water has become disquietingly quiet; or it's like a hotel umbrella or like when a fat child stands next to his bicycle or as if the landlady is sniffing around for gas or like the shadow of a cameraman on a photograph or like a window seat.
INTERROGATOR C: And how is it *really?*
INTERROGATED: No different than usual.
INTERROGATOR C: And how is it usually?
INTERROGATED: Just the way it is.
INTERROGATOR C: And what's the way it is?
INTERROGATED: As usual.
INTERROGATOR D: What does "usual" mean?
INTERROGATED: "Usual" means "not now."
INTERROGATOR D: So usually it isn't like now?
INTERROGATED: It's like now.
INTERROGATOR D: What do you mean by "now"?
INTERROGATED: "Not the usual."
INTERROGATOR D: So now isn't like the usual?
INTERROGATED: Now it's as usual.
INTERROGATOR D: And usually?
INTERROGATED: Usually not.

> *A heavy object falls into the water. A violin is bowed.*

QUESTIONER: Didn't you waste your time on him?
INTERROGATOR A: Once when he used a play on words we belted him.
QUESTIONER: Did he tell you what you wanted to hear?
INTERROGATOR B: We stared at him to make his breathing irregular.
QUESTIONER: Certainly you treated him very politely?
INTERROGATOR E: He held his hand in front of his face, for instance,

and that showed he had hostile intentions.

QUESTIONER: Did you try to become his friends so you could confuse his thinking?

INTERROGATOR A: We carefully filed our fingernails, while we questioned him.

QUESTIONER: Surely you suddenly kept changing your positions while you questioned him, so that he had to keep turning around to face a new questioner; and you wore him down that way.

INTERROGATOR B: We often asked him how he felt.

QUESTIONER: And surely you spoke softly for a long time?

INTERROGATOR E: He was so shocked he stopped yawning immediately.

The ocean waves.

QUESTIONER: Do you like to walk on Persian carpets?

QUESTIONED: The carpet was too shorthaired for me to grab on and hold tight.

The ocean waves.

QUESTIONED: Sugar?

Or telephone poles?

No, a mass of aphids in the naval of a corpse. No, a swarm of bluebottle flies is squashed along with the dog dirt when someone slips on it, right? Or have the wasps landed on the cake we often find on Sunday afternoons in shady garden restaurants, or in theater lobbies? No, this black spot on the wall is dog pee.

Or jelly beans?

Maybe even oregano?

Or snail slime after all?

Is that what you want to know?

The ocean waves.

QUESTIONER: Can I help you?

How can I help you?

Is there too much of a draft?

Should the desk drawer be closed?

Should I turn down the radio?

Do you often suffer from this fear of being touched by words?

Do you want to wash your hands?

INTERROGATOR C: Are you the happy owner of this apple?

INTERROGATED: Is who what?

INTERROGATOR C: Are you the happy owner of this apple?
INTERROGATED: Am I what?
INTERROGATOR D: The happy owner of this apple?
INTERROGATED: What kind of owner?
INTERROGATOR D: The happy owner.
INTERROGATED: The happy owner of what?
INTERROGATORS C, D: This apple.
INTERROGATED: Which apple?
INTERROGATORS C, D: This one.
INTERROGATED: Who?
INTERROGATORS C, D: You.
INTERROGATED: Who what?
INTERROGATORS C, D: You the owner?
INTERROGATED: Who what of what?
INTERROGATORS C, D: Are you the happy owner of this apple?
INTERROGATED: Why?
INTERROGATORS C, D: Why what?
INTERROGATED: Why do you ask?

    A door slams. A truck drives past. A door slams again.

INTERROGATOR A: We won't get any further this way. We're tried being nice long enough.
INTERROGATOR B: When he denies it, that's proof he's keeping something quiet. When he won't look us in the eye, that's proof he denies it.
INTERROGATOR A: His ears stick out. That's a sign he's obstinate. He acts like he doesn't know anything, so he does know something.
INTERROGATOR B: He acts like he's telling the truth, so he's lying. He has a weak chin, so he's not telling the truth.
INTERROGATOR E: On top of that he has a piercing look, thick lips, a broken nose, a retreating forehead, and foreign-looking cheekbones; besides, he falters when he speaks and gets caught up in contradictions; and to top it off, he bites his nails, he has a stupid look, thin, cruel lips, a nose like an eagle's beak, his forehead's too high, and he speaks much too smoothly to be trusted.
INTERROGATOR A: He hasn't got any earlobes.
INTERROGATOR B: He hasn't shaved, or combed his hair.
INTERROGATOR E: His unkempt appearance shows his mind's gone to pot.
INTERROGATOR A: He's sensitive to light.

INTERROGATOR B: He shuns the light.

    The violin sound.

QUESTIONER: Should I turn out the light?

QUESTIONED: Each time before they beat me, they went into this routine showing me how they take off their jackets and—

QUESTIONER: Should I dim the light?

QUESTIONED: —and then carefully hang their jackets on clothes hangers and—

QUESTIONER: Should I turn on the night-light?

QUESTIONED: —and even button up the buttons on their jackets one by one and—

QUESTIONER: Should I leave the light like this?

QUESTIONED: —and then loosen up their fingers and look pityingly at their fingers and—

QUESTIONER: Cuff.

QUESTIONER: Cuff?

QUESTIONER: Unbutton their sleeves, I mean.

QUESTIONED: You might call it "cuff." Or: "strong-arm." I also heard the expression "marathon" put in. Someone added "junk pile." Another put in: "I just stepped on a rotten muskmelon." And still another added "pulp." Those who *put in* something were the self-assured ones; but those who *added* something *else* were the gloomy ones. Or you can also hear it said that they were "stumped."

    The wind. A harmonica. The wind. An accordion.

QUESTIONED: Have I mentioned yet that the white spots I saw on the floor had dripped from the throat of someone who had been choked to death? Or that they immediately showed me their family albums, which were so full that they couldn't stick any more of the pictures in? Have I already told you how much relief and happiness I felt when I put on the shirt on which I had just sewn a button? Did I mention the wonderful dimness in the room? Have I told about how one of them said the features of a relative in a photograph were "like a woodcut"? Have I mentioned the stamp that had missed being canceled? Or the soft butter that hadn't plopped on the floor at all? Or the blackjack? Or the ring with the thorn? Or the ladybug in the fly of my pants?

QUESTIONER: When you squeeze someone's throat harder and harder, you finally hear something crack, don't you?

A resounding chomp on the apple. The roar of the sea.

INTERROGATED: I can't walk straight with both hands tied.

INTERROGATOR A: He can't walk straight with both hands tied.

INTERROGATED: I *found* this newspaper clipping.

INTERROGATOR B: He only *found* this newspaper clipping.

INTERROGATED: I can only repeat that I don't know anymore.

INTERROGATORS C–E *(a little mixed up, not speaking in unison)*: He can only repeat that he doesn't know anymore.

INTERROGATED: I only stepped on a hose.

INTERROGATORS A–E *(speaking rather out of unison)*: He only stepped on a hose.

   Pause.

INTERROGATOR A: Who do you think you're dealing with?

   Pause.

INTERROGATOR B: Try to remember.

   Pause.

INTERROGATOR C: What drove you out in weather like that?

   Pause.

INTERROGATOR D: You'll be eating out of our hands yet.

   Pause.

INTERROGATOR E: Just you leave the thinking to us.

   Long pause.

INTERROGATOR A: If anyone cracks jokes around here, it'll be us.

   Long pause.

INTERROGATOR B: We can get very disagreeable.

   Long pause.

INTERROGATOR C: Why are your feet turned in?

   Pause.

INTERROGATOR D: Why are you hiding your thumbs inside your hands?

   Pause.

INTERROGATOR E: Why are you swallowing so hard?

   Long pause. The sound of crows cawing.

QUESTIONED: Suddenly the word "snow" occurred to me.

   The crows caw.

INTERROGATOR A: You'll stop laughing soon enough, mister.

   The crows caw.

INTERROGATOR E: You'll stop laughing soon enough, kid.
> *The crows are cawing.*

QUESTIONED: Suddenly the words "giant slalom" occurred to me.

> *The crows are cawing.*
INTERROGATOR C: This one's mine.
INTERROGATOR D: Yeah, he's mine.
> *The crows are cawing.*

QUESTIONED: Just when I finally wanted to open my mouth they started questioning me again.
QUESTIONER: How do you like my tie?
QUESTIONED: Wherever I tried to put my hand, it bothered me.
QUESTIONER: Does it also happen to you when you go out the door, that you turn around once as you shut the door?
QUESTIONED: They were all family men, and they used toothpicks while they questioned me.
> *Gargling after brushing teeth.*

INTERROGATOR A: It's unusually humid, isn't it?
> *Pause.*
INTERROGATED *(hesitantly)*: Actually, it's quite comfortable.
INTERROGATOR C: You feel all right, don't you?
> *Pause.*
INTERROGATED *(hesitantly)*: Actually, I'd rather sit.
INTERROGATOR E: The birds are singing nicely today, aren't they?
INTERROGATED *(very hesitantly)*: To be honest, I like going barefoot best.
> *A very quiet motif on the organ.*
INTERROGATOR A: Do you like it here with us?
INTERROGATED *(very hesitantly)*: No.
INTERROGATOR E: Could you please hand me the lighter?
INTERROGATED *(very, very hesitantly)*: No.
INTERROGATOR C: Would you please open the door for me, I have both my hands full of luggage.
INTERROGATED *(after a very long time for thought)*: No.
> *The quiet organ motif.*

QUESTIONER: How did the flyswatter—
They laugh.
QUESTIONER: Sorry.

They laugh.
QUESTIONER: What did you want to—
They laugh.
QUESTIONER: You start—

They laugh less.
QUESTIONER: Talk—
They no longer laugh.
QUESTIONER: So talk, already.

QUESTIONER: Say what you wanted to say.
QUESTIONER: Until you tell me what you wanted to tell me, I'm not telling you what I wanted to tell you.
QUESTIONER: So the point of the pistol bullet is—?

QUESTIONED: The point of the pistol bullet is—

QUESTIONED: I beg your pardon.

QUESTIONED: What were you about to—

QUESTIONED: Please, after you—

QUESTIONED: What were—

QUESTIONED; You wished to say something first, sir?
QUESTIONED: I beg you to tell me first.
QUESTIONED: Sir, until you tell me what you wanted to tell me, I shall not tell you what I wanted to tell you.
QUESTIONED: So how did the flyswatter—?

A short, not funny, one-note solo on a recorder. Then a paper sack pops. A baby's rattle.

INTERROGATOR A: So your armpits started itching when you got scared.
INTERROGATED: I wasn't scared.
INTERROGATOR A: But your armpits itched?
INTERROGATED: Only once at night.
INTERROGATOR A: So you *were* scared.
The baby's rattle.
INTERROGATOR B: Do you have an apple on you?
INTERROGATED: I don't eat apples.
INTERROGATOR B: So you *do* have an apple on you.
The baby's rattle.
INTERROGATED: I have—

INTERROGATOR C: —Poked yourself in the ear with a knitting needle?

INTERROGATED: The page in the telephone book—

INTERROGATOR C: —was torn out by you?

INTERROGATED: The telephone cord—

INTERROGATOR C: —was tied into a noose by you?

INTERROGATED: The room—

INTERROGATOR C: —you won't leave it in the same condition as when you arrived.

> *The scream of a parrot.*

INTERROGATOR A: Doesn't he look different the minute one talks to him a little?

INTERROGATOR B: Isn't there something touching about him?

INTERROGATOR A: Isn't he convincing the minute he opens his mouth?

> *The scream of the parrot.*

QUESTIONER: Why don't we just sit down?

QUESTIONED: Why don't we just sit down?

QUESTIONER: We both said the same thing at the same time.

QUESTIONED: We both said the same thing at the same time.

QUESTIONER: Why don't we just sit down.

QUESTIONED: Why don't we just sit down?

> *They laugh because they said the same thing at once.*

QUESTIONER: We both said the same thing at the same time.

QUESTIONED: We both said the same thing at the same time.

> *They laugh because. . . .*

QUESTIONER: Isn't that funny?   QUESTIONED: Isn't that funny?

> *Pause. Then they laugh because they. . . . and now with the identical sounds of laughter, whereupon they immediately break off again. The paper sack pops. A whip cracks. Someone gargles after brushing teeth.*

INTERROGATOR E: Do you like to walk in the middle of the sidewalk?

INTERROGATED: Do *you* like to walk in the middle of the sidewalk?

INTERROGATOR E: I asked if *you* like to walk in the middle of the sidewalk?

INTERROGATED: And you, sir, do *you* like. . . ?

INTERROGATOR E: Do *you* like. . . .

INTERROGATED: And *you*, sir . . . ?

INTERROGATOR E: *You.*

INTERROGATED: If *you* like to take a walk in the middle of the sidewalk, I like to walk in the middle of the sidewalk, too.

> *Paper is quickly torn in two. Geese gabble. Something smacks the water.*

INTERROGATOR D: And do you like to walk in the rain?

INTERROGATED: Do I like to walk in the rain?

INTERROGATED D: Do you like to walk in the rain?

INTERROGATED: Why should I like to walk in the rain?

INTERROGATOR D: Do you like to walk in the rain?

INTERROGATED: *Do* I like to walk in the rain?

> *Paper is quickly torn in two. A whip crack. A train travels over land briefly.*

INTERROGATOR C: Why do you have specks of blood on your hands?

INTERROGATED: Why do I have flecks of mud on my hands?

INTERROGATOR C: Why do you have specks of blood on your hands?

INTERROGATED: Why do I have pecs like a muscle man's?

INTERROGATOR C: Why do you have specks of blood on your plants?

INTERROGATED: Why do I check my hair on my hams?

INTERROGATOR C: Why do you swear when you care for your plants?

INTERROGATED: Why do I prefer linen underwear?

INTERROGATOR C: Why do you plait the strands of your hair?

INTERROGATED: Why can't I stand to see suffering anywhere?

INTERROGATOR B: Yeah, why can't you stand to see suffering anywhere?

INTERROGATED: Because I have specks of blood on my hands.

> *An owl screams. A foghorn.*

INTERROGATOR C (*pointedly*): How much longer will you go on abusing our patience?

INTERROGATED: A clam chowder long.

INTERROGATOR B (*pointedly*): When will you finally be sensible?

INTERROGATED: On the festival of the celebration.

INTERROGATOR B: Why do you hold tight to your *chair* when you speak?

INTERROGATED: Because . . . (*pause*) when I speak I hold *tight* to my chair.

> *A screech owl cries. A car tries vainly to start.*

INTERROGATOR A: Why is there a hair stuck to the wall here?
INTERROGATED: Is there such a thing as odorless flypaper?
INTERROGATOR A: Why is your handwriting so shaky here?
INTERROGATED: Do you have matches for the fireplace?
INTERROGATOR A: Why did you speak of the cat's naked ear?
INTERROGATED: Do you sell peach preserves?
INTERROGATOR A: Why do you clap your hands in an empty room?
INTERROGATED: What do you mean by that?
> *The tiger hisses. A brook splashes. Water gurgles. Whistle.*

QUESTIONED: The garden hose just fit in my mouth. Their fists never hit the same place twice. The light bulb didn't pop. I envied myself-of-a-minute-ago. Because their power was so limited and I was the only one in their power, they were all the more avid to take advantage of it. They stroked all the furnishings with their fingertips and then looked at their fingertips with contempt. Once I heard snow chains rattling outside, or trumpets blowing, or gun salutes, or the rain, or gun salutes after all? They kept replacing words with prettier words, and the right word was always just on the tip of my tongue.
> *The wind. A horse whinnies. The storm. A dog growls. A tin can clatters. A parade instrument snorts. Chain rattling. A bunch of keys. A lighter is clicked several times. Morse code for "hello." Ringing of glasses. The whistle between two fingers.*

QUESTIONER: I didn't understand you.
QUESTIONED: What did you say, sir?
QUESTIONER: What did you say?
QUESTIONED: Come again?
QUESTIONER: What?
QUESTIONED: Huh?
QUESTIONER: Hm?
QUESTIONED: Forget it.
> *A beautiful violin solo, short, with sounds like "Ah," "Oh, yes." "That's it." "Ohhh," "Mhm" mixed in.*

QUESTIONER: Now say after me.
QUESTIONED: "Now say after me."
QUESTIONER: Not this sentence.
QUESTIONED: "Not this sentence."

QUESTIONER: Not that one.
QUESTIONED: "Not that one."
　　The following dialogue with increasingly long pauses.
QUESTIONER: No.
QUESTIONED: "No."
QUESTIONER: Stop it.
QUESTIONED: "Stop it."
QUESTIONER: There's no help for you anymore.
QUESTIONED: "There's no help for you anymore."
QUESTIONER *(laughs)*
QUESTIONED *(imitates his laughter)*
QUESTIONER *(laughs a little)*
QUESTIONED *(laughs a little)*
QUESTIONER *(laughs once)*: Ha. *(annoyed)*
QUESTIONED *(laughs once)*: Ha. *(annoyed)*
QUESTIONER *(only makes one more sound in his throat, a quick short throat-clearing sound)*
QUESTIONED *(only makes one more sound in his throat, a quick short throat-clearing sound)*
QUESTIONER *(is silent)*
QUESTIONED *(is silent)*
　　The same beautiful, stately violin solo without mixed-in sounds, held for some time.

The "Hörspiel" has ended.

Translated by Robert Goss

Jürgen Becker

Jürgen Becker was born in Cologne in 1932. He spent a few years in the German Democratic Republic and returned to West Germany in 1950. After school and university training, he left the academic world without completing his studies. He held positions with the West German radio station in Cologne, was an editor and director of publishing houses, and in 1974 became a program director of radio-play productions. He has settled down as a free-lance writer near the city of Cologne. He was a writer-in-residence at the Villa Massimo in Italy in 1965–66, traveled to America, and has received numerous literary prizes.

Comparable to Peter Handke's interest in the possibilities of language, Jürgen Becker is fascinated by the instrumental power of speech and his first prose texts (*Felder [Fields]*, 1964, *Ränder [Margins]*, 1968, *Umgebungen [Surroundings]*, 1970) are experimental and avant-gardist in nature. Neither traditionally conceived characters nor plots play a role in these texts and they can be understood as counterproposals to the customary novel. The abundance of ironic and critical observations on prevalent linguistic patterns in ordinary discourse is predominant in his and many other literary works of the 1960s and 1970s. The deconstruction of human behavior, of prejudices and animosities, is the objective in analyzing the vagaries of speech at a concrete time and place. The study of language as a consciousness industry, however, does not always appeal to the average reader, and the detailed deliberations of Becker's prose works are no exception to this fact. He gained a broader public through his second text *Margins* and his radio plays *Bilder (Images)*, *Häuser (Houses,* included in this volume*)*, and *Hausfreunde (Friends of the Family)*, all of which were published in 1969 and accepted for broadcast by several German radio stations. Parallel to the prose texts as contraventions to traditional forms of fiction, the radio plays refuse to adhere to accepted norms of individualized voices and a developing action. The voices remain anonymous and any characteristic features have to be extracted from the multivoiced discourse. *Zeit ohne Wörter (A Time without Words,* 1971) offered prose texts with photographs. Jürgen Becker also published a stage play (*Die Zeit nach Herriman* [*The Time after Herriman,* 1971]), and continued to write prose texts (*Erzählungen bis Ostende* [*Tales to Ostende,* 1981] and *Die Tür zum Meer* [*Door to the Ocean,* 1983]). He has come out with a number of collections of poetry. His works, at once descriptive and reflective, capture the palaver and chatter of human voices, and are manifestations of contemporary minds. The texts register the destructive forces at work in our industrialized cities. They mourn the spoiled landscape, the spiritless world of consumerism, and the unfriendly and insensitive relations among human beings.

The doubt whether an experience can still be produced in the manner of traditional genres informs Jürgen Becker's thoughts on how to sit down and write at all today. James Joyce taught him how to see; other writers helped to let him find his own form. There is a host of images, sounds, and thoughts that must be captured and shaped into authentic voices. It is not the conventional story that is the core of Jürgen Becker's writings, but the construction of linguistic events based on the subjective experience, observation, imagination, thought, and reflection of the writer. Life and art have to be fused into what Becker calls "intermedial praxis." This frame of mind will lead to a realistic consciousness allowing him to register the contradictory nature of reality, our psychological responses, the pressures of social existence, and the evocation of utopian possibilities, thus describing the conditions shaping our consciousness today. In his radio play *Houses,* the plurality of German voices of different ages, gender, and class articulate their impressions, frustrations, opinions, and prejudices. The kinds of words and fragmentary sentences, slogans, and clichés used to make themselves heard tell a tale about the present mood among citizens.

Structured in a circular motion, the end of the radio play is connected to the beginning. At the opening of the play a person is pleased to stay forever in the house near the woods. In the second scene a voice complains about the noisy neighbors and their barking dog. At the close of the play a plaintive voice comments on the dreadful calm and isolation after the yelling neighbors and the barking dog have gone. And the last person we hear announces the departure from a decaying house that is no longer surrounded by the forest. He is eager to escape the gray and heavy air. The entire play, however, moves openly in many directions: from the country to the city with its urban sprawl, from imaginable to unimaginable houses, from monologue to dialogue and multivoiced discourse. There is the voice of hope, of desire, of anger, and of fury; the voice of the disillusioned, of the radical revolutionary, and the reactionary boasting about the glorious days of the last world war, the breaking of resistance, and extermination of the "lower elements." There are political connotations when people refer to the new house rules proclaimed by tenants to keep out disagreeable lodgers and unwelcome visitors to save the status quo. There are the voices of the lonely and the gregarious. And whoever says "I" and remembers a parent's house, speaks with a thousand tongues and different ideological commitments. The person who has some hope left, temporarily escapes the urban wasteland to go hiking through the hills, but cannot stop talking incessantly. The finale is a protest to leave it all behind, to stop the decomposition and decay of the cityscape. In *Houses*, Jürgen Becker achieves "intermedial praxis" in an exemplary fashion through live voices that are convincing and lead to an awareness about the contemporary world.

M. H. S.

HOUSES

—I won't leave here. Ever.

—What? You want to—you want to stay here? Always?

—I want to stay here forever. It's quiet here. You can breathe here. The woods are nearby. The fields are green. It's dark at night. Can we see people? Hardly any people. Here we'll stay. One more time: we'll stay, forever, here.

* * *

—There goes that dog again, barking, I'm going to have to potshot it sometime soon, all my complaining doesn't make a bit of difference. Now they're all throwing their windows open again and starting to shout, all of them, and there go all their doors flying open again and they're all shoving out in the open together and hunting it around the garden. Now they're all yelling in the garden: Where is it anyway? Where? And all the ones in the window yell: There it is, no, over there! The dog that barks all the time, where is it? There it goes through the hedge, crashing around, now it's in the bushes, everybody's yelling, now they're climbing the trees, and there's the first one flat on his back on the ground again, shouting, shouting. Now here comes the dog, no one sees the dog, there it goes in the house. Hey, there it goes in the house. Now the dog's in the house and they're still shouting in the garden, no, now they're coming back screaming to the house, into the house, now all the doors are slamming shut, now all the windows are slamming shut, the ambulance'll be here soon. Worse, worse every time.

* * *

—We know, yes, we know you'll only come back to the city when it's burned down again. That might be very soon. Or you might have to wait a while longer. Or things might turn out very differently. That is, the city'll come out to you, understand? All of a sudden a kind of supermarket will be standing where your cabin's still hidden in the greenery. And then, yes, because it'll keep on like that, where do you go then, where are you going to be alone then, left to yourself and forgotten by all of us?

* * *

—Can we visit you some time?

—Can we make our recommendations sometime?

—Can we point out how we're able to help you sometime?
—We really want to help you.
—Our recommendations are really only recommendations.
—People always look forward to our visits. We're always welcome.
—Or are you suspicious because of a bad experience?
—Or have you stopped hoping that things will get better?
—Or have you already taken care of all your needs?
—What you've never heard of today is what you'll have to have tomorrow.
—If you think the situation can't be changed, you've just stopped hoping.
—A suspicious mind destroys all trust.
—And you want to go on saying no?
—And you want to refuse to change your mind?
—And you won't go along?

* * *

—Some of them were there again this morning. Very early.
—Did they look through everything again?
—This time they flipped through the pages of the books.
—Did they take any away?
—They're not interested in the books.
—What were they after?
—Well, what would they be after?
—What did they say?
—Not a word. They only flipped pages. Just flipped the pages.

* * *

—Do you think it's her new boyfriend?
—This is the third time today.
—And always at the same time.
—And always when she's alone.
—She's not alone today.
—That's why he didn't bring flowers.
—But he parked his car in the same place.
—But today it's a different car.
—Then it's a different friend.
—Then it's the one from the south.
—But he doesn't have a car.

—Maybe he does now.
—He can't afford a car.
—He only came twice anyhow.
—You can't see a light either.
—They've pulled down the blinds.
—The blinds are always pulled down.
—You can't hear a thing either.
—They're being extra quiet.
—Maybe nobody's there at all.
—We haven't seen anyone so far.
—There'll be another one along.
—And we'll see him.
—He won't slip past us.
—We'll know him when we see him again.
—Then no one can fool us again.

* * *

—Have you ever bothered about a thing? Have you once lifted a finger? Do I sit around the whole day? Does it all have to fall on me the whole time? Have you ever once indicated that you give a good goddamn? Has anything ever come out of you that looks like the least little bit of initiative? Is it all going to be shoved off onto me again? Do I have to be the one who does everything all by myself again?

* * *

—Just set fire to the whole mess!

* * *

—First floor. Second floor. Third floor. Fourth floor. Fifth floor. Sixth floor. Seventh floor. Eighth floor. Ninth floor. Tenth floor. Eleventh floor. Twelfth floor. Eleventh floor. Tenth floor. Ninth floor. Eighth floor. Seventh floor. Sixth floor. Fifth floor. Fourth floor. Third floor. Second floor. First floor.

* * *

—Burgmann doesn't live here anymore?
—No, he doesn't live here now.
—Where does he live now?

—Nobody really knows.
—And why doesn't he live here anymore?
—Nobody really knows that either.
—Something's wrong with Burgmann?
—Yes, something's wrong with Burgmann.
—But what?
—Well, nobody really knows what.
—Hasn't anyone heard? Hasn't anyone seen him?
—Sure. Burgmann comes by every day.
—Hasn't he ever said anything?
—No, he's never said anything.
—And: asked?
—He's never asked anything either.
—No, no, didn't anyone ever ask *him* anything?
—No, no one ever asked *him* anything.
—Why doesn't anyone ever ask him anything?
—Everyone's waiting for someone else to ask him something.

* * *

—Are you happier now? Now that you're gone, no one comes around anymore. Sometimes I call up, but I hang up again right away. It's terribly empty here. The cat just scratched at the door. Do you remember the sound? When you finally come back, nothing will be changed. Are you alone a lot? No, you never were able to be alone. If anyone ever came around, he'd be sure to ask for you first. Are you going to stay where you are now?

* * *

—It's to become a new city.
—Well, we always voted the idea down.
—You vote against everything on general principles.
—At any rate, something was tried here that was unusual and challenging, something that never had been tried before.
—And it's all been gone through in other places a long time ago.
—You should hear what the people who live there have to say about it.
—Careful now, they're just waiting for the chance to sound off.
—At first, anyhow, they were all proud, happy, and grateful.
—Yes, but nowadays—and for a long time now too—but nowadays,

the talk is all about a highly aggressive reaction to anonymous ruling power.

—It's really only the weather, the influence of weather conditions.

—Everybody gets tired and irritated some of the time.

—Then *you* try to get along with all the idiots who are always giving us such a hard time.

—And don't forget to draw a fence line.

—Well, since it was a barracks area, anyway, it has changed a lot.

—Drizzle, it's supposed to drizzle.

—Just wait a while. I mean, in a couple of years when the stand of young trees, for instance small groupings with birches. . . .

—The people here are completely uprooted, totally isolated from everything, restless inside, without any ties, uncentered. They don't have any more contact to themselves inside than they do to you and me.

—So when the increase in crime is brought up, it really should be recognized that the locations where future disturbances can form—will form—have already been pinned down.

—Right, right, the situation here can always be taken in at a glance.

—So let's not jump to conclusions. In summer when there's a little green here and there, it'll all look a lot different.

* * *

—Yeah, Mr. Hasenkamp's living here again. When he jumped out the window that time he only sprained his ankle, and because that made him so mad, he went and jumped off the bridge, but it didn't do him any good, they fished him right out, and he's living here again.

* * *

—Just act like you want to buy something and nobody'll notice you.

* * *

—When it's summer again, that's right, in summer. We'll clean it all out, in the garden, in the house, everywhere. You'll see. Yesterday we fixed the terrace. We'll go to work on the rain gutters today. Tomorrow—wait a minute—oh yeah, the basement is next. Everything else is going pretty well. When we can get to it, the shutters, the garden door, the fence. I mean, if you don't stay on top of things from the word go, it does't take too long and you can't stop it, you can't hold it back, it's all falling down. You know, it happens all the time. It's already almost too late to put it all back together again.

* * *

—At night. But not really.
—Sure. He could be here at night. He comes nights all the time.
—But—but not anymore.
—And the light. I leave the light on outside all the time, at night.
—I know. But now, finally—
—And his room. His room, look at his room. I clean up every day, I make his bed every night. When he comes home, he can go right to bed. His pajamas are always fresh and there's some fruit there too, and a bottle of mineral water. He always drinks mineral water, he won't drink water out of the faucet.
—But all this trouble is. . . .
—Everything, the whole house is ready for him. I never sit in his easy chair. His slippers are the only ones next to it, and the reading lamp is on, the ashtray is clean. Last week I ordered a case of port. I cook for him, not much, he doesn't eat much anymore, only a salad at noon, sometimes a little soup, he still likes turtle soup or oxtail. Oh look, there's no fruit. I'll have to get some. And on the weekend, what did we have planned for the weekend?
—Nothing.
—What?
—Nothing. Now just listen to me. . . .
—Oh you, I know what you think. You think what they all think, that he's not coming back. They all think that and they all try to prove it to me. No, no, no. But what, what was it, on the weekend, what did he say about the weekend?

* * *

—We really should write, or call up first, so maybe we could drive there, because . . . listen . . . all those offers, we ought to at least take a look at them, I mean, if we've decided, then we have to do something about it and not just talk all the time, how nice it would be and that everything would finally be different. I mean, we have to really get moving. Because the way it is now, I don't know, it can't go on like this any more. I mean, I can't keep it up much longer, it's more than I can stand, it really is, I can't, really, I can't anymore, I just can't.

* * *

—Here are the new house rules.
—Yes. Better than the old ones.
—Now no one will be making noise anymore.
—We'll all be walking around on tiptoe.
—Talking quietly. Or whispering.
—Sometimes you don't need to say anything.
—The new house rules are working on the first day.
—Unwelcome visitors are staying away.
—We're left to ourselves.
—We're staying at home.
—Everyone's seeing to it that everyone's keeping the new house rules.
—So we don't get the mess we had before.
—It was unbearable.
—They all thought they could do whatever they wanted.
—Now we all want the same thing.
—The house has some order to it again.
—You can walk into the basement or the attic without breaking your neck.
—No more disagreeable housemates.
—Since the new house rules are in force, we don't have anyone to bother us.
—We really don't have anyone who's negative about the new house rules.
—And we have a new super.
—We think of him as our guarantee that the new house rules won't be ignored.
—The old super was a weakling.
—The old super's weakness helped destroy the old house rules.
—The old house rules failed miserably.
—From that you can see how smoothly the new house rules are working.
—Because we picked the new managers.

—Yes. Without the new managers it would have all stayed the same.

—Without the new managers, no one would have come to terms with the new house rules.

—No, without them we wouldn't have ever gotten where we are. Where we owe everything to the new house rules.

—No one doubts it anymore.

—No, everyone's agreed.

—Yes, everyone agrees now that our house needed new house rules.

* * *

—Tear it down. The best thing is to tear it down. Right away.

* * *

—I'm living right out in the forest now.

—Isn't that a little lonely?

—It's supposed to be lonely.

—And isn't it too dangerous?

—Yes, very dangerous. But that's why no one comes around anymore. At last.

* * *

—The black bird the cat brought into the house sat in the dark cellar corner. It sat there with its torn wings without moving, and didn't touch any food. When it was dead, it lay there for days, and even the cat didn't look at it anymore. One day it was suddenly gone, and we still ask each other who got up the courage to throw out the black bird.

* * *

—Never. No.

—Maybe you'll let me explain it again.

—It's been explained enough, that won't change a thing. I say no.

—Just one more word.

—All right.

—Well. . . .

—That's it. Not another word.

—But. . . .

—That's it, I said. I told you, no more discussions. I told you I won't have it. I won't have it in my house. And that's the way it stays.

* * *

—And then hide. Run and hide.

* * *

—And in the evening the new house was up. Who'd have thought it?

—The workers at the site next door stood there with their mouths open while the crane put up one structural element after another in the time their bricklayers took to put down a couple of rows.

—The first outer wall, twelve meters fifty-six centimeters long and three meters fifty centimeters high, was already erected on the standard brick foundation at 7:50 A.M. Of course there was no unfavorable weather that morning.

—The construction crew made every move count. They put up a house in the North German region almost every day.

—Shortly after 8:30 the next wall was already swung into place and anchored on the foundation. This was possible because the mounts were already built into the wall elements. Then the construction crew had plenty of time for breakfast.

—And that's how it went. Hour by hour, one structural element after another. We stood there and imagined we'd already moved in and arranged the furniture the way we planned. But at five o'clock a plastic sheet was spread over the roof against unexpected rain because the roof tiles were still missing.

—At 4:29.

—What?

—At 4:29 a plastic sheet was spread over the roof against unexpected rain because the roof tiles were still missing.

—Anyway, the construction crew quit work promptly at five.

—Naturally it was a few more days and weeks before every part of the house had doors and was ready for occupancy and finally matched the specifications in the description of the 100 percent rationalized construction mode.

—But for a long time now we've known that our new house, so advantageous in the uniform quality of its standardized structural elements, is only another temporary stopover for us. Day after day we keep finding all kinds of shortcomings to complain of, familiar and unfamiliar ones, big and little ones, irritating and insignificant ones.

—But we aren't impatient, and we don't want to be unfair.

* * *

—Because we're living in an age of change.
—In a society that is continually transforming itself.
—Where everyone has a chance.
—Or else people would be killing each other.
—The way it used to be.
—With axes and pointed sticks.
—Clubs and rocks.
—In caves.
—In the forests.
—Bears.
—Wild plants.
—Cold.
—Ice.
—Dark.
—Desolate.
—Empty.
—Nothing.
—Everything.
—Like when it started.
—Step by step.
—Putting stone on stone.
—Loaded down and toiling.
—Full of hope and despair.
—In the fight against nature.
—Against prejudice and overpopulation.
—Glorious and progressive.
—Freed at last and with all the rights of a citizen.
—With pay raises and a shorter work week.
—So we could save for our own home.
—Where we can live any way we choose.
—So. We get up together every morning, eat breakfast together, and drive in our car together to our places of work in the city.
—And if you want to visit us, dear listeners, we're here for you anytime, and we'll fully acquaint you with all the details of our plan without obligation.

* * *

—Get out fast, before the fire spreads.

* * *

—The round house. The red house. Perhaps, the dilapidated house. The windowless house down that way. The clean house. The picture-window house in California. The snowed-in house, in the old days. No, the log house at the edge of the big meadow. The secure house. The colorful house. The easily destroyed house in the middle of the village. Possibly, the empty house. The beautiful house used to stand there. The floating house. The restful house of rest. Up above, the invisible house of the lord. When the house that burned down was still burning. The house that is locked up nights. The house that acts instead of talking. I mean the last, the unmanageable house. That was once the happily married house. The secret house. The only house in your heart. The wandering house. The influential house of the zodiac. The unimaginable house people always talk about. First there was the round house, then came the red house. It's the disappearing house that can't be found anymore.

* * *

—We'll change all that.
—You'll change all what?
—The conditions of ownership.
—Aha.
—It won't be much longer, not much longer that these gentlemen will live there. Not much longer, and these gentlemen will have to make room.
—Who for?
—These gentlemen will see, one fine day, who is standing at their doors.

* * *

—I'd like to be able to look out on a lively street.
—I'd like to stop having to hear the heating go on in the basement.
—But I'd like to know right now where all the exits are.
—And I'd already like to throw everything out the window.
—I'd like to stick my nose in all the pots and see what's cooking.
—I'd like to have something that would finally set me free from always having to have everything right away.
—I'd like to see to it now that there's a good mood in these rooms.
—I'd like to set up a few fortified points in the yard, just in case.

—But I'd like to ask how it would be possible to pick this house up and move it away quickly.

—And I'd like us to be thankful for it all.

—For the last few days I'd like to have a new roof over my head.

—I'd like to have people in the house who are usually not at home.

—I wouldn't like for everyone to think—oh well, you know how fast everyone is to think that.

—I'd really like to set it on fire.

—But I wouldn't like to break in.

—And I'd like a—no, I *could be* happy in a tent, too.

—I'd like for you all to finally put all your things where they belong.

—I'd like to blow you all out the window.

—I'd like to get away in the evening when it feels like the ceiling's about to fall on my head.

—I'd like to be master in my own house again.

*　*　*

—It's getting really impossible to live here without more room and more freedom, or a chauffeur and a gardener, a cook and a bodyguard, or a better view where you could really wallow in a sunset, or a couple of coasts nearby or, better, a private beach right at your feet, or more flight connections so you could go far away when you wanted, or you could get more out of the seasons and the roof would finally get fixed, or the sky above would have a deeper, fuller blue, or it would all belong to us so we could do what we wanted with it, yeah, you'd have to change a lot, or change it all, to make this stupid neighborhood bearable.

*　*　*

—When the whole business goes up in flames, then they'll see what a pile of shit it is.

*　*　*

—We have to call your attention to. . . .

—I know already.

—If you already know, we don't understand why you haven't done anything about it.

—I have. I've done it already.

—But we must call your attention to the fact that nothing has changed.
—You said it.
—Then we must demand. . . .
—You don't have to. I'll take care of it all.
—Then may we hope that, in future. . . .
—You don't have to. It all stays the same. Nothing ever changes.

* * *

—And then he just disappeared?
—Then he just disappeared. He let the place go to rack and ruin, completely, totally, then he just disappeared.

* * *

—Haven't you started to think you'd welcome a visit from us?
—Isn't it obvious that your situation hasn't improved at all recently?
—Haven't you had occasion to say at least once that something is badly needed to free you from your domestic miseries?

* * *

—The crash woke me up.
—I ran right to the window.
—And I ran right out in the street in my nightshirt.
—Then we saw what Santa brought.
—All our cars smashed.
—The kid did one hell of a job.
—He was standing there trembling.
—I called the cops right away.
—Now I can go ahead and shoot myself, he said.
—And the dawn started coming up.
—The birds were already singing.

* * *

—Tina needs quiet. Harry wants to try out his football. Annie's screaming in the kitchen. My stomach is queasy. And the cat wants out. It just wanted out, but when it got out it wanted back in. Now Annie's still. Paul said he was coming for a visit. I told him we have to walk around on tiptoe because of Tina. Harry kicked his football over the fence. Annie goes in the bathroom and runs the water. The hamster isn't rattling its cage because it's sleeping. Now we can see the neighbor lady waving over the fence. I sent Roger away. Nancy's no longer among the living. This time last year I wasn't around. Half the town was in an uproar over the shots. Tina has housework to do. Nobody believes anything I say, and when it's all over, I don't know how I'll go on either.

* * *

—A long time ago this all used to be forest here, beautiful thick forest with animals, real animals. Then it was all fields, great rolling fields and meadows, green, glowing meadows with trees on the riverbanks. Later houses were built, individual houses, hidden away, small, here a village, there a village. Then the city came nearer. On the hill there the villas of the rich. Down on the riverfront was the harbor. Out here were the first factories. Then everything was bombed to ruins and ashes and for a while it looked very much like the meadows and forest were coming back. But the city spread farther than anyone can see long ago and goes on growing. It's already growing together with the next city, the villages over there are being torn down, the suburbs are already up for urban renewal, in the background they're building up to the sky, no one has any memory of what it looked like a few years ago, much less earlier, and that's good. No one's learned a thing. Soon the meadows will be back and then the forest.

* * *

—Stay outside, don't come back in.

* * *

—The gentleman next door can describe our housewife's bathing suit in detail.
—What we had for lunch has already been thoroughly discussed.
—All around us they know the names of our evening's guests the day after.
—It all gets back to us too, but it's really never worth knowing.
—They're imitating our love life all around us.
—Next thing they'll be watching television over our shoulders.

—A little while ago a neighbor called up to tell me where the saltshaker was that got lost.
—Tomorrow they'll be saying again we're talking loud enough for them to understand every single word.

* * *

—Scribble a little house from all the parts we've scribbled for you, and if you feel the need for a little tree to go with your little house, scribble that in too.

* * *

—A navigator lives here, next door to him a data tabulator, behind him a transportation engineer, and upstairs a stewardess. A plastics shaper moved in there, a mining engineer calls this place home, the neighbors down that way are a milling machine operator, a lady who sets up the gizmos that make cardboard cartons, a tax advisor, an excavation crew chief, he's a real fighting drunk. Over there, uh . . . over there lives a consumer advocate, right behind him a receptionist, the high-tension lineman got his a while back. The jockey has moved on too. Down below him an insulation expert makes himself comfortable—for heat and cold and sound, next to him a real nice customer, a guy who paints porcelain and glass, then a surgical tools designer, a drill-press operator, a wood shaper, a saddlemaker. That there, yeah, nobody knows what he does, pretty suspicious, usually he just sits around the house, then over there is a well driller and over there an air-conditioning man. Good folks. Can't say a thing against them, not even against the two hairdressers back there. Way back that way—no, way back there—is standing empty, we'll have to wait.

* * *

—What did they find? Just what they were looking for: pudding powder and a cigarette lighter.

* * *

—I'm going into the living room. Farewell.
—You won't get far.

—Then I'll sit in the dining room and wait there.
—It won't do you any good.
—I wanted the cellar to be cleaned up too.
—In the cellar no one will hear your cries.
—I have to lock the garage.
—It's locked.
—Then I'll look around the garden, whether I have to mow the grass tomorrow.
—It's too late for that.
—The window in the bathroom.
—It's open and it can stay open.
—Should I make something to drink?
—You don't need to ask any more questions.
—There's a thriller on the tube.
—This is thrilling enough.
—Then I'll just stand and wait.
—You won't have to be patient long.

* * *

—The way we used to smoke them out, you know, first we'd set the fires, and then we waited for them to show, from their cellars and from under the roof, you know, and then they'd come out, too, they'd hop out the windows by the families, and the ones that came out on the balconies, we'd pick them off so we could watch them fall, you know, systematically, just as systematically as we combed the lower elements out house by house, and made them show themselves, by smoking them out, always the most effective method, or by breaking their resistance by force of arms, yeah, that's the way we always did it.

* * *

—Don't tell me it wasn't the right thing. Aren't we better off now? Is there anything left to complain about? How did we used to live? What kind of neighborhoods did we live in? Did we ever get asked how we felt about it? Is anyone trying to keep us from being happy now? Are we supposed to start letting someone shove us around again?

* * *

—I'm a have-not, and I have not a thing to lose.

—I realized long ago that an inheritance is not just a gift but above all an obligation.

—I think of my house primarily as my means of production.

—I am—and I remain—distrustful of modern manufacturing methods.

—I couldn't live that way either.

—If they tried to dispossess me I'd blow it all to bits first.

—I'm not the one to want to live with you either.

—I'm purely a hotel type.

—But I can't be alone anymore.

—I still prefer the generous dimensions of the old Berlin apartments.

—I only feel right when I'm surrounded by kitsch.

—I'm a basement baby.

—I'm the sole owner and operator of a never-never land.

—I want to get out of here.

—I'm never at home wherever I go.

—I only got this far by pinching every penny till it had scars.

—I'm telling you: it's a crime that your kind has it so good.

—But I'm giving you half of everything for yourself.

—I feel this irresistible pull back into my ivory tower. Does that make me some kind of fascist?

—I can't pay the next month's rent.

—I'm a bedroom community widow.

—I should have married my landlady when I had the chance.

—I cook, I clean house, I dig in the garden, I paint walls, I pick up, I make beds, I wash the dishes, I iron, I nap an hour in the afternoon.

—I'm the manager here.

—I want to go up to your place with you.

—My wife wears the pants in our family.

—I'm running out on all of it.

—Or I'll call the police.

—I was afraid in the dark rooms of my childhood.

—I'm afraid I'll end up in a home when I'm old.

—I'd like to carry my house around on my back like a snail.

—I'm crawling back into my mouse hole now.

—I'm jumping out the window. It's the twelfth floor!

—I'm looking for another planet. This one's getting too full and too loud.

* * *

—Every one of the accused comes from a good home.

* * *

—No, I really didn't forget you, I honestly intended to invite you over, but then Polly invited Fred and Billy without telling me first, and they took it on themselves to bring along Eisenstein and his new heartthrob, then the Lussmanns surprised us by saying they were on their way, and even Polly said we'd have to act like we were deliriously happy, and all of a sudden I remembered we owed Dr. Brill and that old goat of his. Polly gave me such a hard time about her afterwards. Yes, and I couldn't call it off with Kunstmann— what a bore!—and that good ole country girl he got married to, and by the way Tiny showed up with her fella, the one you can't stand, so the place was packed with all kinds of impossible people, let me tell ya, who'd've liked nothing better than to shoot each other dead, a terrible evening, Polly nearly had a breakdown after and we almost came to blows again, naturally I was totally sloshed, otherwise I'd've never stood it, let me tell ya, just be happy, just be happy, and Harriman wasn't even there.

* * *

—There were hardly any chimneys here in the hill country even a hundred years ago, the smoke just had to find its way out the windows and doors by itself.

* * *

—And what gives these rooms their exceptional attractiveness?
—The sparing use of furnishings and the limited range of color.
—And what makes this simple fisherman's cottage into nothing less than a palace?
—The archway, the whitewashed walls and the meticulously grown plants in boxes.
—And what is a relic from the past?
—The canopied bed.
—And what do we think of as the center of the kitchen?

—The semicircular stone washbasin.
—And what is it we don't mind giving up here?
—Any kind of modern comfort.
—And why is that?
—Because we long for everything to be natural.

* * *

—My parents' house was hidden behind pine trees in a quiet valley.
—My parents' house is the house I've never gotten away from.
—Mine was sold at auction.
—I don't have any.
—My parents' house was in Pommerland.
—Where was yours?
—I was born in a Boeing flying over the Atlantic.
—So that was the house of your birth.
—I've never forgotten my parents' house.
—In my parents' house there were constant whippings.
—My parents' house broke up early.
—I don't care how bad or how good it was, nobody better try to say
  anything against my parents' house.
—My parents' house stood in an old German colony.
—In my parents' house there were always pianists around.
—I never knew my father.
—Somday my parents' house will be the parents' house of my
  children.
—When I count back, I get five.
—There were five in your family?
—No, my parents changed houses five times when I was little.
—I kept running away.
—I kept getting thrown out.
—My parents' house was the Ordensburg.
—In my parents' house politics was never discussed.
—We had chickens, rabbits, ducks, geese, a goat and, always, cats.
—My parents' house was guarded by a dog.
—There was a sentry box in front of my parents' house.
—My children will never be able to say, "That was our parents'
  house."
—I can only remember bunkers, railroad cars, cellars, and barracks.
—We still spend our vacations in our parents' house.

—It was like the sun never stopped shining in my parents' house.
—My parents didn't have a house.
—My parents' house was their parents' house too.
—Mine burned down.
—My parents just blew it all.
—In my parents' house nobody ever voted Socialist.
—From early on, art has been my parents' house.
—People keep holding my parents' house against me.
—This smell takes me back to the way my parents' house smelled.
—I've always been homesick.
—I've never felt at home anywhere.
—My parents' house will be in heaven.

* * *

—So he built garages, set out gardens, a swimming pool for his guests, he bought a horse, hired an orchestra, ordered only good weather, the whole schmeer, everything, and what happens? The garages are empty, the gardens are overgrown with weeds, the swimming pool has dead birds floating in it, the horse is starving, the orchestra hasn't been paid, it keeps raining and raining, it was all for nothing.

* * *

—Thus the position given each house was a reflection of the pride and independence of the people living in it. No one took notice of what others were doing, everyone laid out his floor plan with the showy side of the house wherever he pleased. The garden started right at the edge of the house and was bordered with trees. A great nut tree, often even an age-old linden or oak, sheltered the half-timbered house with its long branches.

* * *

—Stay inside of or only visit, step out of, forget, maybe restore or, better, tear down completely and start over again, buy, look for and find, foreclose on, turn upside down, pass on to your children, shoot at, renovate, wind up going back to, furnish and make a muddle of, desert, burn down, carry around on your back, watch nights, have guarded if necessary, lose, fence in, never let out of your sight, revisit, bombard, protect as a historical monument, remember with pleasure, decorate with flowers or throw stones at, take down and ship away, see again, describe, place at someone's disposal, lock in the morning, unlock in the morning, refuse to tumble into the water, nevertheless blow sky-high, rearrange, seal, put under the auctioneer's hammer, search, visit secretly and secretly leave, paint, storm and defend, walk away from, mention briefly in an article, rediscover in the gray of dawn, never set foot in again, never leave again, board up completely.

* * *

—Yes, I'm here.
—Then I'll come over too.
—But I'm going away again.
—Then wait.
—I'll be back.
—Then I won't be here.
—Then you wait.
—I'll be back.
—Then I won't be there.
—Then I won't come over at all.
—I'm not even here.

* * *

—These rock throwers, these rock throwers down there.

* * *

—How do I do it, how do I get this nail into the wall, which wallpaper gives a room that personal touch, where is linoleum tile preferred, what am I supposed to do with all these lawn mowers, how is a suitable and fully effective lighting system planned, what am I so worried about, what should we eat for lunch today, which kind of paint is washable, what am I doing with this hatchet in my hand, who are we going to invite for tomorrow, how do you get a harmonious agreement of color in rugs, curtains, and upholstery, what are these bamboo stalks doing here, where will I lay my head tonight, what should I do first?

* * *

—In our neighborhood there are many exotic races and nations.
—My neighbor shook his fist at me over the fence today.
—We never saw our old neighbors again.

—You never have friendly neighbors.

—The lady next door, I could tell you stories. . . .

—Our neighbors live on the next island.

—Our neighbor would still say hello yesterday, but not anymore.

—I hope the neighbors are first.

—There's a story about something that happened here that can't be told without making the whole neighborhood sound bad.

—These animals, these pigeons, these cats, this barking, this yowling in the yard, these radios, these lawnmowers, these slamming doors, these screaming kids, these motors warming up in winter, these exhaust fumes, these power saws.

—In our neighborhood we took care of our own problems.

—Another neighbor's complaining.

—They don't have anythig else to do but mow their lawns, clean their windows, clip their hedges, beat their rugs, wash their cars, air their bedding, sweep their floors, clean out their rainspouts, weed their gardens, rake their leaves, shovel their snow.

—Our neighbor is letting his place run down completely.

—Just the way it always used to be with our western and the way it is now with our eastern neighbors.

—Oh well, if you could live in a neighborhood like that.

—Anyone who has such a terrible time with his neighbors must have a terrible time with himself.

—Now we're the only ones who haven't made it into the leisure class.

—There they are, standing around talking again, and I bet they're talking about us.

—Back when everything was so bad, there were real neighbors.

—A true neighbor has the spirit of neighborliness.

—Have you ever had one of those oh-so-convenient affairs with a neighbor lady?

—If they only knew who we voted for!

—The initiative can only come from the neighborhood.

—The neighbors didn't hear a thing.

—We have to move out before the neighborhood gets wind of what's happening.

—I bought it all up so I wouldn't be surrounded by neighbors some day.

—If your neighbor suddenly started throwing rocks, or if one fine day he said, I need this piece of land and knocked over your fence, or if he attacked your wife in broad daylight, or started anything else that would make it impossible to live side by side peaceably, well, what would you do then, would you stand around negotiating all day long?

—Nobody around here knows a thing about any of the others.

—You're a total asshole, you know that?

—Neighbors? I only know the doorbells.

—Right. They were wonderful neighbors.

* * *

—It's not round, it's not old, it's not ugly, you can't just ship it somewhere, it's not blue and it's not green, you can't roll it up, it's not exactly new, it's not made of sticks and it's not made of snow, it doesn't float, you can't fly it, it's not very pretty, it doesn't grow in the woods, it doesn't melt in water, it's not cold in summer, it's not guaranteed unbreakable, it's not a mountain range and it's not a wandering sand dune, it's not white, it has no heart, you can't chase it or catch it, it's not indescribable, it's not the middle of the world, it's not the path to another land, you don't have to have it, it doesn't make you sad, it doesn't leave you crying, it's not just anything at all, you can't forget it, it can't lose things, it's not unattainable, it's not mine.

* * *

—Get out! Get out!

* * *

—When I'm home again, then I'll take care of everything, yes, then I won't leave you sitting alone anymore in the evening, then I won't get excited about every little thing, but I'll be easy to get along with again, I'll clean up the basement and shine my shoes like I used to, then I'll catch up on everything I've been putting off and start fixing the garden fence where it leans without waiting around, I won't smash any more porcelain and I won't throw the baby out with the bath water, it'll be like old times again, we'll eat breakfast together again, we'll make plans again, I'll clean the hairs out of my comb after I've used it, I won't tip so big any more, I'll stop being so sloppy, I'll fold the newspapers neatly after

I've read them and put them in the magazine rack, I won't drive you crazy any more with squeezed-up toothpaste tubes, I'll stop asking you whether anything's any use, I won't be suspicious of you for no reason, I won't try to catch you in excuses anymore, you won't want to scratch my eyes out anymore, I won't threaten to slap your face anymore, we won't be a sad example in public anymore, we won't be acting like everything was perfectly all right with us anymore, we'll try to coordinate the interests that are pulling us apart, we'll pull together like we used to, want to grow old together like before, go to Sardinia together in September, yes, and I'll always send you flowers when I'm away and once I get back home I'll never, never be away from you again.

*　*　*

—So you got it straightened out.
—Yeah, we clued them in.
—We told them off.
—We let them know who it is that's living in a glass house around here.
—They'll tend to their own knitting from now on.
—We don't just let every dog lift its leg on our doorstep.
—It was like being in a crazy house.
—Like cavemen.
—That's why we had to do a litle table pounding.
—And move the furniture around a little.
—But you have to sometimes, to get some quiet in the place.

*　*　*

—The man who only has four apple trees to tend doesn't need a shed to house his equipment.

*　*　*

—Well, it all starts with leveling the building site, and then comes the excavation first of all for the foundation. Then the ditches have to be dug for the sewer pipes, maybe a settling tank, maybe drainage to control the water table, whatever. Moving right along, the water and gas mains and the house-current line, then let's not forget pouring and sealing and plastering the cellar walls and cellar ceiling. A cellar needs cellar doors too, cellar windows, cellar stairs, right? So that's the cellar. Next step. A house has outside walls, they don't stand around unfinished, you have to cover them with siding. Inside, so there can be rooms, partition walls and Sheetrock, you have to add that in. The floor gets its floor covering, let's say tile. Ceilings, ceiling tile. And we're already thinking about a roof. You have to cover the timbers and put down roofing, it has to hold against the storms this far north. How to keep all the rainwater from collecting? The gutters have to slope down to the drainpipe, understand? Then the doors. The front door, the inside doors, French windows, balcony doors. And when there's doors there's windows. Window frames, sliding windows, storm windows, whatever, and you have to immediately decide on regular or insulating window glass. Like I told you, a house consists of all its problems put together. And then another dilemma. Venetian blinds, steel roll-down blinds or hinged shutters, huh? But there's more. Stairs. Outside stairs, inside staircase. Pull-down stairs to the attic on balanced weights. Have we built the chimney yet? Or what kind of heating would we want to build in? An old-fashioned coal burner? Not a chance. An oil heater? Everybody's got one. Forced-air gas heat? I just don't know, gas always makes me feel kind of creepy. So. Electric? Expensive, you can take my word for it, expensive. And hot water is a problem all its own. And just all the installing, electricity, drains, the kitchen, the bathroom and half-bath or guest bathroom, right? That's not the luxury item it used to be. I mean, did my father have built-ins? Did he have a garage, a terrace, balconies? Nowadays, wall surfacing, painting, wall-to-wall carpeting and all that, it's just understood. But now we're really rolling. Building permits, blueprints, architect's fee, inspection costs, party for the construction crew, service charges, credit rating, interest rates, points, down payment, mortgage, insurance, taxes, all that has to be paid for, right? It all has to be saved up for. And who does all the garden work, who cuts the hedges, who rakes all the leaves, who mows all the grass, right? Who's always there to do it all, nope, not me, not on your life. I'm for staying right where we are.

* * *

—This is the guest room.
—I always used to have to sleep on the crack between the mattresses when we had guests.
—When was the last time anyone invited us over?

—If you live so far away, you really can't expect people to surprise you every day by dropping in.

—Our guests can stay as long as they want.

—There they go again with their bourgeois bullshit about hospitality and a guest's traditional privileges.

—I was a guest too, once.

—I know a story where a guest gets his.

—This is the guest house.

—And we're to the point now where we don't invite any more to stay.

—We usually ask who all is coming, and then most of the time we turn it down.

—When we had guests we were always going off alone.

—Holes burned in the rug, glasses broken, records scratched, the lamp knocked on its side, the sink full of dishes, the air full of cigarette smoke, it happens every week now.

—That used to be a house where guests were always welcome.

—We always come home with a couple of stolen glasses.

—We never noticed that some of the girls weren't really girls.

—And of course as usual the ones who stayed the longest were the ones we didn't invite.

—That's because they spoil their guests too much.

—The hostess was the first to take her clothes off.

—I prefer to be the guest no one knows.

—And who was the host?

—The one who started fighting afterwards.

—We'll never go there anymore.

—I'll only be a guest in your house from now on.

—They took over the entire house! We moved to a hotel.

—Wait till they all get here.

—But they're all here now.

—Then we'll lock up and push the button.

—All we have that brings it back is our guest book.

* * *

—I'm telling you, there wasn't one brick left on top of another.

* * *

—The glow, this glow over the roofs.

* * *

—Where the two poplars are, back there.

* * *

—"Come on into my house."

* * *

—And what *is* that house number?

* * *

—The doors slammed. The windows clattered.

* * *

—Get up, get out of here, we're going hiking. Close the shutters, lock the door, we've been laying around inside long enough. The road leads into the country, the country lies before us. Look, a farmyard, and another one, a village. The city fades into the valley haze at the foot of the hill. Now we see a ruin, princes ruled here, kings banqueted, the emperor's son stayed a night. One plane after another coming down low overhead to land at the airfield nearby. An inn, finally an inn. I hear the clock strike from a church tower but I can't see the church tower. Are we homesick already? I don't remember a settlement on the banks of this stream. Impressive schoolhouses, well-built hospitals, good solid indoor pools. You might not think so much of city hall. Now we come to a fence that forces us to follow it through the middle of the woods. Every forest should have a forester's house. What a great place this would be to build on. And there's another castle, the evening sun shining in its windows. I'm sure the lady of the castle rises from her grave every night, expecting the return of her knight errant. How restful this green is on my eyes. Let's gather brushwood for our stove at home. This is the forest the local peasants ran and hid in when the French armies came. So, now we're on our way home. Streams of traffic rushing from business and shopping districts back to the residential and bedroom communities. Sudden fog causes a tremendous series of pileups. On the same highway Napoleon built to take his tremendous army to Russia. My father used to drive a horsecart down it. I wouldn't mind seeing a movie, but where can you find a movie house in the wasteland at the edge of town? All the houses have lights on. We'll be home soon now. So. Now we're at home. Anything changed? Everything's just the way we left it.

* * *

—Why don't you turn on the lights?

—It's not dark enough outside yet.

—Everyone else has their lights on.

—Not over there, and not in back either, across the street somebody just turned the lights off, and the Wiegensteins are still on vacation, their lights are never on, he's just closing his blinds, Mr. Hasenkamp is coming home, I can see a star, there's a car with the lights off, yeah yeah, you're avoiding the light for a good reason, *they've* had *their* lights on for days, the blind need no light, that's the light of a TV set, Mrs. Schwarzkopf doesn't have the money for the light bill, many years ago the city had gas light, and during the bombings nobody was allowed to let a light glimmer through, now someone's turning on the lights there.

—I'll turn the lights on now too.

—It's dark now outside too, wait . . . I'll turn the lights on now.

* * *

—He always said he wouldn't come back to the city, that is, he said he'd come back when the city was burned down again. Oh well. Then I always told him, it could happen anytime, but you might have a long wait too. Oh well. It didn't happen that way at all as it turned out, but very differently, the way I always told him, that the city would move out to him more or less, and where his cabin used to be hidden in greenery the new shopping center is going up, a huge one with acres of parking, and right near, where the farmhouse from the year seventeen hundred something used to be, the drive-in movie will be, the same backers, I think. Oh well. So now he's apparently gone, just gone, split, took off, emigrated, disappeared, without taking a thing, hasn't kept in contact, strange, don't you think? Oh well. He was a strange one from the beginning.

* * *

—Come to me. I'm all alone now.

* * *

—So. Can we visit you sometime now?
—You've been waiting all this time for us to finally get back.
—We don't want to force you into anything.
—We only want to do as you wish.
—And you do have wishes.
—Don't you have any wishes?
—Don't you wish for us to visit you?

* * *

—Nothing happens anymore at all. Since the dog stopped barking, you never hear a thing. This peace and quiet is enough to drive you crazy. I've got to liven things up around here. How about a dog, a dog that barks? Naturally only when somebody comes around. Is anybody going to come around? Somebody ought to announce that somebody ought to come back around, the sooner the better. What a life we used to have around here. Chasing the dog around the garden, that was fun. The barking. The yelling. Since all that stopped—hey, who made all that stop? Yeah, who made it all stop happening around here?

* * *

—Right. I'm leaving.
—But you wanted—didn't you want to stay forever?
—The house is falling down and there's no more peace and quiet. I can't breathe here. The air is heavy and gray. The woods aren't nearby anymore. The fields are gone. You can see people all the time. There aren't any mountains. There isn't any sea. The snow doesn't come this far. The rain is dismal. The night hardly starts and doesn't rightly end. The day is always the same day. It's too warm here. I'm freezing. I always say the same thing. I never hear anything different. I never see anything. I'm going to start decomposing soon. I've got to make it stop. I'm not staying here. I'm leaving here.

Translated by Robert Goss

Reinhard Lettau

Reinhard Lettau has born in Erfurt in 1929. He studied comparative literature first at Heidelberg then at Harvard, where he received his PhD in 1960. He taught at Smith College from 1957 to 1965. For a time he lived as a free-lance writer in Berlin, where he was a prominant participant of the student movement of the 1960s. Before he was evicted from the country, he accepted a position in America. Since 1967 he has been professor of literature at the University of California at San Diego (La Jolla). In the fall semester of 1979 he was poet-in-residence at the University of Essen, Germany.

Reinhard Lettau first became known for his minimal prose texts *Schwierigkeiten beim Häuserbauen (Difficulties in House Construction, 1962)*, followed by short sketches centered on an invented, abstract character called Manig, who provokes and tests the world. There are fifty-four scenes in *Auftritt Manig (Manig Comes on the Scene, 1963)*. In 1968 Reinhard Lettau published *Feinde (Enemies)*. These texts come alive through the sudden effects of the unexpected witty turn of phrase as a response to the discrepancies between our imagined expectations about human behavior and the sociopolitical reality. The most important element is language, and the playfulness of the literary discourse is sustained by the comic gesture. Perhaps, "Comedy is the only thing that can still reach us. Our world has led to the grotesque as well as to the atom bomb." (Friedrich Dürrenmatt, "Problems of the Theater," in The German Library, volume 89, p. 255)

A compilation of newspaper articles documenting the time of the antiwar demonstrations in the United States appeared in 1971, *Täglicher Faschismus, Amerikanische Evidenz aus 6 Monaten (Daily Fascism, American Evidence from Six*

Months). It is a collection that exposes evidence of race discrimination, suppression of protest marches, and the manipulation of public opinion. The publication did not meet with general enthusiasm. *Immer kürzer werdende Geschichten* (*Stories that Get Shorter and Shorter,* 1973) are reprints and contain some additional short prose pieces.

In 1977, Lettau published his first radio play, *Frühstücksgespräche in Miami (Breakfast in Miami),* which was chosen as best radio play in 1979 and received the Prize of the War Blind. A recent work, *Zerstreutes Hinausschauen* (*Looking Outside—Distractedly,* 1980), is a collection of essays on political events, comments on literary trends, observations on literary texts, and his reflections on the process of writing in the modern world. In 1988, he published a slim volume of prose, *Zur Frage der Himmelsrichtungen (On the Question of the Points of the Compass).*

In the spirit of his good friend and mentor Herbert Marcuse, Reinhard Lettau once said that there are stories in wartime—referring to Vietnam—which are not suited for literary treatment because they ask for immediate and active participation. However, the transposition of experience, knowledge, and the collection of documentary evidence can show something in a literary text and "that is a very good thing" (as Reinhard Lettau remarked in a talk with Jürgen Becker). *Breakfast in Miami* was not conceived as a narrative or play for the theater with a conventional dramatic plot, but as a radio play to recall a political phenomenon, the arrival of deposed dictators of Latin American countries in Miami and their various voices as heard and documented in "ongoing dialogues." As a radio play, *Breakfast in Miami* lives, like Handke's and Becker's plays, from language and sound. The conversations of erstwhile dictators gathered around a table in an old-fashioned hotel in Miami are dictated by a knowledge of the insidious power of people who are in control of military and civic affairs. In fifty-four episodes the absurd logic of the Chairman, President, Colonel, Generals, and their American academic advisor has the uncanny ring of authenticity. These are the voices manufacturing opinions for public consumption. The dialogues also reveal the swiftness with which foreign countries recognize the dictators' legitimacy (scene 6). This fact is supported by the source material added at the end of the radio play. The language of "the servants of reason" (34) has the air of the text of a bizarre soap opera, interrupted by the actual reading of the soap opera (17, 23, 33). But in each scene the discourse of the former dictators reinforces the logic of a language of oppression. To solve their problem of communication with the people, those in power have to cultivate a language that can be learned and applied in order to explain the show of force (40) as a demonstration of love for the people.

As in his prose texts, the comic mood predominates but the playfulness of juxtaposing witty and eccentric statements has a deadly serious subtext. The version printed below was slightly revised by the author for this edition.

M. H. S.

BREAKFAST IN MIAMI

SETTING

Elegantly furnished breakfast hall in an old hotel in Miami, deep South motifs in the decor. Half-opened terrace doors, view of the park, blooming magnolia tree, flagpole with US flag. From outside, birds twittering, traffic noises, boat horns. Interior, table settings, etc., sumptuous, silver coffee and tea pots, ornate fruit bowls, pitchers for ice water, etc.

At every new entrance, whenever the French doors to the main lobby of the hotel are opened, thin, artificial, yet live sounding music can be heard, especially tangos. Also noises from perhaps two dozen of the dictators' relatives waiting outside with suitcases, large hats: laughter, songs, fights. They may also interfere by knocking against the doors or disturbing the waiters going in and out.

CAST

All in civilian clothes with the exception of two especially designated scenes. The civilian clothes should in the course of the play gradually become less formal and more vacationlike, suggesting a development from military stiffness to a laxity assimilating the surroundings. For example, shirts with floral patterns, "fashionable" large collars, etc.

The characters, when speaking or moving, should give a realistic, serious, authentic impression, yet freeze abruptly afterwards into stylized poses. No beards.

CHARACTERS

THE CHAIRMAN, JUAN BUGOSLAWSKY, *old, hard of hearing, sleepy, being addressed as "Mr. Chairman" or "Your Excellency", likes aphorisms, often lifts finger before speaking, needs help getting up, occasionally plays with a flyswatter.*

PRESIDENT ARMULIO MANUEL ROSA, *thinks of himself as a retired bourgeois-democratic politician, is addressed as "Mr. President", tries to be "progressive," is half-bald, fat. Boss of the Harvard sociology professor waiting outside. Opportunist.*

COLONEL JESUS SCHNEIDER, *tiny, fat, coarse; gesticulates adamantly.*

GENERAL WESSIN Y WESSIN, *lean, dark, aristocratic type, cynic, romantic, rises late.*

GENERAL MIGUEL MIMOSA, *colorless.*

GENERAL LUIS TORRIJOS, *stupid.*

THE PROFESSOR, *academic advisor, frequently summoned, smooth, good-looking, super-WASP.*

Characters appearing only once: the businessman JOSEPH (THE BARON) BARBOGA, PETER (HORSEFACE) LICARDI, CARLOS (LITTLE MAN) MARCELLA, LINCOLN CELLINI *and* GENERAL DAVILA *with an* ADJUTANT; RELATIVES. *These characters as well as* GENERAL TORRI-JOS *can be played by the same actor so that the play can be performed with a cast of six or seven. In that case, one of the two gangsters in scene 15 would have to be played by the actor later playing* GENERAL MIMOSA, *and the* ADJUTANT *could be played by the actor playing the* PROFESSOR.

Act I

1. Short Conversation about the Question of Who Arrived Last?

CHAIRMAN: You are the second to last dictator, aren't you?
WESSIN: No. The last.
CHAIRMAN: Are you sure?
WESSIN: Of course I can't be absolutely sure. I can't be standing at the border constantly.

2. On the Number of Deputy Prime Ministers

SCHNEIDER: I had twelve deputy prime ministers.
WESSIN: I think it is better to have no deputy prime ministers.
ROSA: I am also for no deputy prime ministers at all.
CHAIRMAN: How long were you dictator?

3. How to Protect Oneself against Kidnappings

SCHNEIDER: Someone kidnapped my wife while she was laying a cornerstone!
CHAIRMAN: What kind of cornerstone did she lay?

SCHNEIDER: It happened just before the laying of the cornerstone. *(pause)* Did you also have problems with political kidnappings?

ROSA: You know damn well that part of my junta was kidnapped after a Wagner premiere. Therefore, I published a list of helpful hints so that the people, who were all living in fear of being kidnapped, could protect themselves.

SCHNEIDER: What type of advice?

ROSA: To begin with, I recommended vigilance and mistrust, also in connection with servants and staff.

WESSIN: What about the servants and staff themselves? Did you have any hints for them on how to protect themselves from being kidnapped?

SCHNEIDER: In the course of my dictatorship, no servant was kidnapped, since they understand how to protect themselves better than we do.

4. Example of a Coup d'Etat

ROSA: My coup d'etat was easy. At the end of August, when several members of our junta had not yet returned from the mountains and others, as is advisable for September, had already left for the country, I invited the two junta members who had stayed behind in the capital, General Efraim Guachalla and Admiral Alberro Albarracia, both of whom never left for the sea until October, as is proper anyway, into my headquarters and from my window I pointed out army units, including armed peasants, parading by outside. Then I said: "As you see, I am not alone!" After that, both men set out for a foreign embassy. The only problem with the coup was that the peasants did not lay down their weapons.

5. About the Distinction between Main and Secondary Enemies

CHAIRMAN: What do the Chinese mean with their distinction between main and secondary enemies?

SCHNEIDER: The main enemies are of course us.

ROSA: I don't believe that. They mean the largest countries and the not-so-large countries. The largest countries are the major enemies and the small ones are the minor enemies; for example Luxembourg is a minor enemy of China, and so on.

CHAIRMAN: How do you explain then that certain superpowers lie in the same bed?

WESSIN: They lie in the same bed, but their dreams differ.

ROSA *(calls)*: Professor! Could you come in for a moment?

PROFESSOR *(enters)*: Actually I am an air marshal.

ROSA: As you like. We are groping in the dark regarding the distinction between major and minor enemies in the foreign policy of some of the superpowers. Please enlighten us!

PROFESSOR: Difficult for us to understand because we have few or no enemies to speak of in the world. But some countries have so many enemies that they wouldn't know where to turn, so to say. Therefore they must classify their enemies for purposes of clarity. This results in groupings that indicate some enemies are themselves the enemies, perhaps even the archenemies of other enemies. When, for example, the long-range goal is a revolution of the entire world, then the major enemy is not the one who would, if the revolution did indeed take place, which is not the case, oppose it vainly anyway. . . .

CHAIRMAN: Why not?

PROFESSOR: Because, Your Excellency, the enemy in question cannot fight against a revolution that has not yet taken place, therefore is harmless.

SCHNEIDER: In that case, who would the major enemy be?

PROFESSOR: The major enemy would be the one who, since he also desires revolution, might spoil it right after it had succeeded, i.e., I conclude. . . .

ROSA: How does one know ahead of time that someone wants to spoil something that does not yet exist?

CHAIRMAN: If one is under suspicion of spoiling something in the future, it cannot be said that he is spoiling something in the present, for at present nothing exists as yet that can be spoiled. That means that in both cases the superpowers have no enemies, do they? They live in a world without enemies?

PROFESSOR: No practicing enemies, Excellency. That is accurate. *(silence)*

CHAIRMAN *(to Professor in private)*: What is your personal attitude on this question?

PROFESSOR: Favorable, Your Excellency. Shall I present the maps. . . ?

ROSA *(after exchanging glances with* Chairman*)*: All right, Professor, you are excused.

> Professor *exits.*

CHAIRMAN: Brilliant!

ROSA: Perhaps a bit eager.

WESSIN: With such a Harvard professor outside my office I could have remained in power longer!

ROSA: Sometimes I have a suspicion he is only from NYU.

CHAIRMAN: What was that about the air marshal? Didn't he say that he was an air marshal?

ROSA: He always wanted to be one so I gave him the title on the flight here.

WESSIN: In the officers' club we used to make the following observation about such cases: "The higher the monkey climbs up the tree, the more you can see of his ass!"

6. About the Recognition by Superpowers

ROSA: I recognized the new order in Chile before any of the superpowers . . . even China!

WESSIN: But normally the superpowers recognize us faster than we recognize ourselves!

SCHNEIDER: The American president recognized me even before my coup!

CHAIRMAN: How did he find out about the coup? *(laughter)*

7. How to Get Elected as Dictator in True Elections

CHAIRMAN: How did you manage to win an authentic election?

ROSA: I had the advantage of being dictator. The elections I called were won with simple honesty, nothing more. I made a speech in which I said the following, in essence. I said that I heard that the voters want a different candidate, not just a different face. In that case, I said, I am well suited, since I am not like myself but am instead entirely different than myself. Naturally I still appear in the same bodily form, I said, but here—and then I tapped myself on the head—here much has changed, and who doesn't believe in change.

8. First Announcement of an Idea

General Wessin y Wessin, *making a late appearance, dashes in and takes a seat, then stands up again immediately.*

WESSIN: I have an idea!

ROSA: It would happen so early in the day that you think you've got an idea.

CHAIRMAN: What sort of idea is it?

WESSIN: Your Excellency, it is implicit in the nature of this idea that it cannot be communicated immediately.

CHAIRMAN: You mean the idea is that it is incommunicable?

WESSIN: No. The idea is one that cannot be communicated in the form of a headline or under pressure.

SCHNEIDER: I take it the idea is supposed to be an especially fine one?

ROSA: Will you permit us to come back to your idea later?

WESSIN: Actually not. I must instead request that you show your good faith by waiting until I myself announce the idea and it becomes possible to express it freely and spontaneously.

ROSA: If that is so, why did you even claim you had an idea in the first place? You should have postponed your announcement and kept your idea and the attempt to convey it to yourself!

WESSIN: When I said that I had the idea I thought I could also present it; only while I was saying that I had the idea, did I begin to sense that the idea would not come very easily to my lips.

CHAIRMAN: So you needed the experience of wanting to say something in order to realize that you couldn't?

WESSIN: That's a somewhat simplified version of the matter. When I said that I had an idea, I had it only after I had said that I had it.

ROSA: Disgusting! *(he hesitates)* Didn't you also once have a building erected and after it was completed you forgot what it was for?

WESSIN: We had forgotten the purpose of the building already after the first ground breaking. From then on the whole thing was pure experimentation!

CHAIRMAN: Utopian situation!

9. About Success with Women as well as Murder on the Deathbed

ROSA: Is it true that you made quite an impression on the ladies during your dictatorship?

SCHNEIDER *(laughing)*: That is probably true for everyone here. I suspect that both things belong together. How can one be a dictator without this personal magnetism?

WESSIN: On the other hand you have to admit that women lose that certain something after one knows them for a while. They may be very good-looking until, one day, they get an unpleasant expression on their face. *(short silence)*

ROSA: The Dulce Encanta is said to have murdered her husband on his deathbed, you know!

WESSIN: Did he die from it?

ROSA: They say she killed him while he was dying.

SCHNEIDER: Good timing. No one could get suspicious. Safest alibi one could imagine.

CHAIRMAN: But how do we know that the general was dying? *(pause)* After all, a bed is a deathbed only after it has been a deathbed.

WESSIN: Has the murder weapon been discovered?

ROSA: The murder weapon was nagging.

WESSIN: But nagging doesn't kill.

ROSA: Not all at once. Only long and repeated nagging. Maybe she had been nagging for years and then in his dying hour, when he saw her coming in thought: "Now she's going to nag again!" *(silence)*

SCHNEIDER: My wife never nagged.

CHAIRMAN: There is something wrong with a dictator who lets his wife nag. To be a dictator in public and at the same time let your wife nag you at home—inconceivable.

SCHNEIDER: I believe it is Anglo-Saxon. My wife had no time to nag because of the public duties to which she was dedicated. She visited hospitals, etc., and won the title "Woman of the Year." Furthermore, in her honor I declared the day we first met a national holiday.

10. First Example of Structuralism

CHAIRMAN: In your country, when there was shooting, did people also run wildly across intersections and squares?

ROSA: First of all, it was often only fireworks that went off in the heat. But in spite of that, you must consider that in all our countries, people run in similar patterns across intersections and streets! There's something for structuralists to work with!

11. About the Difficulties of Renewing Old Business Connections

CHAIRMAN *(straightening himself)*: I find myself in a nice frame of mind today. I'm really in a good mood. *(Professor enters)*

CHAIRMAN: Please show Mr. O'Neill in!

PROFESSOR: Your Excellency, in the first place his real name is Aniello and in the second place he was here already yesterday.

CHAIRMAN: Without leaving a message?

PROFESSOR: Business affairs called him back to Washington.

CHAIRMAN: Did he give you any excuse?

PROFESSOR: He said, "I apologize!"

CHAIRMAN: Was that good enough for you?

PROFESSOR: I pointed out that an apology would have to include an explanation of his sudden departure.

CHAIRMAN: How did he react to your objection?

PROFESSOR: He answered that he would be happy to give an explanation.

CHAIRMAN: Did you ask him why he didn't come forward immediately with one?

PROFESSOR: Yes, I also asked him that. He countered that he had not included an explanation in his original excuse in order to avoid giving the impression that it was excusable, thus needing no excuse—but simply a few words alluding to the excusability of it all. In response I waived my right to an explanation of his reasons and accepted his original apology.

CHAIRMAN: For that you owe us an apology!

PROFESSOR: I apologize!

CHAIRMAN: For what?

SCHNEIDER: Strictly speaking, for asking such a question, you owe us a new apology.

12. About Popularity in One's Own Country

WESSIN: Were you popular with your own people?

ROSA: If you believe in opinion polls, I was the popular man. The newspapers I read also indicated that I was a popular dictator. But as you know one can't rely on newspapers.

WESSIN: So, were you a popular or an unpopular dictator?

ROSA: My people love freedom. They want liberation. But without a liberator.

SCHNEIDER: But that's impossible.

ROSA: My people are like children. You can see that. There is my successor! *(calling to* Mimosa*)*: How are things back home?

> Rosa *rises and goes to meet* Mimosa. *Both hug while about twenty people with suitcases, etc., push into the room from the outside.* Professor, *who was pushed into the room with the dictator's relatives, stands with arms outstretched just in front of them. The newly arrived* Mimosa *motions the relatives away.*

MIMOSA: I requested that you wait outside, remember? This is an official session. Can't you see that?

OLDER WOMAN *(stepping out)*: Don't you recognize your sister Augusta any more?

ADDITIONAL VOICES: Don't forget your promises! What about the White House Reception?

VOICE *(from the table)*: This is a business breakfast—can't you see that?

> *Meanwhile* Chairman, *with the help of those sitting on either side, stands up and turns to the relatives with a raised index finger.*

CHAIRMAN: Meticulously obey all directions! *(relatives exit with* Professor*)*

13. In Praise of Idylls and Observations on the Importance of Being Symbolic

CHAIRMAN *(while all present are listening quietly, gestures freezing, he begins dreamily)*: Strangely enough I feel more secure thinking about what is past than I do thinking about what is happening now. That is why I enjoy reading a book so much. The events contained in it have been decided; no one need interfere any more. I can hardly imagine anything more relaxing than to have a table moved into the garden, drink coffee, and read a book. And swat flies humming around my wife. *(silence)*

WESSIN: Those are deep thoughts you have there!

ROSA: I believe there are also symbolic thoughts contained in it, Your Excellency!

CHAIRMAN: What did he say?

WESSIN *(into the ear of* Chairman*)*: He said there were symbolic thoughts.

CHAIRMAN *(leaning back)*: What's a symbol anyway?

ROSA: A symbol is if something means something other than it usually means, for example, something higher, edifying.

CHAIRMAN: You are posing a difference between common meaning and symbolic meaning? How does one recognize the latter?

ROSA: Up to the observer, Mr. President.

CHAIRMAN: You mean there are no guidelines?

ROSA *(calling)*: Professor! *(he enters)* To the best of your knowledge, have guidelines been issued on the meaning of symbols, flag, blood, etc.?

PROFESSOR *(bows)*: Gentlemen, guidelines could certainly be issued in such matters. For example, if the government palace has Greek columns, it means firstly that it is a palace with Greek columns and secondly that it is a country with a great past. . . .

MIMOSA: Instead of imitating columns, why can't one simply mention the idea of a great past in a speech?

PROFESSOR: Because a column that stands there has more power of persuasion than a speech, which vanishes into thin air—unless you would have someone yell "past" or "tradition" every time people are passing a place where there is no column. Too lean. People want something they can touch.

14. About the Question of the Presence of Bankers in Cabinets

ROSA: If you insist on discussing aesthetic questions, I admit that I find those sand-colored steep-brimmed officers' hats worn in our countries also very ugly. But how arrogant to judge by one's own aesthetic standards! Sometimes, when I put on my uniform, a servant draping it with medals and ribbons, when I looked into the mirror, I almost became sick. Once, appearing at breakfast, my wife said to me: "You win because you are ugly. One can't fight with someone who looks as ugly as you do—the sight of you weakens the enemy. When you stroll through the streets, you have already won because your enemies become nauseous by the thought of having to touch you in battle." This opinion of my wife was naturally an exaggeration, a product of ill humor. Admittedly our uniforms are ugly, but the people treasure them just the same. Our people are small in stature. For example I, if I get up from my chair, am smaller than before. But back to our discussion. Even our corpulence makes us seem more trustworthy. I had a secretary of state who grew thin from worrying about foreign-policy matters. We could not show him anymore, he ceased to be convincing. If I had my way I would rather wear a simple uniform, or, even better, the gray double-breasted suit of the bankers.

SCHNEIDER: Immediately after my putsch I named all the cabinet members field marshals. In response, the cabinet laughed and the minister of commerce said he did not want to be a field marshal. "Perhaps you would rather be an admiral?" I asked. When everyone shook their heads I said, "Then we shall design new uniforms—you don't like the old ones!" "No!" they said. "We desire instead for you to take off your uniform. It looks better, phenomenologically." Later, after I was forced into exile, the former members of my cabinet simply returned to their respective banks.

ROSA: If you gave in to the bankers in the first hour, you were only a pompous shell!

WESSIN: Listening to you, one could give in to the impression that in our countries the bankers were in power, not us. Never yet in my life have I exchanged words with an economic leader. Besides, I prefer the company of real men. If someone came in to see me and started to talk about economy or finances, I kicked him in the ass. After all, we weren't Marxists who can only talk about money. Do you honestly think that I could have collected followers and strengthened my base if I had stepped into somebody's living room with the words: "Oh here can you see Dow Jones and Chase Manhattan! Three cheers for mortgages and machines! Long live power plants and dividends!" Can you imagine what the family would have thought of me?

SCHNEIDER: Marxists and industrialists in the same breath!

WESSIN: The books of both groups are dominated by statistics. One counts its own profits, the other counts the profits of the others. Thus I have a choice between greed and envy. Caught up in these alternatives the true questions of humanity are forgotten. Both groups of people, fighting shoulder to shoulder, to be sure, defeated me!

15. About the Difficulty of Throwing Off Shackles

CHAIRMAN: In Eastern Europe they have finally thrown off their shackles!

SCHNEIDER: Now they will have to work, like everybody else!

WESSIN: In some countries they have to work even with shackles. The Chinese work with shackles!

ROSA: They had their chance. They could have thrown off their shackles. But they sat and sat on that Square and sometimes they got up and waved.

CHAIRMAN: Correct! For fifty days they waited for their removal.

WESSIN: So did the government. The government also waited for their removal.

ROSA: We removed them before they reached the government building. *(Pause)*

SCHNEIDER: I had them removed before they got up!

16. Further Discussions about the Economy and about Dealing with True Opposition Parties

MIMOSA: So in your country you had abolished the economy. But there must have been some money; who managed it?

WESSIN: I did. I followed the principle of self-supervision by submitting to myself a control report of my work, usually at the end of the day. The next morning I either dismissed it or signed it. Sometimes as president I would, after checking the books, have to cross out profits I thought I had earned the previous evening as bank director.

MIMOSA: Then at noon perhaps you could, as chief of state, occasionally book sums as credits that you thought you had lost as bank director?

WESSIN: Correct. Sometimes even five minutes after I lost them as a banker. *(pause)* Self-control, you know, is the most difficult control, because no matter how it comes out, you lose!

MIMOSA: Or win! Sometimes you win!

WESSIN: OK, you win, but you never win without losing and vice versa, and a winning, which goes with losing, adds up to losing, as in math. I just didn't want to bore you! I thought you knew!

SCHNEIDER: As far as the economy was concerned there was only one principle to which I paid the closest attention, namely that 100 percent of the national income was distributed among 100 percent of the people—after all, that's the main thing—the proportions regulate themselves automatically.

ROSA: I was more progressive. Milton Friedman was my economic advisor. Like a miracle healer. In Chile he forced the inflation rate down to 174.3 percent. Besides, I had a real opposition party. I don't know if you were aware of that?

SCHNEIDER: But your opposition party had only two members, didn't it?

ROSA: Enough to say "Yes"!

CHAIRMAN: Is it true that your government responded to legislative proposals of the minister for internal security with the words "Yes sir!" while the opposition just got up and said "Yes"?

ROSA: Yes. However, that "Yes" was a polite "Yes," not hissed forth from grinding teeth as you just did.

WESSIN: Did the opposition party sometimes say "No"?

ROSA: Yes. In such cases we placed the floor leader of the opposition party at the top of the speaker's list. The Americans were about to reduce our military aid—all parties joined in a unanimous "No" vote.

CHAIRMAN: Which agency in America, government or the World Bank? *(silence)*

ROSA: I think it came directly from the World Bank.

CHAIRMAN: It appears to be simply a postal question whether the check comes from Washington or New York.

WESSIN: It's also connected with the elections in America. Sometimes you have to turn to Nelson Rockefeller, other times he has no say and you must speak with David Rockefeller—in other words, it's a family affair.

CHAIRMAN: Just like in classical tragedy!

A tropical downpour begins suddenly, continuing into the next scene.

17. A Reading of the Soap Opera

PROFESSOR *(enters, taking a short bow)*: Your Excellency, gentlemen! Erica went out last night with Jeff as she was angry at Nick's pursuing Christine. Monica offered to restore Erica to Nick again. Don fell into a deep depression when Joyce behaved in a way indicating that she may not be returning his feelings. . . .

CHAIRMAN: I didn't know that Don and Joyce had already met!

ROSA: But one could see it coming, Your Excellency.

PROFESSOR: . . . when, returning from group therapy, he found Connie in Ron's arms and suspected the worst! This was shortly after the episode where Tom thought that Don had slept with Lulu, but then found out that she was engaged to Mac, although Charlie's picture was found in her wallet. I remind you of the angry outbreak that occurred when Connie intimated that Paul had something going with Wanda.

The rain stops.

18. About Scientific Avant-gardism

MIMOSA: If one considers the high theoretical level of our discussions, disregarding some exception, it is astonishing that we did not all become university professors!

SCHNEIDER: I was! In my country the president of the republic is automatically the leader of the university!

ROSA: I have an explanation for our intellectual drive. In the first place, while in office we had no time to spend on problems that really moved us, so that our own intellectual impulses are gushing forth. Secondly: I can hardly imagine a better preparation for a university teaching career than that of a dictator. Of course, I'm not referring to those professors who are constantly talking about so-called ideas and, as a consequence, have allowed whole provinces of pure thought to become barren. In my country one could distinguish between two types of intellectuals. One type spoke incessantly and on top of that in an impolite voice about so-called subject matters—the other concerned itself exclusively with the far more complex question of how to get close to this, and, in case this succeeded, which admittedly did not occur, how to turn them back and forth. I admit this latter group called itself funny names such as *(covers his mouth)* ethnomethodologists, semioticists, etc., as in pharmacy. Still, one could learn a lot by listening to them.

SCHNEIDER: In my country they called themselves structuralists. By that they meant that different things can look alike, for example, a meatball and democracy, but these people were upright supporters of the state.

19. About Resignation as a Political Weapon

ROSA: Didn't you ever resign once in the course of your dictatorship?

WESSIN: No. I merely threatened to resign a few times. I am of the opinion that there are too many resignations in our countries. I have heard about leaders who resigned fifteen times during their dictatorship.

MIMOSA: That was me. I resigned a total of fifteen times, though three times in a row—all in one day. So two of these don't really count.

WESSIN: And you didn't get the impression that this political weapon becomes dull?

MIMOSA: On the contrary. During the first resignation it was still a little ticklish. The first resignation is always the most difficult resignation. One lacks skill in recognizing the right mood of the people. Just after the formal declaration of my resignation there was an unpleasant silence. Then cries of protest arose and the agitated crowds of people came to the palace. When I later stepped out onto the balcony and, after some waving of my hand, shouted loudly over the raucous chanting of the crowds until these faded in the distance, and when I then, in well-chosen words, placed myself again at the disposal of the people, then my government had become stronger than before, and I am tempted to say that he who does not learn how to resign can never be a good dictator.

WESSIN: But the last time you resigned, they took you by your word, didn't they?

MIMOSA: Correct. The president of the republic broke his promise and accepted my resignation. Other possible risks are: if one resigns for too long and appears as pouting, or if demonstrations are too small or, as in my case, too large, or if the national guard gets panicky or if a gun starts shooting. *(silence, nodding)*

CHAIRMAN: Did you always resign with your whole cabinet?

MIMOSA: The cabinet always resigned spontaneously with me. Naturally there were gentlemen who had no desire to resign. One time a group of cabinet members sitting in the background chanted: "We do not want to resign!" I did not take that particular group with me when I read my resignation speech.

20. About Sleeping Late and about the Utilization of Natural Resources

MIMOSA: You are late!

ROSA: You are always late.

WESSIN: For a while now I have had difficulties getting used to this blinding brightness called daytime. Birds twittering and problems: the alliance of these two. Besides, I've been up reading Castañeda all night, inspiring.

SCHNEIDER: A general who can't get out of bed!

CHAIRMAN: Originally, what was your military education? Were you not educated for the general staff? They sleep in.

WESSIN: You, when you get up early you only act as if you had something to do. Or which orderly was by your bed this morning with which cable? Which head of state on the telephone?

ROSA: I am writing my memoirs.

WESSIN: You can't call that work!

MIMOSA: I agree. Don't you miss the pushing and shoving around your person when history was made? Reservoirs, state visits, earthquakes, etc.?

CHAIRMAN: Earthquakes?

WESSIN: You enjoyed those, eh?

ROSA: They did fill the coffers of certain people.

SCHNEIDER: All I ever got were planeloads with wool blankets and powdered milk.

MIMOSA: I admit that we sometimes exaggerated an earthquake here and there. We didn't have any other natural resources.

WESSIN: They say that you once, well, conjured up an earthquake?

SCHNEIDER: In the first place, it was in a distant province; in the second place, it eventually did occur; and in the third place, it lasted a rather long time.

WESSIN: Three times lucky!

21. About the Ugly Sight of Smoking

VARIOUS *(to* Wessin*)*: Please stop smoking! Yes, it is harmful!

WESSIN *(laughing)*: Why shouldn't I smoke?

ROSA *(disgusted)*: Because a dictator who smokes is an ugly sight.

SCHNEIDER: . . . drinks too. A dictator who drinks is also ugly. Same with meat.

CHAIRMAN: Meticulously follow the health measure decided upon!

22. Examples of Justified Suspicion

ROSA: And when did you become suspicious?

WESSIN: This Savedra was deaf, but during conferences he always sat far away from me!

ROSA: And you? How did you become suspicious?

MIMOSA: That's quite a story. I had a conference. Several provincial posts needed to be filled. Various individuals outlined their position in short papers. The decisions were made to my satisfaction when I was called out of the conference room for another appointment. On the way there I suddenly realized that I had been tricked at the conference.

CHAIRMAN: How did you know that? Why did you get suspicious?

ROSA: Well, in all this rush I had left some papers behind. So I turned around on the spot and hurried back into the conference room, which I had left only seconds ago. Before I even opened the door I could hear laughter roaring within, which abruptly stopped as I entered. Laughter that stops when you enter—that's *bad!*

CHAIRMAN: I would also have had second thoughts in that situation.
A tropical downpour begins suddenly, continuing into the next scene.

23. A Reading of the Soap Opera

PROFESSOR *(enter, takes a short bow)*: Your Excellency, gentlemen! Nick informed Erica that no matter how much she was upset about her role as a sex object, she was apparently not angry enough to break off relations with him completely. John decided to claim Clarice since Jeff got cold feet. Joyce transferred her interest from Bob to Jim. Phyllis presented Neil with a Mercedes for his birthday. Matt informed Maggie that she had debased him for the last time. Gina promised not to betray to Adam that Jill had injured herself while in an intoxicated condition. George asserted that Ellis was only being used by Edith. Merle did not commit suicide.

The rain stops.

24. About the Distrust against Oneself

MIMOSA: We admired your caution, even in dealing with close advisors. Apparently you observed strict vigilance even with your most trusted collaborators, otherwise you could hardly have succeeded in uncovering so many conspiracies against your person.

ROSA: I have to preface my actual answer to your question with the self-critical observation that I may have uncovered some conspiracies that actually were not conspiracies. It is like sometimes you think somebody is Jewish but later it turns out he never was. In any case, I assumed the habit of examining the thoughts I had had on a given day while falling asleep at night—as a rule not too many since one doesn't have much time during the day to think while ruling. If I noticed on these occasions that I had placed confidence in a specific person, I then asked that person for a confession.

SCHNEIDER: How did you recognize the traitor?

ROSA: There are simple traitors, i.e., gentlemen who voice contradicting opinions, then there are traitors of the second order, i.e., gentlemen who lie, and finally there are supertraitors, i.e., gentlemen who say nothing at all. For example, I spotted one traitor because he was tossing compliments in my direction. Another one I caught when he commented rather loudly about my facial expression on entering the cabinet room. He alleged a nasty formation of wrinkles above my eyes.

WESSIN: I would imagine that both praise and censure died out soon wherever you went?

ROSA: Silence too. I am also not fond of hearing silence, perhaps because I cannot put myself in the position of an individual who would, so to say, voluntarily wish to be a dictator.

MIMOSA: How come?

ROSA: Because like all real revolutionaries I come from a good family, thus am incorruptible.

25. More about the Difficulties of Establishing Fresh Business Connections, as well as observations about the Climate

PROFESSOR: Your Excellency, Carlos (Little man) Marcella is at the door requesting an audience.

CHAIRMAN: What is his real name? Little Man or Marcella?

PROFESSOR: Marcella. The other name is a nickname.

ROSA: And why again no Mr. O'Neill?

PROFESSOR *(to Rosa)*: Mr. President, Little Man Marcella is a public figure, at home in economic circles, representative of Rizitello's, who is the right-hand man for Jimmy (the Weasel) Fratiano, who is a personal advisor to Lincoln Cellini. *(to Chairman)* Cellini himself speaks almost exclusively with O'Neill.

WESSIN: It seems we are getting further and further away from O'Neill.

CHAIRMAN *(to Professor)*: Show the gentleman in at once!

LITTLE MAN *(sitting, fanning himself)*: It's hot here!

ROSA: Like home. In our countries it's always hot.

LITTLE MAN: In the States people like it though. They are happy about it. They call it vacation.

MIMOSA: But for us it's no vacation. It's like this all year for us.

LITTLE MAN: What you spend your whole life doing is something we can only do once a year for two or three weeks. We tell ourselves: to be stupid once a year is enough. After that it's back to work!

SCHNEIDER: Stupid?

LITTLE MAN: Not meant as an insult! I mean in your countries everything is luscious. Reaching up in the air you have a handful of bananas. There is twittering, chirping, blowing into trumpets, stamping of boots with clanking spurs, under hats throwing shadows over whole provinces. Victories are celebrated over animals that have no weapons—but for all that, there is less thinking. I am tempted to say: a glance at a barometer anywhere in the world and one knows the form of government!

SCHNEIDER: You don't approve of our form of government, do you?

LITTLE MAN: It's certainly not ideal for business, that's for sure!

WESSIN: Business turns a country upside down. Where there is commerce there is no order and anarchy triumphs. Besides, commerce gets in the way of troop movements!

ROSA *(to* Little Man*)*: The general is irritated and suspicious of progress!

LITTLE MAN: General Wessin, I can understand the bitterness of your tone. I know how it is: all of a sudden an individual is not needed anymore. This also happens in business. For example, one of my closest associates lost his usefulness and disappeared on a business trip.

ROSA: You mean you simply lost your best man?

LITTLE MAN: First of all, I do not have a best man, such a thing does not exist in business. All my associates are my best associates, I myself am very best associate! *(laughter sets in hesitantly, then spreads among the table; then, clearing his throat)* Rinaldo Cozzi got lost on Hawaii. From there we received a cable: "Delicious! Send us more!"

WESSIN: In Colonial times cannibals still used to be illiterate!

CHAIRMAN *(lifting his finger)*: What is your line of business?

26. About Artistic Avant-gardism

MIMOSA: People here talk as if a dictatorship were one long sorrow, nothing but grief and suffering. Certainly it was that also but in reality there was, aside from all the work, a lot of joy!

SCHNEIDER: As a leader you have to spoil yourself. I, for example, was firmly rooted in the world of fine art and surrounded myself with poets; their audacity is refreshing. One of them once informed me, while intoxicated, that he could never espouse one cause because that would mean that he would have to oppose another cause. I found that clever.

ROSA: Me, if I could be reborn on earth, I would like to become a liberal. It would be fun to oppose everything. One always has friends.

SCHNEIDER: I think it's adorable how poets act as if they were against themselves when in reality they are only against each other. We can learn from them in that respect. In my country, for example, a young man wrote a pamphlet against literature in which he demanded the expulsion of dreams from the libraries onto the streets! A delightful idea. But hardly had his name gotten around than he himself composed a book with a classical title reminiscent of spring; and what's more, the book was about himself.

ROSA *(gravely)*: My opinion on this is as follows: Art must above all be big and everywhere! Out of the museums! Let the people experience it! The whole nation as one big, nonending artist! All its activities one collective work of art! *(amazed silence)*

WESSIN *(stuttering)*: You mean, everything is art—for example if one eats breakfast that is a work of art? Or driving a car?

ROSA: Gentlemen, you must admit that driving a car in our countries is truly an art. By that I mean that it is intentional. Art is, if one does something unnecessary intentionally. We intentionally wait until the buses are overflowing; we choose the narrowest, most dangerous roads, make sure that the tires are worn thin—and after advising the driver to devour the road, we stick a bottle of tequila in his hand, wish him bon voyage and wait for the reviews!

WESSIN *(disdainfully)*: That is extraordinarily avant-garde!

SCHNEIDER *(pondering)*: I have to admit that censorship becomes obsolete with this kind of art. *(silence)*

WESSIN: So, I see that I represent a reactionary viewpoint. I am apparently the only reactionary at this table. As far as art goes, I believe that is chiefly concerned with human feelings. Of these there are altogether two: sadness and happiness. I therefore brought back with me two songs that an ensemble sang for me when I was on a goodwill mission abroad. *(he stands up)* The sad one began: "Where are you going little girl, in the forest?" and the happy one went: "Jubilating fellows, I'm one of yours!"

27. Introduction to Philosophy

Gentlemen motionless, lost in thought.

CHAIRMAN: Games lose all suspense when the rules have been so calculated that a person must always win when he plays. In winter you can stand in front of a window and set up rules so that you win if you breathe on the window. Now if you do breathe on it, you can turn to those around you and say "I won!" The applause you receive from that is practically meaningless.

ROSA: Or one could also say: "I am now observing this sugar bowl," but afterwards one could communicate to the audience only that part of one's observations of the sugar bowl that is verifiable visually, withholding the advance knowledge gained by previous experience, for example the knowledge that the sugar bowl has a bottom that is invisible unless one lifts it.

CHAIRMAN: With such comments we would soon find ourselves deep in the realm of philosophy!

28. More about Sleeping Late and Why There are No More Ladies

ROSA: Enter the lover of the night!

WESSIN: Gentlemen, still, you can see, cups are somersaulting out of my grip, objects jump off into air—but it has to do with my upbringing. I was educated, as you know, for the general staff, i.e., to ask questions. A good general staff officer is, so to say, a child on duty. How can I, if I want to pose a good question, tear myself—without transition—into a wakeful state of alertness? One's questions, if one is immediately strong for the day, conceded too much to the day and are therefore uninteresting.

ROSA: Why don't you provide us with an example of an interesting question?

WESSIN: Just now, on the occasion of fastening my cuff links, as I was attempting to gain a preliminary overview of the day, I presented myself with the following question: Why is it that there are no ladies any more?

SCHNEIDER: But I am living with some.

WESSIN: I mean real ladies.

MIMOSA: Maybe there are no more ladies because there aren't any more gentlemen either.

SCHNEIDER: It used to be this way. You could say to a lady: "You are a lady!" And the person in question really would be a lady, in time.

WESSIN: I think it's because women want to be men. Apparently they assume that we like ourselves, otherwise they would not assume we would like them if they are as we are.

CHAIRMAN: Maybe it gets boring if one is liked all the time, so they decided to give up the whole thing and, just as us, not be liked anymore by anyone.

Act II

29. More about the Difficulties of Renewing Old Business Connections as Well as Observations on Inner and Outer Freedom

Dark morning gradually becoming lighter in the course of the scene, staggering sleepy entrance of the gentlemen.

MIMOSA: This is the earliest breakfast of my life!

ROSA: Economic leaders like Lincoln Cellini prefer an early breakfast. There is a lot to do. The cry of the rooster in the morning is a call to action. The roosters are their allies!

MIMOSA (*holding a slip of paper in his hand*): The president of the United States during my term of office sent me a message with the following contents: "We do care. I care. I have visited most of your countries. I have met most of your leaders. I have talked with your people."

CHAIRMAN: Would you please translate that?

WESSIN: He can't speak English and claims to be a dictator!

PROFESSOR (*entering*): Gentlemen, Mr. Lincoln Cellini!

CHAIRMAN: You mean Mr. O'Neill is still not appearing in person?

PROFESSOR: Your Excellency, Mr. O'Neill never appears in person. Unless you count goodwill missions.

CELLINI (*seating himself in a dignified manner*): Thank you, gentlemen, thank you!

CHAIRMAN (*to* Professor *while looking at* Cellini): Tell him that we are very pleased about his visit and hope for a satisfactory conclusion of our negotiations!

CELLINI (*to* Chairman, *whereby both nod at each other while* Professor *looks at* Cellini): I received your praise and I am greatly refreshed!

PROFESSOR (*to* Chairman): He heard the greetings and they refreshed him.

SCHNEIDER: . . . very much. He said "refreshed him very much."
Chairman *motions* Schneider *to be silent.*

CELLINI *(laying his hands flat on the table, looking quickly to the right and to the left)*: I like you men! You are real men! *(silence)* Gentlemen, I take it this is a social visit, to get to know each other and renew old acquaintances!

PROFESSOR *(to* Chairman*)*: He says that his visit is basically a social one.

CELLINI: I'm not the government, you know. I'm mostly in business. In this country we have a strict division between government and business, you know! *(laughter)*

PROFESSOR *(to* Chairman *who nods while listening)*: He says he does not come as an official representative of the government but rather as a businessman. In this country, government and economy are strictly separate.

CELLINI: As you know, politics and economy will bloom only in true democracies. If you followed this advice you might still be in power down there!

PROFESSOR *(to* Chairman*)*: He says that economics and politics flourish only under free democratic societies. If we had followed that guideline we would still be powerful. *(*Chairman *yawns, nods sleepily)*

SCHNEIDER *(smiling)*: Mr. Cellini, democracy is a superstition based on statistics. To introduce democracy in our countries would be like offering a reformed alcoholic a glass of whiskey. *(during the following words,* Chairman *begins to fall asleep)* Besides, with freedom it is as it is with poverty. There is an inner and an outer freedom. Like all exterior things, outer freedom is not as valuable as inner freedom. A traditional song of the Germans proclaims *(he stands up)* "Thoughts are free"—with this, this great nation wants to indicate, that freedom is basically an inner quality.

MIMOSA: Mr. Cellini, it has really not been stressed enough what an overwhelming significance the interior has in comparison with the exterior. What's inside is also more profound. For example, in your country people are free on the exterior, but inside, the emotions are raging—you are volcanic and on the brink of an explosion! Look at the way you are drumming the table!

CELLINI: I'm not at all on the brink of an explosion!

ROSA: As far as freedom is concerned, Mr. Cellini, it is a great idea. *(in private, seriously)* Besides you, I guess I am the only democrat at this table. Freedom suffers because it is invisible. One can buy nothing with it, so it has few fans. With freedom it's like this, it's as if you approached someone secretly who has no financial means at his disposal and whispered in his ear: "I have an idea that will help you out of your predicament! Become rich!" *(pause)* And besides, Mr. Cellini, what have you accomplished with your freedom? Look out the window! Why do people who are free erect buildings that are so ugly? Why do the streets look swept empty of people? Are they all in their living rooms, crippled by freedom? Thanks a lot! I would on this occasion like to repeat my people's favorite slogan with which they loved to greet me: "Down with freedom!"

> Cellini, *smiling at* Rosa *as he spoke, had been pouring champagne and continued pouring, while continuing to smile so that the whole tablecloth is now soaked with champagne. After this, he gets up and leaves, smiling wordlessly.*

CHAIRMAN *(waking up startled from a snore)*: Continue the negotiations tenaciously! *(continues sleeping; silence)*

ROSA: I think he was a bit angry!

WESSIN: Mr. President, I know these Anglo-Saxons. They are reserved when it comes to showing their feelings. With his behavior, including exit, he meant to say: "I am rather impressed with you! I admire you!" *(pause)* Professor?

PROFESSOR: He was irritated. *(to Rosa)* Your negative comments on freedom were especially insulting to him!

SCHNEIDER: Such topics of discussion are too philosophical for Anglo-Saxons.

ROSA *(sad)*: Colonel Schneider, you are talking like a racist!

WESSIN: Ethnocentric, as it is called nowadays. Ethnocentric.

30. About Swimming against the Current

General Luis Torrijos *enters.*

CHAIRMAN: Where did you come from?

ROSA: We certainly didn't expect you to show up here!

SCHNEIDER: Are you here for a state visit or was there a putsch against you?

TORRIJOS: There was too much swimming against the current, a slogan I myself announced. Suddenly everyone was swimming against the current, or at least far too many.

SCHNEIDER: Why didn't you simply also swim against the current?

TORRIJOS: That's why I'm here. For example, last weekend I directed my private secretary to request an audience with the American ambassador. The secretary, however, swam against the current and said on the spot, without leaving my office, "Your order has been carried out, sir. I have asked the American ambassador for no audience."

CHAIRMAN: In that case you should have always demanded the opposite of what you wanted, for example: "Please do not ask the American ambassador for an audience!"

TORRIJOS: I did that. In response, the secretary reported to me that the ambassador had granted my request for no audience. So I didn't know whether or not I was allowed to go.

SCHNEIDER: I would have gone regardless.

TORRIJOS: I did, but the ambassador was not there. *(after a pause)* He was often not there.

SCHNEIDER: I always went directly of the CIA station chief!

ROSA *(waving Schneider off, to Torrijos)*: Why didn't you simply ask for the opposite of what you wished and then add: "But for heaven's sake, don't forget to swim against the current?"

TORRIJOS: To this the secretary replied, with a certain amount of justification, that the explicit admonition, to swim against the current, when strictly obeyed, meant that one should actually swim with the current.

WESSIN: Did he accompany you to the airport?

31. About Suffering, while Dining with Beautiful People

SCHNEIDER *(looking around the table with his chin down, while repeatedly knocking rhythmically on the table with a spoon)*: My putsch was a revolution, I'm not sure whether you were aware of that? *(leaning back)* Can you imagine, therefore, how I suffered when, on my way to an appointment, reclining in the back seat of my car, I saw the shacks and huts race by outside? And when I later drove up at a palace, its steps trimmed with traitors bowing, making my way through rows of beautiful people with alien smiles, when I finally had reached my destination—some supper—I was still weakened by the sight of my own countrymen outside their simple quarters and I knew then, gentlemen, that, deep inside me, I belonged to them. . . . Deep inside I belonged to them, not to the fancy people, and I spoke only for them, though admittedly in disguise. The arrogant manner in which I was often treated in the drawing rooms made this painfully clear!

TORRIJOS: And their awkward diction! And the procedures and extras with which they burden the simplest events, such as eating! How to put the saltshaker down, all that nonsense with flowers as if they had anything at all to do with soup! The avoidance of certain subjects at the table in favor of conversations about former centuries! Again and again the so-called eighteenth century! Again and again silver birds on the mantelpieces, but on the walls there are etchings of soldiers whose uniforms the gentlemen cannot account for!

SCHNEIDER: Yes, and the dignified beards, white, of the bankers, trimmed, suited for conquerors. Their limping because, God knows why, they choose to walk with canes! And the weak expression on their faces, perhaps to protect themselves from getting slapped!

WESSIN: If they were really so much smarter than us, why didn't they march in formation?

32. Second Announcement of an Idea

WESSIN: Again I have an idea!

ROSA *(pointing at him)*: Look who's got another idea!

SCHNEIDER: We can hardly imagine that you, of all people, should have an idea!

CHAIRMAN: Didn't you have an idea before?

MIMOSA: . . . whose characteristic it was that it could not be communicated?

TORRIJOS: . . . which, incidentally, is nonsense, because whatever one thinks one can communicate!

ROSA: Furthermore, if the essence of the idea was that it could not be communicated then you have betrayed the idea by informing us that it could not be communicated. You are a traitor of the idea!

Wessin *stands silently, perplexed.*

CHAIRMAN: Is this a brand-new idea or is it the old one that could not be communicated?

WESSIN: It's a new idea!

SCHNEIDER: Let's have it!

WESSIN: I can't.

SCHNEIDER: Why not?

WESSIN: It's only a new idea insofar as it's the old idea in another situation. To be sure, the idea is just as unchanged as ever, but we, its potential listeners, have changed, so that the idea, while calmly remaining itself, has become radiantly new in relation to us!

CHAIRMAN (*raising his finger*): Learn from ideas!

> *A tropical downpour begins suddenly, continuing into the next scene.*

33. A Reading of the Soap Opera

PROFESSOR (*enters, takes a short bow*): Your Excellency, gentlemen, after Brook caught Benny in a compromising position with the upstairs maid, he agreed to spend a weekend with Danny. Phoebe started to drink heavily. Kyle admitted to Maggie that his wife was blind but that she knew how to use that handicap against him. Rita admitted that she had been with Roger when Cyrus was dying. Jason invited himself to be Laurie's host at Elli's dinner for Edith and Richard. Iris was thunderstruck when she heard that Corinna's mysterious cousin was none other than David. Sharon canceled her rendezvous with Gerry because of his relations with Lyz, but she agreed to give it another try with Russ. Heather took a great number of sleeping pills. After being rejected by Peg, Jack turned to Joanne who responded to his needs.

> *Rain stops.*

34. About the Abolition of Wars due to the Introduction of Similar Uniforms and Why There Had Been Eternal Peace in Latin America Ever since

Gentlemen motionless, lost in thought

TORRIJOS: Our true passion, the military. As a cadet I pictured myself at the head of a small unit, riding at dawn into another country, now I'm sixty and have not experienced a single war. The enemy never came.

SCHNEIDER: We once had a genuine war after a soccer game. Both sides won.

CHAIRMAN: Wars are going downhill.

MIMOSA: When we are being reproached for having no wars, i.e., needing no army, we are being accused really of two things. Firstly, that we do not attack others, secondly, that others do not attack us. But it is after all not our fault that no one attacks us. Let's examine the reasons for this. No one attacks us because we are peaceful, but also because we are strong. Vice versa, it is similar. We ourselves do not attack others because they are too weak and we feel sorry for them; furthermore because they are too strong and we would lose.

WESSIN: But what about a senseless attack?

Silence, then suddenly:

SCHNEIDER: I think it is because of our uniforms that we have no more wars. You have to be quite an expert to tell our enemies apart. And even experts I have seen floundering. Once, at the airport a visiting head of state, while inspecting the guard of honor, lifted the cape of a flag officer to check if he really was one of my men. "They are truly my men, comrade!" I called over to him. Now imagine these same troops marching into another country! What confusion! Can't you see them running toward each other with spread arms, calling: "You are us!"

Silence, nodding of some of the gentlemen.

ROSA: The fact that our uniforms all look alike is a visible manifestation of the firm alliance binding our armies. This unity transcending national boundaries strengthens us, but at the same time irritates the enemy, who must now refrain from the usual invasions. War has become senseless. The enemy who does not understand this must fight without armies.

SCHNEIDER: Sometimes even without weapons!

ROSA: Without weapons?

SCHNEIDER: In my country the enemy had no weapons, as far as I know. *(silence)*

WESSIN: Isn't that an advantage?

SCHNEIDER: It sounds that way. But in reality it meant that driving through the country one never knew whether an enemy was present or not because actually no one was shooting, or at any rate, no one was shooting back.

WESSIN: Then all you had to do was distribute arms to the enemy!

SCHNEIDER: The idea of distributing arms to the enemy was debated but rejected because we told ourselves that this was probably what the enemy was waiting for, I mean for us to make a mistake. *(silence)*

TORRIJOS: If there was never any shooting at you when you were driving through the country, how could you actually know that you had enemies? Perhaps all your worries were unnecessary, and you had no enemies?

CHAIRMAN: Did you ever meet an enemy personally?

SCHNEIDER: The enemies who were led to my office insisted there were none. We had to persuade them to admit it. But even then everything sounded invented. Sometimes they became emotional, which I detest. Then one couldn't understand anything. In other words, the enemy doesn't talk. He stutters, he moans, he cries, he screams, but he does not talk. If you want to find out what he wants, you have to put the words in his mouth, but even then he shakes his head, probably he didn't like the way it was phrased. *(silence)*

TORRIJOS: Maybe it was fear that made him speechless?

SCHNEIDER: You're right, the enemy is not courageous, one cannot show him around without embarrassing him. Therefore to protect his dignity I did not exhibit him, not in public. One has to respect the dignity of the enemy, for whom it must be dishonorable to be found in an unfavorable situation. But even if the enemy is alone, he insists just the same that he cannot speak, firstly because no one hears him, secondly because no one believes him, and thirdly because it is unnecessary for him to talk. He alleges that he does not need to talk because we, when we talk ourselves, no matter about what, come up with strong arguments against ourselves. For example I, when I say: "The National Assembly is hereby convened!" have allegedly indicted myself. *(laughter)*

SCHNEIDER: In short: until this day I don't know what the enemy has against me. You don't believe me? Please call the professor in for an interrogation!

TORRIJOS: But Colonel, sir, the professor is not an enemy!

SCHNEIDER: We'll tell him afterwards! *(calls)* Professor! *(to the others)* Just for an example!

35. Proof of the Speechlessness of the Enemy

SCHNEIDER *(to* Professor *who has just entered)*: Speak!

PROFESSOR: Sir?

SCHNEIDER *(standing up)*: Please speak!

PROFESSOR: I don't understand!

SCHNEIDER *(to others)*: He doesn't understand me! *(to Professor)* I have in my hand a document from Major Texeira de Oliveira! *(At the mention of this name, everyone freezes. From here on* Schneider *speaks his sentences rapidly, with longer pauses between them. Slowing down of actions almost to slow motion.* Schneider, *pacing back and forth with his hands folded behind his back:)* You still recognize the name Texeira de Oliveira, don't you?

PROFESSOR: Of course, Colonel!

SCHNEIDER: You recall then that he exists? *(to the others)* He has just remembered something! *(to Professor)* What does that name mean to you?

PROFESSOR: Colonel, Your Excellency, Major Oliveira is responsible for information that is collected.

SCHNEIDER: So! We are making some progress! And you thought his arm wasn't long enough to reach all the way up to Miami, huh? *(to the others)* Oliveira is often active in Indian territories far from the capital! *(to Professor)* But Oliveira has representatives! He is not all lost in desolate native territories, admit it! *(silence; to the others)* He doesn't wish to admit it! *(silence)*

PROFESSOR: Colonel, to the best of my knowledge I don't know what I'm supposed to confess!

SCHNEIDER *(to the others)*: So, in the best of his knowledge, he does not know all the things he should confess! *(close to* Professor, *whispering)* We need time to think this over, don't we? I can understand that! *(suddenly aloud)* Didn't you repeatedly express yourself against Oliveira's thinking? *(silence;* Schneider, *looking at his own hand)* Keep still! Don't move! *(to his foot)* Foot, do as I say! *(looking up)* As you can see, I'm in control of myself! *(wipes perspiration from his brow, then with a gesture of resignation:)* Gentlemen, I am exhausted. Too weak for this sort of thing! *(pause, then, pointing to* Professor*)* At other times so eloquent, but now out of steam! At home, in the faculty club, remarks were made in his presence, remarks about patriots!

ROSA *(causing* Professor, *who is on his way out, to stop for a moment, without turning around)* Air marshal! We are just kidding! It was just a joke! Everything's all right!

Professor *exits. Silence.*

WESSIN: That was supposed to be a joke? We made better jokes in the casino!

ROSA: I think he is guilty!

TORRIJOS: But he is not a real enemy!

SCHNEIDER: That's exactly the point! Just imagine a real enemy!

36. About the Antielitist Nature of Censorship

CHAIRMAN *(swatting a mosquito)*: Flies, the true fascists!

TORRIJOS: We had real freedom of speech and of the press!

ROSA: I consider it hypocritical to proclaim freedom of speech and freedom of the press when the people can neither read nor write.

TORRIJOS: But they can speak!

ROSA: Your answer is elitist. How can an illiterate population acquire the information and background they need in order to speak intelligently? Freedom of speech and of the press are only for the elite; therefore can be abolished. I would do this even if everyone were indeed able to read. After all, newspapers are only written for people who can get up from their reading immediately and act on what they have read; or else newspapers are for people who have given up on life, since they have apparently resigned themselves to letting everything happen around them without lifting a finger, as in a dream or the movies, where people also don't act. "Tell me, what is it you have forgotten today?" I used to ask my wife who read the papers daily. "I forgot everything I forgot, darling," she answered. "Didn't Israel or the pope do something? No hurricanes, no asshole staggering around on the moon?" *(as if waking suddenly from a dream, wiping off a tear)* Happy days!

MIMOSA: There was censorship in my country, but no one noticed it because it wasn't reported in the papers. After all, it wouldn't be much news to come out with a headline: "Still Censorship Today!" You might as well run a headline saying: "Today Is Today!"

CHAIRMAN: In contemporary Russia there are actually headlines like that. I once saw the following headline: "Numerous Saucepans Were Manufactured Last Week!"

37. About the Unrest while on State Visits Abroad

General Toro Davila *enters, followed by a younger* Adjutant *who resembles him. Both in uniforms as* Schneider *in scene 13, but their gestures are calm and dignified.*

DAVILA *(has taken his seat, to* Adjutant *who held his chair for him, without looking at him)*: Thank you, thank you! *(*Adjutant *exits)*

MIMOSA *(excited)*: General Davila! Where are you coming from?

WESSIN: You haven't been deposed, have you? Have you come here to check how things are if one is deposed?

CHAIRMAN *(motioning* Wessin *off)*: General Davila, how is your family? How is Mrs. Davila?

DAVILA: Thank you, Your Excellency—everyone is fine. You do have it pleasant here!

TORRIJOS *(agitated, interrupts)*: How is my country?

DAVILA: Wonderful! Your country is doing wonderfully! The news of your removal went over the provinces like a comforting spring breeze.

ROSA: What brings you here?

DAVILA: A hemispheric summit meeting that is not half as agreeable as being with you.

CHAIRMAN: Gentlemen, a toast to General Toro Davila! *(they drink)*

DAVILA *(looking around)*: This is the good life! *(smiling, he adds:)* I shall propose at the summit that they all move into this place and rule their countries from here!

WESSIN: Yes, if you make this your seat of government and you get overthrown at home you don't even have to drive to the airport!

SCHNEIDER: Maybe change rooms! *(laughter, then silence)*

CHAIRMAN *(to* Davila*)*: How does it feel to be in power still?

DAVILA *(smiling)*: One is restless, Your Excellency, especially at foreign conferences. Frequently, one is overthrown at home while abroad for a conference.

MIMOSA: I always took my whole cabinet with me on trips, as well as general officers all the way down to major general, colonels, some of whom were not even in the cabinet yet, plus other leaders of parliament. There was no one left to make a coup!

> Adjutant *rushes in and hands* Davila *a telegram.* Davila *glances over it quickly. Complete silence at the table.*

DAVILA *(hurrying out the door)*: Gentleman, I bid you farewell!

SCHNEIDER *(getting up halfway)*: Are you still in power?

38. About the Difficulty of Expressing Simple Thoughts

TORRIJOS: The great Chinese leader announced recently in the hall of the people that there was unrest under the skies and that the situation was excellent. Isn't that a contradiction? Either there is unrest, in which case the situation is not good, or everything is all right, in which case there is order.

MIMOSA: Maybe he intended to say that the disorder was good.

TORRIJOS: In that case he could have chosen a simpler way of expressing it, such as "Disorder is good!"

39. Third Announcement of an Idea

WESSIN: Gentlemen, concerning my idea, there has been a new development. I can now say with near certainty that I shall never be able to communicate this idea at all. No point to wait any longer!

CHAIRMAN: I was looking forward to your idea!

TORRIJOS: Why can't you communicate it?

WESSIN: If I knew that, I would probably be able to tell you an awful lot, including the idea itself!

ROSA: Is this your last word? I mean, is it conceivable that you could one day come in and say: "I have an idea; here it is?"

WESSIN: Unthinkable. Unless it were an entirely new idea! *(silence)*

SCHNEIDER: Why is it that you express your thoughts in such a complicated manner?

WESSIN: Because my thoughts are complicated. Complicated thoughts cannot be expressed in simple language.

CHAIRMAN: If that were true, it would be the end of all communication departments!

WESSIN: It is! Nobody had told them yet.

TORRIJOS: It's my opinion that a thought that cannot be expressed because it is too difficult should not be expressed. In other words, we shouldn't say what we can't say.

MIMOSA: I consider this question superfluous because whatever can't be said is something people should keep to themselves anyhow. Furthermore, if a person can't say something the question of whether or not he should say it is moot.

CHAIRMAN: I'm now confused.

TORRIJOS: Then I'll try once more. He says that the people's difficulties of understanding ideas cannot be alleviated with the help of grammar or style. He says that a difficult thought, if expressed elegantly, simply becomes more mysterious.

ROSA: He says that everything that is not understood by the masses is not worth thinking.

MIMOSA: I did not say that. If that were true, there would not be much left to think about.

40. About the State of Emergency as a Linguistic Problem and Legislative Questions

ROSA: The question of the state of emergency is, like almost all questions, a purely linguistic one. Declaring a state of emergency is another way of affirming the normal conditions that prevailed up to that time. Now there are some wise guys who claim that if the state of emergency lasts too long it becomes the rule, and if we didn't terminate it, we would be undermining the meaning of the word emergency, i.e., language would suffer under this state that should therefore be ended.

TORRIJOS: In order to solve this confusion, I declared the state of emergency twice in a row, i.e., I declared a state of emergency within the state of emergency. The emergency of the emergency allowed us to return to the rule and language was once more allowed to blossom.

WESSIN: A fallacy in the service of national language?

SCHNEIDER: As conservatives, the biggest problem we have is letting the people know that we love them. In other words, the problems we have with some of the people are nothing more than problems of communication. We all have an unfortunate tendency of calling a spade a filthy, black shovel, so to speak.

ROSA: But it is possible to express laws in clear language. In the field of communication, which flourished in my country, this is called "mediation." One goes on the assumption that the public will agree with anything that is mediated. I placed at the beginning of my deliberations the experience that laws result from reality.

SCHNEIDER: A truly inductive system of justice?

MIMOSA: Reality must be our teacher in the writing of laws. Example: Once in the provinces Guanabara and Minas Gerais, the enemy won in true elections—expected swarms of anchovies had not arrived in time. I had the winner of the election arrested. From this practical experience I deduced law number one, according to which enemies who win should apparently be arrested.

MIMOSA: Whatever is healthy we learn from reality, not from thin air!

41. About the Disappointment of Being Adult as Well as the Necessity of Reintroducing Poverty

TORRIJOS: I must tell you, I am disappointed with life. *(laughter)*

WESSIN: No wonder, if you've just been deposed!

TORRIJOS: No, apart from that, i.e., I'm disappointed generally. Listen! *(pensive, motionless sitting of the others)* As a child growing up, I had vague but definite ideas of what it would be like to be adult. Not that I went around with the idea that I deserved unending glamour, but at least I thought I would be permitted it: dates with ladies in furs, hotels at intersections where many boulevards come together, but as I was growing up, this world that had been flickering before my eyes faded away, and since then I find that wherever I go, things have already happened, as if someone, bowing, whispering to me: "I'm terribly sorry, sir, but the party checked out two minutes ago, destination unknown!" And instead, in the lobby all I can see are blue-haired ladies from America, tourists in pink pants that sparkle, you know, like on a trapeze in a circus. Or terrifyingly checkered jackets, even luggage they carry themselves. And fat. Colonel Schneider, in comparison to them, is an exhaled comma. Eyes sunk into rosy faces whose milk glow drills you into the ground. As a child I saw myself sitting in a lobby, a real lady arriving followed by a line of luggage-toting servants. Sometimes I thought secretly that perhaps all this never really existed, was all merely invented, like in the beginning of mysteries, but only in the beginnings. Since then I have noticed that if ever a thing was really beautiful, then it had already been the climax in the entire history of that thing. Perhaps we are conservatives only because, for the sake of order, we wish to bring everything that had been promised to us to a standstill just long enough so we can see it once; after that they can make their changes!

MIMOSA: I'm afraid all that is passé. In order to experience all that, you would have to reintroduce poverty.

SCHNEIDER: Are you referring to interior or exterior poverty?

ROSA: A leading personality in German letters has defined poverty as a beautiful glow that shines from within. *(silence)*

TORRIJOS: In my country the enemies of the state took cover in religious orders and in priests' cassocks, to perpetrate crimes against the law. Revolutionary bishops have turned me into an atheist, but we should not say too loudly that God is against us.

SCHNEIDER: He helped me. I preferred flying to Rome over flying to Washington. In Rome, you only have to kiss the ring. *(laughter)*

42. About Questions of Logistics

TORRIJOS: My view of problems is the following: For problems there is always a solution. Once people are cognizant of this fact, the world looks different. All problems are basically of a logistical nature, namely: "How do I get from A to B and back?" The following hypothetical situation will illustrate this. If we were to look at the world from some distance with sharp eyes, not much more of our activities could be seen than persons moving back and forth at various speeds. That, then, is what it all amounts to: that we are all at unspecified times headed for unspecified places.

SCHNEIDER *(murmuring)*: Pure physics!

TORRIJOS: This is how it was with me. When the logistics were mastered, all was mastered. Then I sat in the center of everything that had been mastered, exhausted from the labor that had created the order around me and had all sorts of foolish ideas, like the prince in a fairy tale.

WESSIN: Limp. I find that limp!

ROSA: Well, in such cases you get off your ass and make some innovations, for example you can think of a new name for the party, say "Alliance for Renovation," that will broaden your power base because people love nothing better than unity and something new. It's as in art, when you get applause only under the condition that it is completely new, never mind the content. The secret of my success was that I continually made new things: new flags, new titles, new buildings, new people, also often and suddenly new appointments. Once the foreign minister came to me and said:

"Good morning, Mr. President. I bring you the reports from our foreign missions!" "No," I said, "dear Claudio, today you are chief of the pastry association. Elfie will help you. Or what about harbor master?"

MIMOSA: You are like a child tossing toys all over!

ROSA (flattered): As a dictator you always remain a child. The child is a preformation of the dictator. I as dictator preserved some of the innocence of a child. Do you have something against children? Our most precious good! The child is the future! And you aren't going to have objections to the future!

43. Path to the Inside

CHAIRMAN: Good morning, gentlemen, how are you this morning? (silence)

WESSIN: Mood bleak, Your Excellency!

TORRIJOS: In need of a fresh start!

MIMOSA: But we started from the beginning just yesterday!

TORRIJOS: Doesn't count. Nothing came of it!

WESSIN: Do we have to start from the beginning every morning?
    Silence. Schneider enters, walking solemnly, like a sleep-walker, blissful smile, dressed in a white robe, hippie-type necklace.

ROSA: Colonel Jesus Schneider as a late riser!

SCHNEIDER (sits down; suggestion of a grouping a la Last Supper): I have meditated all night! (lights incense)

ROSA: Put that thing out! It stinks!

SCHNEIDER: It helps me touch my inner reaches!

WESSIN: Inner reaches?

SCHNEIDER: I approach my inner reaches and get in touch with myself!

WESSIN: Disgusting! You touch yourself?

SCHNEIDER (mysteriously): Your Excellency, gentlemen. I have found my own inner rainbow, the rainbow of peace! Human beings suffer due to forces emanating from the unconscious. These must become conscious! Our problem is that we are too occupied with others, not enough with ourselves. I have composed a poem about this and shall now present it. (he gets up, plays a few notes on a flute, then recites)

Now the time has come
to discover and love
the beautiful being
I really am
and not the person
I have been programmed
to think I am.

ROSA: I have to admit, this poem vibrates with me!

MIMOSA: There are certain thoughts contained in it!

PROFESSOR: And you, Wessin?

> *Silence.* Wessin *lifts hands in a gesture indicating that he wishes to speak, but is motioned to be silent as* Schneider *again plays a few notes on the flute. After this, again silence.*

SCHNEIDER: I don't think General Wessin is sufficiently holistic in his thinking yet.

WESSIN: Holistic?

SCHNEIDER: Holistics consist of three parts: Firstly, striving for health; secondly, cosmic clarity; and thirdly, be positive!

TORRIJOS: General Wessin, throw off some of your inhibitions for once. You owe it to yourself! We owe it to ourselves!

WESSIN: All right, I'll throw off some inhibitions! *(he stands up; silence)*

WESSIN: Can you give me a hint as to how one goes about such a thing?

SCHNEIDER *(seriously)*: Try crying, it feels good. Trembling, stuttering. Or take a swing at something. Or maybe a primal scream! *(silence)*

> Wessin *screams. Then applause and cries of:* Bravo, dear Wessin!

SCHNEIDER: Now you are uninhibited!

MIMOSA: Do you get a sense of self-realization?

ROSA: Now he's got to get inside.

WESSIN: Inside?

SCHNEIDER: Yes, with the help of breathing.

ROSA: Conscious breathing! Close your eyes! Sit still and let the world be!

> *All close their eyes and begin to breathe deeply and at regular intervals.*

CHAIRMAN *(in a trancelike state)*: Learn from the future!

SCHNEIDER: The future is inside!
ROSA: Inside is love!
MIMOSA: Love is the future!
PROFESSOR: The future is the love that is inside!
WESSIN: Inside is the love that is the future!
> *While the preceding is being repeated:*
> Blackout.

Sources

The idea for the following collection came up only after the play had almost been completed. The material is therefore rather incidental and could be continued ad infinitum. In production some of it could be used for slide projections, or one might compose a playbill in the form of a newspaper with it.

Scene 5

"The higher the monkey climbs up the tree . . ." General Westmoreland in an interview with *Public Broadcast Radio,* San Diego, 18 Dec. 1976.

Scene 6

"For the year 1976 the financial support given to the present military regime in Chile by the People's Republic of China was $100 million." Enrique Kirberg, former president of the Technical University of Santiago de Chile, in a lecture given 19 May 1977 at the University of California in San Diego.

*

In a message dated 2 April 1964 President Johnson recognized the Brazilian military regime of General Castelo Branco even before Branco had completed his coup d'etat against the democratically elected administration of President Joao Goulart: "The American recognition arrived even before Goulart had slipped over the Uruguayan border and before the question of the presidential succession or the constitutionality of the transition had been resolved. The unusual rapidity and unbridled enthusiasm of the recognition tended to confirm the widespread suspicion of United States participation in the coup" from *Brazil in the Sixties,* Riordan Roett, Vanderbilt University Press, Nashville 1972, p. 91; text of Johnson's telegram from *Public Papers of the Presidents of the United States, Lyndon B. Johnson, 1963–64,* United States Government Printing Office, Washington 1965, p. 433; *cp:* M. R. Martin, Gabriel H. Lovett, *Encyclopedia of Latin American*

History, Indianapolis–New York (no date), p. 57, as well as the newly released documents at the Johnson Library in Austin, Texas according to which the coup was supported by strong US naval units. The papers released in December 1976 also showed that the new dictator, General Branco, was one of the closest friends of the US military attaché in Brazil, General Vernon Walters who resigned from his post as second man at the CIA only in 1976. *Cp* Lewis. H. Diuguid in the *Washington Post* and *New York Post,* 27 Dec. 1976.

Scene 7

"The voters want a different candidate, not just a different face" Nixon during countless campaign speeches in 1968.

Scene 16

"Four years ago the president of the World Bank, Mr McNamara, released figures according to which the poorest 40 percent of the Brazilian population earned 10 percent of the national income. That was in 1960. In 1970 the same 40 percent of the population only earned 8 percent of the national income. Comment by the former minister for economic affairs, Delfim Neto: 'One thing is for sure, namely that 100 percent of the national income is distributed among 100 percent of the population, the proportions are not so important. In capitalism there will always be poor and rich people,' " *Spiegel,* Hamburg, No. 1/2, 1977.

*

After Milton Friedman's departure for Israel, the Chilean rate of inflation was 174.3 percent. *Cp: News from Chile, Chilegram,* vol. IV, no. 21 (March 1977)—an official bulletin of the Chilean military government.

*

For an excellent report on "Trilateral Commission" as well as the connections between David Rockefeller, President Carter, and Brzezinski *Cp:* Robert Scheer in the *Los Angeles Times,* 23 Jan. 1977. After a student demonstration against the US attack on Vietnam at Columbia University, Brzezinski observed: "If that student leadership cannot be physically liquidated, it can at least be expelled from the country. . . ."

*

According to reports by William Goodfellow and James Morrell (Center for International Policy, Washington, DC) US reductions of military aid to foreign dictatorships were deceptive because the US dispensed such aid through 15 separate channels. Only four of these were subject to congressional scrutiny and approval. Meanwhile cash continued to flow through 11 government corporations and international financial institutions, *e.g.*, the "International Bank for Reconstruction and Development" ("World Bank"), which in the fall of 1976 sent $115 million to Argentina, an additional $390 million was on the way. One out of every four dollars came from the US. The "Inter-American Development Bank" in 1976 dispensed $198 million to Argentina, an additional $253 million was on the way, with 52 percent of the support coming from the US. In the same year the "International Monetary Fund" sent $315 million to Argentina. Since the US cut their military aid to Uruguay, that regime received $74 million from the "Inter-American Bank" and $30 million from the "World Bank." Such examples could be continued *ad infinitum*. *Cp* also: W. Goodfellow, J. Morrell, "US Aid and Comfort for World Torturers," *Los Angeles Times,* 19 May 1977.

Scene 18

In several Latin American countries Generals have been named to run Universities. The present rector of the University of Chile is General Augustin Toro Dávila *(cp: Chilegram, op. cit.).*

Scene 19

On 1 Dec. 1977 (three months after the first publication of this play) Bolivian dictator, General Hugo Banzer, appeared on TV and, with moist eyes announced his resignation, promising he would merely stay in office long enough to supervise fair elections. After this, he applied for retirement as a general officer, thus causing another 50 highly ranked officers to do likewise in order to make possible a "change of generations" in the Armed Forces. After he had thus removed all his major rivals from positions of power, he accepted the verdict of his newly appointed Army Commander, General Alfonso Villalpando, that the Army, "after deep meditation" had rejected his resignation. *(Cp: Frankfurter Rundschau, 30 Dec. 1977.)*

Scene 29

"We do care. I care. I have visited most of your countries. I have met most of your leaders. I have talked with your people. I have seen your great needs, as well as your great achievements," President Nixon told a dinner meeting of the Interamerican Press Association, "and I know this, in my heart as well as in my mind." (Stuart M. Loory, *Los Angeles Times,* 1 Nov. 1969.)

*

"Democracy is a superstition based on statistics" (Jorge Luis Borges in an interview with Dieter E. Zimmer in: *Die Zeit* [Hamburg], US edition, 19 Nov. 1976.)

*

". . . according to Agee, former (Mexican) President Gustavo Diaz Ordaz preferred meeting with (CIA) station chief Winston Scott rather than US Ambassador Fulton Freeman in the late 1960s . . ." (*Los Angeles Times,* 16 Oct. 1974).

Scene 34

About the so-called "soccer war" between El Salvador and Honduras, which enabled Honduras to silence the unrest in the country, *cp: International Herald Tribune* (Paris), 15 July 1969 and *Süddeutsche Zeitung* (Munich), 26 July 1969.

*

"One has to respect the dignity of the enemy. . . ." General Augusto Pincohet in a GDR-TV interview of the movie *I am, I will Be* (1976). Quoted from memory.

Scene 36

"It's no good to proclaim freedom of speech and freedom of the press if the population cannot read or write." General Alfredo Stroessner, dictator of Paraguay, in: *Der Spiegel,* Hamburg, no. 48/69.

*

"The man in the street does not even know we are under censorship—(the newspapers) cannot mention that. . . ." *AP* report in: *Los Angeles Times,* 7 May 1969.

Scene 37

Heads of state from the following countries were overthrown while traveling abroad in recent years: Panama, Uganda, Nigeria, Ghana, Libya, Congo, Seychelles.

President Mobutu of Zaire, when he gets bored with his 22 villas at home, sometimes flies to one of his villas in France or Switzerland. "But when he flies off in Zaire's Boeing 747, he simply takes along with him everyone of leadership potential. There's no one left at home to stage a coup." Julian Hartt, in the *Los Angeles Times,* 15 March 1976.

Scene 40

"As Conservatives, the biggest problem we have is to let people know we love them." Orrin Hatch, US Senator from Utah, in the *Los Angeles Times,* 13 Dec. 1976.

*

"Why did the Chilean Army declare an Interior state of war? Because it is extremely legalistic. If you want to apply martial law and enforce it, you first have to declare a state of war formally. Because we don't want to rule by arbitrary decree, like a dictatorship, but we insist on a rule of law within the framework of the new form of government, which we are erecting to-day. . . ." (Colonel Petro Ewing, speaker of the Chilean Junta, in an interview with *Der Spiegel,* Hamburg (no. 13/74)—a statement that cannot be surpassed in clarity, brutality, and stupidity.

Scene 41

"The government cannot permit that its enemies hide in religious orders and priests' cassocks to perpetrate crimes against the law." General Alfredo Stroessner, in: *Der Spiegel,* no. 48/69.

Scene 42

"National Renovating Alliance" (ARENA) is the name of Brazilian dictator Ernesto Geisel's ruling party. "Renovation" *(Rastakhiz)* was the name of the Shah of Persia's ruling party.

*

Former Governor Reagan of California proposed a new name for the GOP in order to improve its chances for future elections (*cp: Los Angeles Times,* 19 Nov. 1976)

Scene 43

The poem was published anonymously in: *Los Angeles Times* (7 April 1977)

Translated by Julie Prandl and Reinhard Lettau

Select Bibliography of Secondary Literature

Arnheim, Rudolf. *Radio: An Art of Sound* 1939: Rept. Salem, New Hampshire: Ayer Company, Publishers, 1986.

Benjamin, Walter. "The Work of Art in the Age of Mechanical Reproduction." *Illuminations: Essays and Reflections,* Ed. Hannah Arendt. New York: Schocken Books, 1968.

Bloom, Margaret. *Die Westdeutsche Nachkriegszeit im Literatischen Original-Hörspiel.* Frankfurt: Peter Lang, 1985.

Brecht, Bertolt. "The Radio as an Apparatus of Communication." *Brecht on Theatre.* Trans. John Willett. New York: Hill and Wang, 1964.

Cory, Mark. *The Emergence of an Acoustical Art Form: An Analysis of the German Experimental* Hörspiel *of the 1960s.* University of Nebraska Studies, new series, no. 45 (1974). Lincoln: University of Nebraska Press.

Döhl, Reinhard. *Das Neue Hörspiel.* Darmstadt: Wissenschaftliche Buchgesellschaft, 1988, vol. 5 of *Geschichte und Typologie des Hörspiels,* Ed. Klaus Schöning, WDR.

Demetz, Peter. *After the Fires: Recent Writing in the Germanies, Austria, and Switzerland.* New York: Harcourt, Brace, Jovanovich, 1986.

Esslin, Martin. *Meditations: Essays on Brecht, Beckett, and the Media.* New York: Grove Press, 1982.

Fischer, Eugen Kurt. *Das Hörspiel: Form und Funktion.* Stuttgart: Alfred Kroner Verlag, 1964.

Frank, Armin P. *Das Hörspiel: Ein Literarisches Studium.* Heidelberg: Carl Winter, Universitätsverlag, 1963.

Frost, Everett C. "Why Sound Art Works—and the German *Hörspiel.*" *The Drama Review,* 31.4 (T116), Winter 1987.

Grün, Rita von der. *Das Hörspiel im "Dritten Reich": Eine Statistische Erhebung und Auswertung.* Frankfurt am Main: R. G. Fischer, 1984.

Hammer, Franz. *Frühe Hörspiele.* Berlin: Henschelverlag Kunst und Gesellschaft, 1982.

Keckeis, Hermann. *Das Deutsche Hörspiel: 1923–1973.* Frankfurt: Athenäum Verlag, 1973.

Klippert, Werner. *Elemente des Hörspiels.* Stuttgart: Reclam, 1978.

Klose, Werner. *Didaktik des Hörspiels.* Stuttgart: Reclam, 1974.

Knilli, Friedrich. *Das Hörspiel: Mittel und Möglichkeit eines Totalen Schallspiels.* Stuttgart, 1961.

Lermen, Brigit. *Das Traditionelle und Neue Hörspiel im Deutschunterricht.* Paderborn: Ferdinand Schöning, 1975.

Mueller, Roswitha. *Bertolt Brecht and the Theory of Media.* Lincoln, Nebraska: University of Nebraska Press, 1989.

Rilke, Rainer Maria. "Primal Sound" *(Ur-Geräusch). The Creative Vision: Modern European Writers on Their Art.* Eds. Haskell M. Block and Herman Salinger. New York: Grove Evergreen, 1960.

Schefner, Horst, ed. *Theories des Hörspiels.* Stuttgart: Reclam, 1978.

Schöning, Klaus. *Neues Hörspiel: Texte. Partituren.* Frankfurt: Suhrkamp, 1974.

———. *Neus Hörspiel Essays. Analysen Gesprache.* Frankfurt: Suhrkamp, 1970.

———, ed. *Schriftsteller und Hörspiel: Reden zum Hörspielpreis der Kriegsblinden.* Königstein: Athenäum Verlag GmbH, 1981.

———. *Spuren des Neuen Hörspiels.* Frankfurt: Suhrkamp, 1982.

———, ed. *Hörspielmacher.* Königstein: Athenäum, 1983.

Schwitzke, Heinz. *Das Hörspiel: Dramaturgie und Geschichte.* Cologne, 1963.

———. *Hörspielführer.* Stuttgart: Reclam, 1969.

Theatre Journal. 43.2 (Fall 1991). Special number on radio drama.

Viehoff, Reinhold. *Literaturkritik im Rundfunk.* Tübingen: Max Niemeyer Verlag, 1981.

WDR Hörspielbuch (Annual Anthology). Cologne: Klepenheuer and Witsch, 1963.

Das Hörspiel: Ein Literaturverzeichnis (1963–1983). Cologne: Westdeutscher Rundfunk, 1976/1983, four volumes.

SoundPlay: Germany/USA

With the exception of Günter Eich's *Don't Go to Al-Kuwaid!,* all the Hörspiele in this volume are included in the *SoundPlay: Hörspiel* series produced by Voices International and distributed in 1991 for national broadcast in the United States by PPS—the Pacifica Program Service (P.O. Box 8092, Universal City, California 91608 [1-800-735-0230]. Major funding for the series was provided by a grant from the National Endowment for the Humanities, with additional support from the National Endowment for the Arts and the Goethe Institute. The series includes:

Bertolt Brecht / Kurt Weill, *The Flight of Lindbergh: A Radio Cantata,* performed by the Stamford Master Singers, conducted by Steven Gross; produced by Everett Frost and Faith Wilding. Production: Voices International.

Wolfgang Borchert, *The Outsider,* directed by Georges Wagner Jourdain. Coproduction: Deutsche Welle; WGBH, Boston; and Voices International.

Günter Eich, *Dreams,* directed by Everett Frost, Production: Voices International.

Günter Eich, *The other Woman and I,* directed by Erik Bauersfeld. Production: BARD.*

Ingeborg Bachmann, *The Good God of Manhattan,* directed by Carey Perloff, produced by Faith Wilding. Production: Voices International.

Experimental Radio Drama Program I, produced by Erik Bauersfeld. Production: BARD.

Ernst Jandl and Friederike Mayröcker, *Five Man Humanity,* directed by Robert Goss and Klaus Mehrländer, and produced by Erik Bauersfeld. Coproduction: BARD and WDR, Cologne.*

Kurt Schwitters, excerpt from the *Ursonate,* performed by Kurt Schwitters. Production: RRG, Stuttgart (1932).

307

Gerhard Rühm, *Ophelia and the Words,* directed by Klaus Schöning and produced by Erik Bauersfeld. Coproduction: BARD and WDR, Cologne.*

Max Bense and Ludwig Harig, *Monologue: Terry Jo,* directed by Klaus Schöning and produced by Erik Bauersfeld. Coproduction: BARD and WDR Cologne.*

Wolfgang Schiffer and Charles Dürr, *Gertrude,* directed by Oscar Eustis and produced by Erik Bauersfeld. Wolfgang Schiffer, dramaturg. Production: BARD.*

Experimental Radio Drama program II, produced by Erik Bauersfeld. Production: BARD*
Ferdinand Kriwet, *Radio.* Realization: Ferdinand Kriwet. Production: WDR, Cologne.
Peter Handke, *Wind and Sea,* directed by Heinz von Kramer. Production: WDR, Cologne.*

Peter Handke, *"Radio Play" (No. 1),* directed by Klaus Schöning. Production: Voices International.

Jürgen Becker, *Houses,* directed by Erik Bauersfeld. Coproduction: BARD and WDR, Cologne.*

Walter Adler, *Centropolis,* directed by Erik Bauersfeld. Production: BARD.*

Mauricio Kagel, *The Tribune,* directed by Everett Frost. Production: Voices International.

Reinhard Lettau, *Breakfast in Miami,* directed by Everett Frost. Production: Voices International.

Helmut Kopetzky, *Moscow Time.* Realization: Helmut Kopetzky. Production: Voices International.

John Cage, *Roaratorio: An Irish Circus on Finnegans Wake.* Realization: John Cage and John David Fullemann. Production: WDR, Cologne.*

Plays marked with a * were broadcast on KPFA, Berkeley, California, beginning in October 1984 as part of the "Hörspiel USA" series originated through the cooperation of the Goethe Institute (San Francisco), West

Deutscher Rundfunk (WDR), Cologne, and Bay Area Radio Drama (BARD) by Erik Bauersfeld, Ernst Schürmann, and Klaus Schöning with the assistance of Robert Goss.

* * *

Note: This anthology of German radio drama has been published in order to make the English translations available for reading and study. They are protected by copyright and may not be acted or read aloud to an audience, recorded, broadcast, televised or performed, or presented in any way, as a whole, or in part, in either amateur or professional productions, without advance written permission from both the author and the translator. In most instances this permission will require the advance payment of a negotiated fee. Listed below are the representatives of the authors and translators included in this volume:

Günter Eich
Peter Handke
    Suhrkamp Verlag
    Postfach 10-1945, Lindenstrasse 29-35
    D-6000, Frankfurt am Main 1
    Federal Republic of Germany
      Telex 413 972
      FAX 75 601 522

Robert Goss
    2627 Fulton Street, 4
    Berkeley, CA 94704

Anselm Hollo
    1501 Orchard Avenue
    Boulder, CO 80304

* * *

Wolfgang Borchert
    Rowohlt Verlag
    Sanford J. Greenburger Associates
    55 Fifth Avenue
    New York, NY 10003

Michael Benedikt
    Anne Borchardt
    Georges Borchardt, Inc.
    136 East 57th Street
    New York, NY. 10022

* * *

Ingeborg Bachmann
    R. Piper Verlag
    GMBH & Co.
    Georgenstr. 4; PostFach 430 120
    8000 München 43
    Federal Republic of Germany

Faith Wilding
    2 Washington Square Village, 16J
    New York, NY 10012

* * *

Jürgen Becker
    WDR Hörspiel Studio 3,
    Appelhofplatz I,
    5000 Köln I,
    Federal Republic Germany

Robert Goss

* * *

Reinhard Lettau
    Grove Weidenfeld
    841 Broadway
    New York, NY 10003-4793

ACKNOWLEDGMENTS

Every reasonable effort has been made to locate the owners of rights to previously published works and the translations printed here. We gratefully acknowledge permission to reprint the following material:

Sanford J. Greenburger Associates for permission to use *The Outsider* by Wolfgang Borchert.

Georges Borchardt, Inc., for permission to reprint Michael Benedikt's translation of *The Outsider* by Wolfgang Borchert.

R. Piper GmBH and Company for permission to use *Der Gute Gott von Manhattan* by Ingeborg Bachmann. From Ingeborg Bachmann, *Werke,* © R. Piper & Co. Verlag, München 1978.

Faith Wilding for permission to reprint her translation of *The Good God of Manhattan* by Ingeborg Bachmann. Translated by Faith Wilding. Translation was commissioned by Voices International for the radio drama series *Soundplay,* to be broadcast nationally on public radio in 1991.

Robert Goss for permission to reprint his translations of *"Radio Play" (No. 1)* by Peter Handke and *Houses* by Jürgen Becker.

Suhrkamp Verlag for permission to use *Traüume* and *Geh Nicht Nach El Kuwehd* by Günter Eich from "Träume." © Suhrkamp Verlag, Frankfurt am Main 1953. *Hörspiel (1)* by Peter Handke from "Wind und Meer. Vier Hörspiele." © Suhrkamp Verlag, Frankfurt am Main 1970. *Häuser* by Jürgen Becker from "Bilder Häuser Hausfreunde. Drei Hörspiele." © Suhrkamp Verlag Frankfurt am Main 1969.

John Calder (Publishers) Ltd. for permission to reprint *Breakfast in Miami* by Reinhard Lettau.

THE GERMAN LIBRARY
in 100 Volumes

German Romantic Criticism
Edited by A. Leslie Willson
Foreword by Ernst Behler

Friedrich Hölderlin
Hyperion and Selected Poems
Edited by Eric L. Santner

Philosophy of German Idealism
Edited by Ernst Behler

G. W. F. Hegel
Encyclopedia of the Philosophical Sciences in Outline and Critical Writings
Edited by Ernst Behler

Heinrich von Kleist
Plays
Edited by Walter Hinderer
Foreword by E. L. Doctorow

E.T.A. Hoffman
Tales
Edited by Victor Lange

Georg Büchner
Complete Works and Letters
Edited by Walter Hinderer and Henry J. Schmidt

German Fairy Tales
Edited by Helmut Brachert and Volkmar Sander
Foreword by Bruno Bettelheim

German Literary Fairy Tales
Edited by Frank G. Ryder and Robert M. Browning
Introduction by Gordon Birrell
Foreword by John Gardner

F. Grillparzer, J. H. Nestroy, F. Hebbel
Nineteenth Century German Plays
Edited by Egon Schwarz in collaboration with Hannelore M. Spence

Heinrich Heine
Poetry and Prose
Edited by Jost Hermand and Robert C. Holub
Foreword by Alfred Kazin

Heinrich Heine
The Romantic School and other Essays
Edited by Jost Hermend and Robert C. Holub

Heinrich von Kleist and Jean Paul
German Romantic Novellas
Edited by Frank G. Ryder and Robert M. Browning
Foreword by John Simon

German Romantic Stories
Edited by Frank Ryder
Introduction by Gordon Birrell

German Poetry from 1750 to 1900
Edited by Robert M. Browning
Foreword by Michael Hamburger

Karl Marx, Friedrich Engels, August Bebel, and Others
German Essays on Socialism in the Nineteenth Century
Edited by Frank Mecklenburg and Manfred Stassen

Gottfried Keller
Stories
Edited by Frank G. Ryder
Foreword by Max Frisch

Wilhelm Raabe
Novels
Edited by Volkmar Sander
Foreword by Joel Agee

Theodor Fontane
Short Novels and Other Writings
Edited by Peter Demetz
Foreword by Peter Gay

Theodor Fontane
Delusions, Confusions and The Poggenpuhl Family
Edited by Peter Demetz
Foreword by J. P. Stern
Introduction by William L. Zwiebel

Wilhelm Busch and Others
German Satirical Writings
Edited by Dieter P. Lotze and Volkmar Sander
Foreword by John Simon

Writings of German Composers
Edited by Jost Hermand and James Steakley

German Lieder
Edited by Philip Lieson Miller
Foreword by Hermann Hesse

Arthur Schnitzler
Plays and Stories
Edited by Egon Schwarz
Foreword by Stanley Elkin

Rainer Maria Rilke
Prose and Poetry
Edited by Egon Schwarz
Foreword by Howard Nemerov

Robert Musil
Selected Writings
Edited by Burton Pike
Foreword by Joel Agee

Essays on German Theater
Edited by Margaret Herzfeld-Sander
Foreword by Martin Esslin

German Novellas of Realism I and II
Edited by Jeffrey L. Sammons

Friedrich Dürrenmatt
Plays and Essays
Edited by Volkmar Sander
Foreword by Martin Esslin

Max Frisch
Novels, Plays, Essays
Edited by Rolf Kieser
Foreword by Peter Demetz

Gottfried Benn
Prose, Essays, Poems
Edited by Volkmar Sander
Foreword by E. B. Ashton
Introduction by Reinhard Paul Becker

German Essays on Art History
Edited by Gert Schiff

Hans Magnus Enzensberger
Critical Essays
Edited by Reinhold Grimm and Bruce Armstrong
Foreword by John Simon

All volumes available in hardcover and paperback editions at your bookstore or from the publisher. For more information on The German Library write to: The Continuum Publishing Company, 370 Lexington Avenue, New York, NY 10017.